THE MOMENT COLLECTORS

SAM MANICOM AND FRIENDS

THE MOMENT COLLECTORS

TWENTY TRAVELLERS' TALES
FROM AROUND THE WORLD

"Life is not measured by the
breaths we take, but by the moments that
take our breath away."

—*Maya Angelou*

SAM MANICOM AND FRIENDS

Print Edition: ISBN 978-0-9556573-9-9

Contributing Authors:
Claire Elsdon
Geoff Hill
Spencer James Conway with Cathy Nel
Shirley Hardy-Rix and Brian Rix
Ted Hely
Lisa Morris with Jason Spafford
Mark Donham
Graham Field
Tiffany Coates
EmmaLucy Cole
Tim and Marisa Notier
Christian Brix
Helen Lloyd
Michelle Lamphere
Travis and Chantil Gill
Simon and Lisa Thomas
Daniel Byers
Geoff Keys
Michnus and Elsebie Olivier
Sam Manicom with Birgit Schünemann

Editors and Proofreaders:
Susan Dragoo
Sam Manicom
Jill Boulton
Birgit Schünemann

Consultant:
Paul H Smith

Cover Design:
Fil Schiannini

Cover Photo:
Michnus Olivier

Illustrations:
Simon Roberts Illustrations

Photography Includes Work by:
Jason Spafford
Simon Thomas

This book is also available on *Kindle*.
Please note: For the *Amazon Print on Demand* version all photos are black and white.

Published by
Adventure Motorcycle Travel Books
Sam-Manicom.com

Contents

Introduction

The Moment Collectors covers a broad spectrum of 20 unique and adventurous tales of life on the road as overlanding motorcyclists—from the hugely experienced globe-riders, to those relatively new to wandering and exploring on two wheels. Each story is told by the motorcycle travellers themselves, some well-known, and others by individuals or couples you may be meeting for the first time.

Our Moment Collectors include published authors of books, magazine articles, blogs, and first-time writers. As they take you exploring five continents—Africa, Asia, Europe, South and North America—each relays a tale representing the kind of inspiring moments only possible by life on the long road.

Several ride two up, some ride in pairs and there are solo riders too. This is how things are on the open road—the full mix.

It's important to us that this international book of travel, by authors from around the world, retains the clear identity of each of them. With this in mind, their styles, spelling, slang and the quirks of authors' nationalities are alive within their chapters. We hope you enjoy this aspect of *The Moment Collectors*.

I'm extremely grateful to them all for sharing such personal high points in their lives.

—*Sam Manicom*

Foreword

by Lois Pryce

This anthology of motorcycle adventures comes at an opportune time during the uncertainty of the Covid global pandemic; a moment in our history within which most of us have been challenged and restricted in ways previously unimagined. A period of revaluation and learning to adapt, which has been spent with a mix of itching to hit the road, reliving past adventures and dreaming of future ones.

I can't be the only one who has been mulling over my past motorcycle travels and wondering if such carefree, freewheeling expeditions will ever be quite the same again. A handshake from a border guard, a hug from a fellow traveller-turned-friend, an invitation into a stranger's home to share a meal or crash on their sofa. All these things, we took for granted. But they are the very essence of what makes independent motorcycle travel so special. I believe that the drama, challenges and delights of the road as described within these chapters will be alive in our futures, but we will have learnt to adapt to the new circumstances. The motorcycle opens up the world in a way that a journey by bus or plane, or even travelling overland by car can never do. It ignites curiosity and camaraderie in others, and inspires openness in all of us, the riders

I truly believe that the adventure motorcycling community is unique in this way. Even if you are travelling alone, you know that somewhere out there are other like-minded folk who are rooting for you, who will step up if you need a hand. They get it. They know why you're doing what you're doing, and you don't need to explain yourself. Being part of this community over the last twenty years has been a heartening experience – I've made lifelong friends all over the world, shared tales, food and beers, laughed and commiserated, and most of all, been helped and helped others along the way.

Motorcycle adventures are not just about feeling the wind on your face, riding into the sunset, or even the physical challenge of tackling a rough road or negotiating anarchic traffic in a faraway city. The best moments come from the people we meet on the road. And I'm pleased to say that many of those people are involved in the creating of this book, from contributing their own stories, to the illustrations, the proof-reading and the design – it's a big ol' global moto family affair, and I sure am glad to you know y'all.

—*Lois Pryce,* London, UK

Lois Pryce is the author of three books about her motorcycle journeys around the world, *Lois on the Loose, Red Tape & White Knuckles*, and *Revolutionary Ride*. She is a freelance travel writer and journalist, and her work has appeared in motorcycle magazines around the  world, in the *New York Times*, the *Guardian*, the *Observer*, the *Telegraph*, the *Independe*nt and many other publications in the UK and the US. Lois is the co-founder of the A*dventure Travel Film Festival* and is a *Ted Talks* Speaker.

LoisOnTheLoose.com

Preface

"Life, it's a blank canvas of moments
waiting to be painted."

—*Anonymous*

Who are Overlanders? Why on earth do people ride away from the comfort and safety of their homes and straight into a constant flow of boundary-stretching challenges in foreign lands, some life threatening?

Are they adrenaline junkies? No, actually, they are just like you. They are courageous, fascinated, kind, generous, and open-hearted. They have simply found another quite wonderful way to explore and to hone these qualities. It's been said that they are rebellious individuals, but the reality is that they all have an incredibly strong streak of curiosity. Motorcycle travellers revel at the buzz of freedom which exploring on two wheels makes possible.

The long road is a rollercoaster of uncertainty, surprises, fear, tedium, delight, pain, and laughter, so both good and bad days. Sometimes it's phenomenally difficult and you'll find examples of that in several of these stories.

The ever-changing mix of our authors' experiences takes you to places where history and geography lessons come alive in living 3D. Each sight, sound, scent and feeling is a vital ingredient as they explore some of the most incredible cultures, and the most breath-taking sights in the world, and yet some encounters are sobering. Travel also shows the sadder sides of life and our motorcycle travellers are both humbled by some moments and are amazed by others.

Overlanders learn that the respect of a handshake, and smiles and laughter, are the international languages which need no words. We hear much of the kindness of strangers; the true stories before you in these pages are the reality.

One of the beauties of international travel by motorcycle, with a hunger to learn and to experience, is that many preconceived ideas are shattered. A person, who has made themselves both open and vulnerable, learns to recognise and appreciate all the quirks and opportunities that tumble across their paths. As they ride from one contrasting and unique moment to another, they learn the true value of perspective, and inevitably become optimistic realists with a passion for this phenomenal planet and its people.

The Moment Collectors is written for those of you who could and should head out to experience this amazing world of ours but need a little nudge. Make it happen. That clichéd saying "It's a whole new world out there" is the wonderful truth.

This book is also written for those of you whose responsibilities stop you from hitting the road at this time. Our full respect is with you. Where would this world be if people did not take their responsibilities seriously? Please keep your dreams alive; we hope that your time will come. We are also sharing these special moments from the long road with those of you who are fascinated by travel but are quite happy enjoying the adventures from the comfort of an armchair. We love your curiosity.

These are *The Moment Collectors*:
Claire, Geoff H, Spencer & Cathy, Shirley & Brian, Ted, Lisa & Jason, Mark, Graham, Tiffany, EmmaLucy, Tim & Marisa, Christian, Helen, Michelle, Travis & Chantil, Lisa & Simon, Daniel, Geoff K, Michnus & Elsebie, and Birgit & Sam

Adventure: "An unusual and exciting experience."
Moment: "A point in time. An opportunity."
—*Oxford English Dictionary*

The Unthinkable Happens

by Claire Elsdon

> "A ship in harbor is safe, but that's not what ships were built for."

—John A. Shedd

My journey to Wad Madani had not been easy. On leaving the Sudanese capital city of Khartoum, I'd taken the wrong turn at some kind of bus station and had ended up shadowing the main road out of town on a parallel track about a field away. The track I was riding on consisted of sun-bleached sand interspersed with tough grasses and took me through the backstreets, behind-the-scenes side of outer Khartoum.

At first, this meant the sour repulsive tang of the local rubbish dump, offensive for its odour, and alarming for the languid packs of dozing street dogs that sprang to attention as soon as they spotted some interestingly packaged fresh meat wobbling past on two wheels. Instantly they leapt into life, the strongest two barking like mad as they made chase on this hapless adventurer. Terrified, I opened the throttle, desperately hoping neither to fall foul of these potentially rabid beasts, nor to suffer the loose, increasingly deep drifts of soft sandy track that threatened to drag a tyre out of my control any moment. Handling soft sand had never been in my comfort zone, but Rover's jaws certainly were a long way from it, so off I sped down the track.

After some time, I suddenly realised that not only had I lost the canine meat-seeking missiles, but also my bearings. Strangely, no one was around to ask for directions, so I looked about for clues. The searing 40°C midday heat was in full force and the exertion from the dog chase had left me feeling like a boil-in-a-bag biker. I could do with some shelter and some refreshment, but first I needed to engage my brain and work out where to go.

I always half-loved and half-loathed these Crystal Maze moments, the real-life challenges where it really is down to just you to work out how you are going to overcome a practical problem. Often, there's some extra challenging factor like extreme heat, lack of water or baffling local language.

Fortunately, on this occasion, way over in the distance, I could just about make out a line of telegraph poles punctuating the horizon in a straight line. It looked as though at some point, if I just kept going, they would cross my path. Most likely, those telegraph poles were laid out along the main road, in which case I had cracked the mission. Somewhat prematurely congratulating myself for my problem-busting skills, I continued down the track with restored energy and had almost made it back to the intersection with the main road when I spotted the unmistakable figure of a well-built, lone and armed Sudanese soldier. He signalled for me to stop.

"What are you doing here?" he demanded before I could even kill the engine. "Don't you know this is a militarised zone? You shouldn't be here!" the soldier yelled, looking furious.

I gulped, feeling instantly alone and rather vulnerable in this otherwise deserted spot. So this had been why there had been no one about. How I wished at a moment like this some friendly faces would appear. Nevertheless, I realised that was unlikely given the circumstances. I was going to have to create some of my own.

I switched the bike off, removed my helmet and cracked out my ultimate weapon: a killer grin. "You have no idea how happy I am to see you!" I enthused, trying to mask my fear by adopting the manner of an ever so friendly but quite out of her depth English woman; a persona that always seems to come easily to me. Fortunately, the soldier visibly dialled down his annoyance when he realised that the offending motorcyclist was, in fact, a woman, and a shadow of amusement began to creep across his face. Perhaps it was childish but the benefits of this "Surprise, I'm a woman!" factor never failed to entertain me and, at times like this, I was especially grateful for it.

Keen to take advantage of this small window of mercy, I kept up the smiles and chatter, thanking the soldier profusely for flagging me down, describing my brush with death with Fangs and Co., and issuing a desperate plea for help with my onward orientation in as appealing a fashion as possible.

The soldier had nodded throughout my tale and now, apparently intent on aiding a damsel in distress, he was delighted to share the excellent news that in just a few metres (as was indeed perfectly clear to the naked eye), I would intersect with the main route and my onward adventures would, quite literally, be back on track.

Awash with relief that the soldier had cast aside his inner warrior for the hero, I thanked him profusely for his help, put the helmet back on and, with a dash of the throttle and a grin in my helmet, reflected on just how much I loved moments like this. With the wrong attitude, that encounter could have easily escalated into a nasty scene rather quickly, but with lots of liberally applied friendliness and respect, seasoned with a healthy dose of luck, it had all turned out okay. Maybe the world isn't such a bad place after all.

An hour or so later, I finally arrived at Wad Madani, a medium-sized city nestled on the banks of the Blue Nile. Known as the honeymoon destination of choice for romantic newlyweds, the place had a welcoming feel, with a relaxed atmosphere and colonial style buildings of faded grandeur lining the walkway along the river.

I was happy to arrive at my lodgings. The slightly crumbling but once undoubtedly beautiful hotel was now ravaged by the harsh Sudanese sun and partially reclaimed by nature. By the time I parked and unloaded the bike in a painted brick outhouse, wrestled my way through the rather overgrown garden with my luggage and hauled it into my simple room, I felt the overwhelming need for a siesta. Hypnotised by the gently whirring ceiling fan and the cool, calm of the hotel room, I stretched out on the bed and shut my eyes.

By the time I woke up, it was dark outside, and I was completely disoriented for time, location or what I was supposed to do next. A grumbling tummy reminded me that it was probably time for dinner.

Still struggling to shrug off my woolly mind, I gathered a small bag containing essentials, together with a Michelin map of North Africa, and headed out onto the street to find somewhere for a bite. A bone-jarring tuk-tuk ride later, I settled down at a restaurant, ordered some food and unfolded the map, which occupied most of my table. As I smoothed the crumpled paper, Sudan came more clearly into view, as did northern Ethiopia. I placed my finger on the location of Wad Madani and traced the route southeast down to the border, noticing there was only one town of any note along the route. I'd heard from other travellers as well as my guidebook that there was little to recommend this town. It was largely a staging post before the push to the border, so I decided it probably wasn't worth a special stop. On the other hand, if I were to keep going and cross the border into Ethiopia, the next obvious stop was Gondar.

I had heard a lot about this place from Eve, who I'd recently met in Aswan, back at the border between Egypt and Sudan. She told me about the historic buildings, the significance of the upcoming Timkat Festival to Ethiopia and the stunning location nestled at the base of the Simien Mountains. I couldn't wait to be there, and if I got there soon it would give me a chance to link up with some other overlanders I'd travelled with recently and who had been good company.

I quickly tallied the mileage from Wad Madani to Gondar and realised that at over 300 miles it would be a big chunk to ride in a single day. Usually, I only cover about 150 to 200 miles per day, a steady pace to enjoy the ride on my trusty 400cc Suzuki DRZ and take diversions and side routes as they came. Trying to travel more than 300 miles and include a border crossing, my first in Africa alone and without a fixer, seemed potentially a challenge too far. But then, as usual, my go-to ignorance-is-bliss mind-set of "How bad could it be?" clicked into gear and the decision was made.

My mind turned straight to practicalities. Covering this much mileage, managing the border crossings, always with the intention of finishing riding for the day before dusk, would mean hitting the road at first light. That would require waking up early, before any shops would likely be open or the hotel served breakfast.

With that in mind I needed to find some basic provisions on my trip back to the hotel in order to be ready for a day of self-sufficiency with bananas, bread, cheese, water and the like. As I rode back to the hotel in a tuk-tuk, I was surprised to find that there were no shops or street stalls visible at all. Usually, towns in this part of the world came alive at nightfall, and this was by no means a small backwater. Concluding that I must have just missed the obvious, I resolved to ask for help.

Back at the hotel, I headed up from the street, through the damp wilderness of the garden and into what would once have been a formal reception area. In these times though, it had been reduced to a rather forlorn, forgotten-looking area in which an elderly wooden school desk had been placed in the middle of the room. This desk hosted an ancient-looking desktop computer covered with a thick layer of dust that someone had haphazardly tried and failed to clean with a cloth, leaving a crisscross of slices through the residue. My luck was in though. A young man, presumably the receptionist, was sitting behind it inspecting the screen with a close eye. He smiled as I approached and gave me a look of bright-eyed efficiency that I hadn't seen in a while.

Encouraged, I enquired about where I might find a shop or stand to buy some basic provisions such as fruit and bread for the following day. "No problem at all," he replied with a cheerful nod, pushing back a red plastic patio chair and deftly hopping from behind his desk, all in a single motion. Without a further word, he paced through the garden and onto the pavement. Fully expecting him to stop and point me down the street to a nearby shop, I was somewhat surprised to see that instead he approached a low-slung, dark-coloured saloon car which was parked in front of the hotel. He got into the driver's side and beckoned for me to get in too.

"I guess something was lost in translation," I thought, as I tried to explain my request again. But the receptionist stood firm. "Sure," he cried, throwing up a hand as if none of this was a big deal at all. "I know a great market not far from here, let's go!" With that he pushed open the passenger side door, as if what had been holding me back up until then had been the burden of opening it.

Of course, the real burden was the battle going on in my mind. On the one hand, the heavily drilled 1980s warning of "Stranger danger" was blaring loudly in my mind, along with full-on comedic disaster siren sound effects. I didn't know this man from a bar of soap. By any good logic I should decline this invitation and yet my instincts, which had been barraged into shape by now, were telling me that this guy, although a stranger, could be trusted. They were also saying that moments like this were exactly what this trip was about.

So, I cast aside the obsession with certainty and control that my previous working life on the trading floor as a stockbroker had drilled into me and went with something a little more risky but potentially infinitely more valuable. I couldn't put my finger on it but an inner voice was telling me to do it, to get into the car. And so, I did.

We pulled out of the parking spot and into the moderate traffic of late evening in Wad Madani. Desert dust sparkled and shone in the car headlights as scents of heat, palm leaves and dates gave the night air a warm, exotic musk. The vibe in the car felt relaxed and the receptionist was eating some kind of seed or nut. This apparently needed to be shelled in the mouth, to discard the dry, slightly sour outer layer before getting to the kernel inside. As we drove north along the river, he opened his palm and offered me some.

I took a few and attempted the shelling process but predictably failed, the bitter taste of the outer shell drying my mouth of any saliva, leaving me struggling not to pull a face. This didn't go unnoticed by my observant companion, who chuckled at my experience while keeping his foot on the accelerator.

As we drove farther and farther away from the hotel, I began to notice that we were passing quite a few mini-mart style shops that would more than adequately serve my needs, but still we didn't stop. My mind began to race. What had I done getting into this car with a total stranger? No one in the world knew I was with him. Where on Earth were we going? Far, far out of town so that he could do goodness knows what with me? Surely any of those shops would have been more than adequate for what I needed? Had I massively misjudged the situation? With mounting fear, I began to suspect I had as he took a few turns, appearing to head away from the main drag. We passed a few more street sellers and still carried on.

My concerns continued to escalate as I reflected that, perhaps, exceptional circumstances called for exceptional measures. Just at that moment, the shiny chrome handle of the passenger door caught my attention. This gave me an idea. I've seen James Bond films, plenty of them in fact, even a few of the *Mission Impossibles*. Presented with a similar level of peril, I was quite sure that Tom Cruise would have little doubt about what to do next. The correct protocol had to be the "pull and roll": simply yank the car handle open and tip yourself full pelt lengthways onto the street (hopefully missing any oncoming traffic) and then roll to the side of the road before running for it. I took a breath, weighing the prospect. Sure, I may well injure myself in the process, I reasoned, trying to convince myself into action, but at least I'd win back some control in the situation (maybe a little wasn't such a bad thing after all). And I would escape my almost certain death at the hands of this assumed psychopath manning the driver's seat.

But then what? The less panicked side of my mind challenged. *So I roll out of the car, and probably get mangled by an oncoming truck. Then I'd lie at the side of the road for a moment in a terrible state. The driver will have noticed I'd just executed a death dive and would simply pull over to ask what the hell I was up to. Some plan!*

No, I reasoned, settling back in my chair, hands clamped beneath my thighs lest another wave of panic should take over. *Let's play the long game, stay calm and keep my wits about me and be ready for what comes next.*

A tense silence descended over the car as we continued on for another few blocks. At last, the car pulled to a halt and the driver proudly announced that we had arrived.

As I peered out of the window, I could see that just to the right stood the most beautiful and extensive selection of fresh fruits. Great hands of yellow bananas had been hung from the top left- and right-hand corners of this wooden roadside stand. A spread of highly polished apples, juicy oranges and various bright red and pink berries were neatly arranged in a beautiful patchwork of colour and texture on a waist-high display. I hadn't seen anything like it for many weeks and took a moment to feast my eyes. This fruit stand had certainly been worth the drive, and I could see now it was rightly a destination stop for any discerning purchaser. Relieved that it now seemed that the driver's plans appeared to have legitimised the extensive trip, I took a calming breath and turned to the business of buying what I needed.

With space very much a premium on the bike, I could only take the barest of essentials, so I asked the vendor for three bananas. The man looked slightly taken aback but then proceeded to take two massive hands of bananas from the stand and place them on his weighing scales. He then confirmed to me that this was indeed three kilos of bananas and quoted the price. My turn to be taken aback, I apologised for the confusion and confirmed that I had only wanted three bananas rather than three kilos of them. The vendor shook his head gravely. Slightly bewildered, I turned to the receptionist for clarification. He explained that all fruits are only sold by the kilo at this stand and so a minimum purchase would be one kilo of bananas. I tried to explain that I couldn't carry a kilo but before I could say much more, the receptionist quickly purchased the bananas from the vendor and presented them to me with a smile. "A gift," he offered graciously. "And is there anything else you would like? Some oranges perhaps, or grapes?" he asked, gesturing at the display.

At this point, panic began to flush my body again as the barely healed scar tissue of my experiences in Egypt came splitting open. I had lost count of the number of occasions, in a variety of locations in Egypt, where men had tried to take advantage of me, or seek an opportunity, or outright assault me. As a single foreign female on a motorcycle, I seemed to be viewed as something of a plaything.

Generally speaking, in Egyptian society a respectable woman should always be accompanied by a husband or male relative. As I failed this particular cultural test, it seemed to be the case where various men assumed I had no honour and therefore was fair game for whatever they liked. Sometimes this behaviour was dressed up in terms of providing a service or buying a gift of some sort, and then later expecting remuneration in some currency or other. At other times, charged-up young men considered they could just take what they wanted without the charade of a trade. This had been a very difficult reality to accept in Egypt and one which, after a particularly bad incident, had shaken my conviction about continuing with the trip.

What would the point be of continuing to ride through the continent to Cape Town if I was going to end up being chased the whole way and frightened of those I met?

Fortunately, I had been able to reflect on this for long enough to realise that, for some reason, I simply didn't believe this would be the case. My instincts told me that had been in part a run of bad luck and in part a harsh learning curve in cultural perspectives.

For example, what I had thought to have been modest and distinctly unsexy attire of long-sleeved, high-necked hiking shirt and khaki hiking trousers was, I discovered, very titillating in comparison to the vast and shapeless djellabas local women wore.

In a remote oasis in the western desert, a kind hotel owner had sensed my compounded ill-ease after many weeks of very difficult experiences and recommended a visit to the local clothing shop. Though bewildered by this recommendation at first, I sensed that he felt strongly about this course of action, so I followed his advice. With some guidance from the shopkeeper, I invested in a headscarf, and a djellaba six sizes bigger than anything I had ever worn. The previously predatory behaviour decreased dramatically as soon as I stepped out in my new clothes, and so I had hopefully concluded that this extremely difficult chapter was behind me. Back in Wad Madani, however, Banana-Gate now blew that theory apart. The all-too-familiar fear of that cat-and-mouse game was upon me once again as I battled to reason why this man would have done this, if not as a down payment on a favour to be called in later.

Flustered, I declined the receptionist's offer of any further fruity purchases. "No problem," he replied and gestured behind us to a glistening palace of a mini-mart, all shiny glass walls with immaculate shelving, the like of which I had also not seen in many months.

"Let us continue to the shop where you may choose what else you will need." Much as I was delighted to see this gorgeous emporium before me, I was desperately keen to avoid any further slippery business involving payments and increasing debts of favour, so I somewhat clumsily insisted, "Thank you, but I must pay for everything!"

My companion nodded and chuckled softly, gesturing that I should lead the way. I continued into the shop with fear-induced adrenalin pumping through my veins. I strode around the shop as though my life depended on it and gathered the things needed at double-quick speed. I paid up, this time thankfully without challenge, and we proceeded back to the car.

"All done?" he asked, reaching for the driver's side door.

"All done," I confirmed a little weakly, wondering what the next instalment of this uncomfortable drama had in store. As I dropped back into the saloon car, I reflected on my situation and tried to find some kind of orientation in the events of the evening. It did seem surprising that the receptionist had driven me this far and had played along with the provision purchasing process at an admittedly lovely fruit stand and shop, if he intended all along to abduct me to a distant location and do something horrible.

But perhaps the twist in the tale was actually going to come on our return to the hotel. Now that I was indebted to him, surely there had to be a nasty surprise in store. I resolved to try to act confident and reinitiate some light conversation on our drive, partly to keep my mind from going into overdrive, but also to help give the impression of confidence and substance just in case he thought I might be a pushover.

As the car pulled onto the street and we started to retrace our route back to the hotel I kicked off our chat with what I considered to be an easy conversation starter: "So, how long have you worked at the hotel?"

"Me?" he asked, before making a dismissive hand motion. "Oh no, I don't work at the hotel!"

"*What?!*" I blurted, instantly failing in my endeavour to remain cool, calm and collected. "But I saw you behind the reception desk; you were working on the hotel's computer!" I reasoned, horrified to realise that not only was this guy not who I thought he was, most likely he was some kind of deviant fraudster who had—what?—broken into the hotel to lure unsuspecting foreigners?! What on Earth was going on?

The man simply laughed as he explained, "No, I am the local tax inspector, everyone hates me! I know the manager of this hotel, so I just went there this evening to check my email at his computer and then you entered. And so now, here we are."

My eyes grew wide as wild thoughts did laps around my mind. So, if this guy wasn't even working at the hotel in question, then this car trip to the shops couldn't even be explained away as being some kind of extended courtesy service of the hotel! Thank goodness he had only bought me bananas, but still, this was surely not going to end well. I resolved that, upon arrival back at the hotel, I'd need to be very strong.

A few minutes later the hotel came into view. With a huge jolt, the front end of the car mounted the pavement as we came to a stop. The tax inspector and I clambered out of the car and walked up to the entrance of the hotel. As he turned to face me, I braced myself for a quid pro quo that I knew I wasn't going to like.

"And so, here we are," he ventured, "safely back at the hotel. You have a very long journey ahead of you tomorrow. Please ride very safely and inshallah, you will arrive well at your destination. It has been a pleasure, and now I must return home. I wish you a very good night". With that, he did a very small bow, turned on his heel and began to walk down the street.

I was in shock and quite dumbfounded. My mind was racing, trying to make sense of what had just happened. Most importantly, I was beginning to process the hitherto unthinkable that this man had actually just been very generous with his time, efforts and even money for no sinister ulterior motive at all. He had helped, apparently wanting nothing in return. This blew my mind and horrified me all at once.

This gentleman who, I now realised, had never told me his name, nor to my shame, had I asked it, had just been so kind while for much of the time I had suspected him of the worst. I feared I had been far from gracious and at times, actually rude. Mortified but realising it wasn't too late to make amends, I chased after him with my groceries still in tow and called out after him, "Excuse me!"

Thankfully he stopped in his tracks and turned around. "Firstly," I started, faltering slightly for the right words, "I'm so sorry, I just wanted to thank you properly for the generosity and kindness you have just shown me. You have really gone out of your way to help me here and I really do appreciate it, so I wanted to just make sure you knew that. Really—thank you. "The man nodded his head and smiled patiently.

"Secondly," I went on, "I am so sorry, but I realise I don't know your name. What is it, please?"

He smiled again, gently laid his hand over his heart and replied, "I am Ahmed."

I returned his smile and nodded. I took a breath. There was something else I just needed to understand. "Thank you, Ahmed. One other thing, and again, I'm sorry to be even asking you this question, but like I say, you have been so extraordinarily kind. Why is it that you helped me so much? I have never known such incredible generosity from a stranger."

Ahmed smiled and shrugged gently. "You are a guest in my country. I must make you feel welcome so I wanted to help you if I could. That is my pleasure. And please, just give away any bananas you cannot carry to someone else. It will be all right. Have a safe journey now, good night." He gave one last patient smile and nod before turning and walking down the street, leaving me to think.

How glad I was that I had met this man. I was so grateful not only for his generosity but also for the lesson Ahmed had reminded me of: how beautiful it is to give with no expectation of receiving, and to treat the strangers with care.

This interaction had been the stuff of spine-tingling marvels. It was exactly why I set off on this road trip in the first place: to embrace the uncertainties and to slough off the protective shell I had worn so rigidly throughout my city life. That shell had been developed as a survival mechanism but kept me numbed from living wholeheartedly the entire time I wore it.

It felt really good to allow myself to take it off, to be open once again to the world around me and rediscover the real beauty of so many within it. Ahmed had demonstrated so vividly that the things of greatest value in life definitely can't be priced up on a Bloomberg terminal. Greed isn't good, and generosity rocks.

As I stood on the pavement, marvelling at the evening's events, and watching Ahmed walking away, becoming a smaller and smaller figment in the landscape, I realised something else: not only had he not been the receptionist at the hotel, but it would appear that the car hadn't belonged to him either! I would have to just thank the universe for the use of the petrol this time.

About the author:

Claire Elsdon is a recovering banker turned biker, who in 2012 quit her stockbroking job to ride a motorcycle the length of Africa. Having lived for the best part of a decade immersed in the highly competitive, often brutal world of the trading floor, Claire was keen to re-examine her beliefs about how the world really worked and what her role should be.

Along the way, remarkable encounters with strangers showed her the priceless beauty of a life lived with courage, community and kindness firmly at its centre. At the same time, a serendipitous voluntary placement in Malawi confronted her with the devastatingly high accident rate amongst motorcyclists including motorcycle taxi drivers and their passengers. Tasked with the challenge of solving the problem, Claire designed and ran her first ever "Love Your Motorcycle" maintenance and road safety class in 2013 and, in so doing, discovered a way of serving her purpose and spreading joy in the process.

Since then, Claire founded a movement called *Pikilily* and moved to Mwanza, Tanzania in 2016 to establish a community-based organisation there called *MJ Piki* (which means "brave motorcycling woman" in Kiswahili). *MJ Piki* trains local women to ride motorcycles and empowers them to earn an income by serving their communities as safe motorcycle taxi operators. In addition, these women voluntarily run safe motorcycling training sessions for the community, reducing crash rates and gently challenging gender stereotypes.

In 2019, Claire moved back to the UK with her family. The fine women of *MJ Piki* continue their work and to date have trained over 3,000 men, women and children in motorcycle safety.

Website: pikilily.com
FaceBook: Claire Elsdon, @MJPikiMwanza and @pikilily
Twitter: @Pikilily_tz and @Clairebikeabout

Far from Home

by Geoff Hill

"Every day is a journey, and the journey itself is home."

—*Matsuo Basho*

I've ridden an Enfield from Delhi to Belfast, Triumphs from Chile to Alaska and around Australia, and a BMW around the world. But I still remember the single happiest moment of my motorcycling life.

It was halfway through riding the 16,500 miles of the Pan-American Highway from Chile to Alaska with former Isle of Man TT racer Clifford Paterson, who had decided that our journey was a recreation of the ramblings of Don Quixote and his faithful sidekick Sancho Panza, so I'd be called "Don" and he "Sancho."

Then he changed it to "Pancho" because he thought it sounded better, just after christening my Triumph Tiger 955i and his Aprilia Pegaso as "Tony" and "April", respectively.

So far, things had gone swimmingly. Well, apart from Tony's engine cutting out mysteriously all the way through the Atacama Desert with what later turned out to be fuel contaminated by diesel. That was a bit nerve-racking, but not as bad as when I crashed in Colombia, almost killing myself and almost wrecking the bike.

With us both patched up, we limped on through Central America.

Late one afternoon, almost at the border between Guatemala and Mexico, we stopped for a drink at a roadside cantina before plunging into the usual inferno of chaos. While idly leafing through the guidebook, I almost choked on my coffee when I noticed that due to terrorism in the Chiapas region, journalists were not allowed in. Not only that, but you needed your birth certificate to bring a vehicle into the country.

When we got to the passport office on the Mexican side, I wrote "Manager" in the space where it said "Occupation," and just prayed to the Lord and the Seven Sainted Sisters of Constantinople that no one would ask for my birth certificate that was 8,000 miles away in my study. Fortunately, no one did, and I emerged an hour later and $29 poorer, but with the windscreen sticker that allowed 15 days to make it to the US border.

However, disaster was just about to strike.

Clifford went in for his turn and came out after half an hour. "They won't let me cross the border. No way, no how," he said grimly.

My heart sank. "Why not?"

"Well, you know the way I had to leave without the original bike registration document because it hadn't arrived from Swansea?"

"Aye, but you have a letter saying you're legally entitled to use the bike. It's worked at every border so far."

"Well, not at this one. I've tried begging, I've tried pleading, I've tried being calm and reasonable, I've tried bursting into tears, and I've tried pointing out that we're raising money for orphans. Nothing's worked."

"Did you try hinting at a bribe?"

"I did. I asked if there was any special payment that could be made for temporary transit, and he said no. He's not shifting. It's original documents, or nothing. I'm stuffed."

He went across the road, found a Canadian-Spanish speaker who had been waiting seven hours for a bus, and went back in to try again. An hour later, they came out with good news of sorts: the Customs official would accept a faxed copy of the document. I looked at my watch. It was 1am at home. I hauled out my BT charge card, and from a phone box called Clifford's mate Yannick.

Incredibly, he was still up, and promised to go to Clifford's office first thing in the morning, see if the DVLA had finally sent the original documents, and fax them.

In the meantime, since we could neither go back to Guatemala or on to Mexico, we rode across the road to a ramshackle building with a peeling hotel sign out front.

"Welcome to limbo, or possibly purgatory," said Clifford as the proprietor showed us into a bare cell with a single bulb, a concrete floor and a resident ant colony. We settled in for the longest night of our lives.

Dawn broke to reveal the worst possible news from Yannick. The registration document had never arrived in the licensing office in Swansea. Like us, it was lost in limbo. Even worse, today was, naturally, a Saturday, so the chances of anyone doing anything about it before Monday were nil. Even then, it would take Swansea weeks, or even months, to chase down a replacement document.

Since we didn't have weeks or months, the trip was over for Clifford; after all we had gone through together, I couldn't believe it. We sat in the sun outside our two-bit hotel, sick at heart and wondering what to do.

"What if Yannick scans a document from another vehicle, changes the details to April's and faxes a copy of that?" I said.

"No way. If we get caught at that lark, it'll mean jail for us both, and I don't fancy spending years in a Mexican jail, thanks very much," he said.

We sat there racking our brains for a solution.

"Listen," he said at last, "it's Saturday morning. There'll be a new Customs official on today. I'll tear a spare page out of the Carnet, which looks official and has my name and all the bike details on it, and pretend that's the registration document."

"That's never going to work Pancho, those guys aren't stupid."

"I know, but I can't think of anything else."

He went back to our room, returned with the page from the Carnet, and walked across the road to the Customs office. I had never seen him look so drawn and weary. His endless optimism, it seemed, had finally run into a brick wall. It was so ironic, after all the tough border crossings we'd been through, that the very last one before The Big Easy of the United States would prove impassable.

I sat for an hour as the sun and the heat rose, until the door of the office finally opened and Clifford walked out, his face impassive. About halfway across the street he could no longer contain himself. Bursting into a huge grin, he produced the elusive sticker from behind his back and held it aloft.

"Get on the bikes," he said. "We have to get out of here before he changes his mind or calls the boss."

We ran back to the room, threw everything in our bags in seconds, started the bikes and leapt on them. I followed Clifford as we rode past the Customs post, my heart pounding. All it would take was one phone call, and we would be hauled back and jailed for attempted fraud.

We raced down the road. For the first five miles I kept glancing over my shoulder, sure I'd see flashing lights and hear the growing wail of sirens. But there was nothing. I glanced nervously ahead, convinced that a Customs official disguised as a tree would leap out from the hedgerow, demand our documents and then have us strung up by the dongles. But there was nothing except the open road stretching all the way to the USA.

As we rode along under the endless blue sky, passing farmers working in the fields, their wives hanging washing and their children playing in gardens bright with bougainvillea, I was overcome with such a sense of relief and well-being that, for the rest of my life, if anyone asked me what happiness was, it was this day.

We climbed through pine forests and dappled glades, each with a resident shepherdess or woodcarver, and by nightfall found a motel by a river.

It turned out to be a love hotel, with a steady stream of couples arriving nervous and leaving happy. I suppose we should have suspected something when we saw how many mirrors there were in the room. Not to mention the rotating food hatch in the outside wall, like a secular version of those found in closed nunneries.

And then, the evening brought good news, and bad, from home. The good was that *Way to Go*, my last book, had been reprinted again because of US demand, and that my brother Trevor would be joining us on a rented Harley for a week along the west coast of the States.

And the bad news was that my wife Cate would not, as we'd originally hoped. She was, as we had increasingly feared, too snowed under by work to get away. I had thought many times during the long hard slog up through South America, of what I would feel when I saw her again in Los Angeles. It would, I had imagined, be the same as the feeling I had every time I saw her after any absence: as if all the love in the world had been squeezed into a heart too small to contain it.

So now I would not see her in California after all, but we would be together again, before sooner became later, and I would have her for the rest of my days. In the border crossing of life, that was worth all the stickers in the world.

For me, the next few days, as we rode the long miles through Mexico to the US border, were in many ways the most heroic of the trip. Men of steel, we rose at dawn and sped north, with flies in our teeth, a song in our hearts and the wind in our hair. Well, except for Clifford, who had lots of wind but no hair.

We were only days from the border with the land of freeways which, unlike in Mexico, lived up to their name and the land of big rock candy mountains, sugar lump trees and ice-cream soda fountains. I could hardly wait.

But I would have to. The more impatient we became, and the faster we wanted to go, the more crucial it became that we slow down and take it easy. I knew only too well from Colombia, where I had been thinking that we had to get to Cali before dark rather than the corner in front of me, of the potentially fatal consequences of thinking too far down the road. So, we curbed our impatience and made up the miles by starting early and finishing late.

At sunrise, we passed trucks loaded with peasants on their way to a day's work in the fields, just as their fathers and grandfathers had done, and at sunset, we passed them again coming home. Nothing stopped us as we ate up the miles day after endless day. Nothing, that is, until April refused to start at a filling station.

"Bloody battery again," muttered Clifford, hauling it out and setting off to the side in order to find a mechanic with some acid. No, the other sort.

"Don't know why you can't get yourself a nice reliable Triumph," I called cheerily after him.

He seemed to take it well, apart from the spanner which missed my head by an inch.

Sadly, there was no acid to be found in the entire village, so we rounded up a team of willing volunteers for a push start, and for the rest of the day, April was left running any time we stopped briefly for a drink.

That night, we found a hotel on a hill to aid in getting April restarted, and Clifford went looking for a charger, only to return with the news that not one was to be found in the whole of Mexico.

He flung himself on the bed in disgust and made the mistake of switching on CNN news. On the screen, presenters were telling us that shopkeepers were rioting in Nepal. Below them, for those who had trouble concentrating to the end of a whole spoken sentence, the same story was summarised in subtitles. Below that again, a continuous stream of words across the bottom of the screen about

20

how Belgium had defeated Russia at tennis, Michael Schumacher had won a Grand Prix and Tiger Woods had done a bungee jump. It was an irrelevant broadcast for the uninterested, and a world away from the reality we had experienced every minute of the day for the past two months.

Next morning, we started April with a push down a hill and, that afternoon, had coffee in a plaza, listening to the cantina owner's tape deck, when it suddenly struck me how similar Mexican rap was to Northern Ireland politics: the same words repeated over and over again, ad nauseum. And that gave me the disturbing and deeply meaningful vision of Ian Paisley wearing basketball boots with the laces undone, baggy trousers and a baseball cap on backwards, muttering darkly into a microphone, "No I say no, no, no, I say no, I say no, Ulster says no, I say no, I say no surrender, *yeah.*"

It was clearly time to move on. I drained my coffee, we got back on the bikes, and by evening were climbing into the mountains, stopping for the night at a handful of log cabins on the edge of a canyon. The canyon was so deep that I rose the following morning to see if I could see the bottom while standing on the edge as the first glimmerings of sunrise crept over the edge of the world. Below was an impenetrable darkness where mist ghosted into what I imagined as Xanadu, where cities twisted and vanished even as they were born. As their walls and turrets burned up in the gathering light, their inhabitants came whirring up out of the darkness, metamorphosing as they rose into hummingbirds. At my feet, they sipped from the yellow flowers growing along the lip of the canyon, their wings invisible.

As I watched, enthralled, there came a sound from behind that almost made me fall off the edge. I turned to find an ancient Tarahumara woman swaddled in an indeterminate number of bright clothes. Above the chaos of faded colour, her face was like a piece of sun-dried driftwood you'd find on a beach and take home to wax and polish for no other reason than the beauty of its shape and texture.

"I am sorry, sir, I did not mean to startle you," she said in slow Spanish. "I come up here sometimes, for the beauty of the morning. And because I do not sleep well since my husband died."

"I am sorry to hear that. When did he die?" I said in my equally slow Spanish.

"It was 44 years ago. I am a little lonely these days because my daughter has not been to see me for a while. She has moved away."

"Where to?"

"To the next valley. They're getting more rain than we do these days. Maybe they are more Catholic."

She sighed and began to walk back up the path into the woods. I walked with her, for no other reason than that it seemed the right thing to do. Her home was a tiny log cabin with smoke curling up through a hole in the roof. Out front lay a kitten the colour of dust, and three dogs so small they should have just clubbed together and become one. I stopped, breathing hard, since at this altitude oxygen molecules are only one a penny, and she beckoned me in.

Inside, a black pot of beans bubbled over a fire on the dirt floor, in the centre of which stood a rough table and chairs. On the wall hung a ramshackle lino print of Christ, his eyes cast up to heaven as if someone had just said something incredibly obvious to him. Perched on the frame of the print was a hotel from a Monopoly game set. The only light was through the hole in the roof and the open door, and apart from the occasional mewing of the kitten, there was not a sound in the world.

"I have been living here since before aeroplanes began. When I saw the first aeroplane, I had already been here half my life," she said. "How many days is it to where you live?"

I tried to work it out, and settled on a couple of weeks, since I had stopped thinking in terms of aeroplanes.

"Two weeks? That is a long way. What is your home called?"

"Ireland."

Her eyes grew vague, "I have heard there is a place across the sea," she said as the kitten strolled in, stretched all four legs in turn and sniffed the beans in the pot, but they were not ready yet. Annoyed, it chased the smallest dog out the door. The old woman turned to me and took my hand.

"May things go well with you, sir. You are far from home," she said.

"And with you," I said, squeezing her hand and walking away down the path.

Back in our log cabin, I found Clifford stirring.

"Get up Pancho, you lazy bastard," I said. "We have to be in Alaska by teatime."

We fell from the mountains to the desert again. Once we passed a milk lorry in which the sunlight exploded off the serried ranks of the silver churns, then from the golden heads of the father and his two sons out front. In the burning heat, their pale skin and blond hair created such a contrasting visual shock that I wanted to stop and check the colour balance on my vision.

They were, in fact, Mennonites, members of the sect founded in the 16th century by Dutchman Menno Simons and who had been going off in a huff ever since. In 1776 they had been granted a home in the Ukraine by Catherine the Great. A century later, ordered to join the army, 100,000 of them went off in a huff to Canada. When the Canadians insisted that they send their children to state schools, they went off in a huff to Mexico where they lived in a community with more banks per acre than anywhere else in the country.

We came upon their dairy and stopped to take a look. There, women in long dresses, their heads bowed, stood stirring pools of milk, the liquid light lapping on the underside of their chins. The single ones wore white headscarves and the married ones black, which didn't indicate that their Mennonite husbands were exactly bundles of fun. In one of the rooms, a woman made quilts while her son played with a laptop. It was a strange vision, of both purity and uncertainty. Were they happy, or sad? It was impossible to tell, for they are among the most silent people on Earth.

We crept away and rode north.

By nightfall, we were in Chihuahua, home of dogs so ugly they are best suited as guide dogs for the blind. A friend had one once that looked like a tumour covered in threadbare grey Dralon. Thankfully, we were unlikely to see any, since they are both nocturnal and wild, roaming the desert in packs looking for coyote to supper on. When found, a coyote was likely to just roll over and die from the embarrassment of being cornered by a bunch of Dralon swatches.

We were riding aimlessly down a dusty street when we found a hotel painted in a shocking shade of pink. So pink, the street would have been better named Blancmange Boulevard. At check-in, the clerk handed me a form asking, "How did you learn of our hotel?"

"From arriving outside one minute ago," I wrote carefully.

In the bathroom, the delights included a small bottle of viscous yellow liquid bearing the legend 'The Original Ma Evans Herbal Shampoo', above which was a line drawing of a matriarch resembling the great-grandmother of the bride of Frankenstein. I switched on the air conditioner and, to the accompaniment of a noise like a thousand asthmatic bees roused from their slumber, the room slowly filled with cold dust. I was going to like Chihuahua.

Meanwhile, Clifford went out looking yet again for a battery charger. After he returned empty-handed, we walked the streets until we found a restaurant that fulfilled all three of our criteria: it was cheap, there were people inside, and they were alive.

At the next table, a birthday celebration was underway and, on a small stage, a mariachi band was playing Johnny Mathis's *When a Child is Born*.

"Bit early for Christmas, isn't it?" I said to the waitress.

"No, late from last Christmas. This is Mexico," she replied.

"God, she's lovely," said Clifford, going off to take her photograph for the book of Pan-American beauties he planned to publish after the trip.

That night, as we were settling down to sleep, there came a knock at the hotel room door. It was Isidro, the boy from the garage down the road where Clifford had inquired about a charger. He had cycled 10 miles home after work, borrowed his father's, and cycled back with it in the dark.

"I will collect it in the morning," he said. "Just leave it at reception."

It was yet another of the countless acts of spontaneous goodwill we had been offered every day of the journey, and what I had learned on all my motorbike journeys. People are essentially good the world over, especially if you also travel with a good heart and keep smiling... especially at border crossings.

As Clifford set to work connecting the charger, I looked idly at the map and suddenly realised we were a mere 300 miles from the border. Later I lay awake, too excited to sleep, like a child on Christmas Eve.

Clifford woke at dawn, reconnected April's freshly charged battery, pressed the starter button, and was met with a silence broken only by the mocking call of the jays in the tree above. Until we found a new battery, it was nothing a push start wouldn't cure, and it hardly mattered, compared to the fact we only had a few more hours in Latin America.

No more wondering what the Spanish for "battery charger" was, and no more octane booster, the last of which was added to a final tankful of fuel, and the bottle ceremoniously dumped in the nearest bin.

No more giant potholes lurking under flooded roads, no more mountains of mud, no more three-hour border crossings in the searing heat, and no more native protests, unless the California Gay Vegetarians Against the Bomb were on the rampage again.

Not to mention luxuries such as toilets with paper and sinks with plugs.

For once, I didn't mind push-starting April, and soon after we were first in the queue for the home of Pancho Villa, or Pancho Villa's villa, if you prefer. In fact, we were the queue.

If the earnest Emiliano Zapata was the Ernie Wise of the Mexican Revolution in 1911, Pancho Villa was the Eric Morecambe. A cattle rustler turned brilliantly innovative bandit, he refused to take anything seriously, travelled with a film crew in tow and allegedly arranged his battles to ensure they took place in the best light for filming. He eventually retired to this 50-room mansion around which his widow Luc Coral showed visitors until her death in 1981.

These days it was run by the tourist office, which had, with no obvious sign of irony, put up signs all over the place banning revolutionary activities such as eating, smoking, drinking, shooting, letting children run wild and sitting on the furniture. Inside, his bed was in the sad state of repair you'd expect from a man who fathered 25 children by several women. But the bed wasn't quite as sad as the Dodge limousine he was driving when he was gunned down during a family vendetta in 1923. The limo sat in the courtyard with a meter on the dashboard showing that the battery was still charged. They sure built them in those days.

Villa, suspecting that he might be killed, had already built a magnificent mausoleum in Chihuahua where he wanted to be buried, but as he was murdered 200 miles away in Parral, they buried him there instead. Two years later, someone dug him up and cut off his head. Today, his head is lost, his body is in Mexico City and his mausoleum is empty. There was a photograph of it in the Chihuahua tourist brochure, accompanied by the inspired caption: "Mausoleum where Pancho Villa is not buried."

We emerged, blinking in the sunlight. The thermometer on the wall read 104°F. I looked at my watch, it was 10am, and time to break for the border.

Then, as if in a last-ditch bid to stop us from making it on the final 100 miles, we were met by a plague of giant caterpillars scurrying across the road. By swerving carefully, we managed to get away with only squashing an estimated 568,432 of them. Then a cloud of primrose yellow butterflies appeared on the scene to do their bit, bouncing off the windshields with abandon. There would be a few tears around the butterfly campfire that night, I feared. Or whatever it is that butterflies do in the evenings.

The miles sped away, and before long we were tearing off our once-precious Mexican stickers and sitting in the queue for American passport control, edging ever closer to the Stars and Stripes fluttering in the breeze on the other side.

"After months of South and Central American border crossings, you don't know how glad I am to see you guys," I said to the border guard.

"I bet you are," he said as he inspected our passports then handed them back.

"What? No three-hour wait? No demands to walk five miles back into Mexico and get copies in triplicate of my dog licence?" I joked.

"Nope. None of those. Welcome to the US", he grinned.

Thank God, I thought. I don't even have a dog.

I started Tony and followed Clifford down Main Street USA, a smile on my face as wide as Fifth Avenue and exactly the same feeling in my heart. I imagined, as every dusty refugee who ever entered this Promised Land, to forge a shining future of his very own brave new world. I'll tell you how deeply moved I was: even the sight of a Walmart brought a tear to my eye.

You see, like love, travel, especially travel by motorbike, makes the ordinary seem extraordinary. From the moment you wake up in the morning and realise all you have to do is to pack your gear and ride off down the road into the deliciously unknown future, without a clue what the day will bring, until the moment you find a little place to stay, somewhere to eat and grab that first cold beer of the day.

Apart from the beer, motorbike adventures are like when I was a boy, when every day was an adventure and a new beginning. Because when we are children, we are reborn every morning, but when we grow older, a little of us dies every night, killed by *what ifs* and *if onlys*, by mortgages and bills, dry rot and rising damp. When we travel, we are children again.

And we also realise that all the stuff we accumulate in our adult life, which we think defines us, doesn't at all. On a motorbike you can only carry very little, and yet have a remarkable time, unencumbered by regrets and concerns. On a motorcycle, every day is an adventure and a new beginning.

And in every moment of those days, I am still a boy on a bike.

About the author:

Geoff Hill is a critically acclaimed author and award-winning journalist based in Belfast. He's won multiple national and international awards for feature and travel writing. In a previous life, he was Ireland's most capped volleyball player.

He writes a weekly motorbike column for the *Daily Mirror* which is a desperate attempt to disguise the fact that he knows bugger all about motorbikes. He's also the editor of *Microlight Flying* magazine, in spite of the fact that he knows even less about aeroplanes than motorbikes.

He's the author of 18 books, including three novels and bike adventure books about epic journeys from India to the UK, Chile to Alaska, around Australia and around the world recreating the journey of Carl Stearns Clancy, the first to take a motorbike around the world over 100 years ago, complete with the original boots Clancy wore on that trip.

He's either won or been shortlisted for a UK Travel Writer of the Year Award nine times. He's also a former Irish, European and World Travel Writer of the Year.

Geoff lives with his wife Cate, a cat called Cat, a hammock and the ghost of a flatulent Great Dane. His hobbies include volleyball, flying, motorbikes, tennis, skiing and worrying about the price of fish.

Facebook: geoff.hill.792
Twitter: @ghillster
Geoff's books are all available on *Amazon*

The Bi-Polar Pole and Joey the Camel Collider

by Spencer James Conway
with Cathy Nel

"There is no failure, except in no longer trying."

—Anon

It is difficult to imagine life getting any stranger than standing in the middle of a South American desert with 5,000 people cheering, while our last-minute recruited Polish cameraman sprinted across a sand dune, naked, followed by half of the Argentinian police force.

Cathy and I were styling it up, as usual, in a top-quality hotel, "hotel" being a ridiculous compliment to this establishment. We were in San Juan, a modern city with wide, tree-lined avenues irrigated by canals, from which it derives its nickname, "Oasis Town". The city is in a fertile valley surrounded by rocky, mountainous desert.

It was such a smart city that it was quite a struggle to find a place so bad, but when costs demand it, it can be done. Our room was a small outhouse on the roof of a Hotel El Dodgy, which I presume used to be a storage or laundry room. The only other use for the roof area was for the washing line, where the decidedly World War II-like sheets and blankets were hung. For some unknown reason there were also 12 truck tyres, five shop mannequins with various limbs missing, and a cardboard cut-out of Queen Victoria. It was waterlogged and lying on the concrete floor, as though Her Majesty had been assassinated.

Our humble abode had bedbugs galore, cockroaches, wet blankets (common, and my one nightmare), no toilet, no running water, and an inebriated, rusted fan hanging dangerously from the ceiling. It was close to 35°C, and despite the altitude and heat we slept well. There was also a rat in the room, who had decided that one corner was his hangout. I thought that rats were supposed to constantly run around—surely the word "scurrying" was coined especially for them. So, it was rather disconcerting when he just sat in the corner, staring us down. It rather freaked me out. I solved the problem by imagining him with red square sunglasses and I named him "Yasser Ara-rat." I did not really mind him after that.

That was a psychological technique that Cathy taught me. She told our children that if they were ever scared of an animal, they should give it a cute name. Five-year-old Feaya had a run-in (luckily, not a full mugging) with a spider and a pre-existing fear of hairy arachnids, courtesy of her uncle and grandmother. Feaya's fear also made her run and hide till the spider was caught and ejected outside. However, as soon as she named spiders, "Charlottes," she was fine.

We woke up sweating like miners and nauseous as novice seamen. We had food poisoning, and Cathy had come off worse. I was not remotely surprised, as the previous evening we had bought some dodgy street food that was about 300 years old. The meat was green, but the hue was hidden well in the dark. Luckily for me, Cathy had been hungrier, and my eyesight better. There was no way she was doing anything but remaining horizontal today.

The problem was that this was not just any day. The world-famous Dakar Rally was coming through. The day before, I had managed to secure a wonderful position with the world's press and camera people.

We'd be in the exclusive press area, situated on a towering rocky outcrop with a flat, high plateau above a spectacular river crossing.

For those who have been living on a different motorbiking planet, the Dakar is an off-road endurance event, with heavy emphasis on the word "endurance." The terrain traversed is much tougher than conventional rallies and the vehicles used are typically true off-road machines, rather than modified road vehicles. The race involves huge sand dunes, mud, camel grass, rocks, boulders and erg. (Google time, I was not clearing my throat). Unlike many rallies where much of the route can be blocked off and monitored, the Dakar throws in other hazards including terrorists and camels. Both are dangerous, believe me.

Let me tell you a quick story. Bear with me, as the relevance of Joey Evans will become clear. A famous Dakar rider and friend, South African Joey Evans, broke his back in a devastating motorbike accident in October 2007. With two races left in a regional off-road racing championship, and his sights set on a win, Joey crashed at the start of the race and was ridden over by almost the entire field of racers. Teeth shattered and his back broken, Joey woke up spitting out his own teeth and unable to feel his legs. Two specialists agreed that he would never walk. The third wanted to fuse his back to take pressure off his spinal cord. But the specialist also gave him hope. His spinal cord was not severed but was severely compressed and there was a chance he could regain some movement. As it was, Joey was paralysed from the neck down.

But the married man and father of four girls was not ready to give up. He then spent two years enduring intense recovery and rehabilitation. Joey not only learned to walk again, he even got back on his motorcycle. Well, he was lifted onto his bike, by incredulous friends.

This was not enough for Joey. He decided that anything was possible and even with his broken body he believed that it was only his mind that could hold him back. He set his sights on entering the Dakar and told only his wife.

"I saw myself crossing the finish line. I envisioned the end, repeatedly. This created a mind-set that it had already happened. I just had to follow the path that would get me there."

31

But that path was studded with setbacks. To qualify for the Dakar, you need to submit a CV with a set number of long-distance rallies and endurance races, at least one of which must be on the international circuit. To meet the criteria and to get ready for the race, by 2013 Joey was competing in 500 and 1,000 kilometre races. It had taken him many years to get back to that level but in 2014 disaster struck again. Joey hit a cow at high speed, in KwaZulu Natal. This is where the reader goes, "For God's sake!" or "I think someone's telling him something." Joey ended up in hospital, this time with broken ribs and a shattered arm. The recovery would take six months.

"It was devastating. When I woke up and could feel my legs, I knew I could handle anything, but I still questioned everything I was doing. What was I putting my family through? And for what?" I asked my wife and she said that "I need to be me." A year later Joey was back at Amageza, a 5,000 kilometre rally through Botswana and Northern Cape. He followed that up with his international race in Morocco, sent his entry in to Dakar and was accepted. Now he just needed 1.1-million Rand. Joey, being Mr Motivator, raised the money, entered and completed the Dakar in 2017 - 10 years after his initial accident - and is a total inspiration, to never, ever, give up.

If that was not enough, God had other plans. In his next rally Joey hit a camel. Camels, in case you have not met one, are big and hard and Joey came off worse, with a split head and superbly spectacular multi-purple bruising. The camel had the hump, (sorry) but Joey, like the superman he is, finished the rally. Once again, the man recovered. And in his next rally, he hit an elephant. OK. That last sentence is false, but I think you get the gist.

Joey has written an amazing book, brilliantly entitled *From Para to Dakar*. It is almost irrelevant what pursuit/sport/job, etc. Joey undertook. He speaks to everyone about overcoming obstacles in life, no matter what they are. He is also extremely humble, which makes the potency of his never-say-die attitude even more powerful. It is inspirational, dedicated people like Joey that are the only ones who will get a sniff of this amazing event; a rally that was started by the "interesting" Thierry Sabine.

Now, let's get a glimpse of what Joey bit off. What a challenge!

In 1976 Thierry got hopelessly lost in the Tenere Desert while competing in the Cote Abidjan/Nice Rally and decided that the desert would be a spectacular location for a rally. He chose a route from Paris to Dakar in Senegal and the world's most difficult rally was born. One hundred and eighty-two vehicles entered the inaugural rally, starting in Paris, with 74 battered machines surviving the 10,000 kilometre trip to the Senegalese capital. Cyril Neveu holds the distinction of being the event's first winner, riding a Yamaha motorcycle. (Yay-maha—my favourite brand since I was two months old.) The event rapidly grew in popularity, with 216 vehicles taking part in 1980, and 291 in 1981.

Tragically, Sabine was killed when his Ecureuil helicopter crashed into a dune in Mali during a sudden sandstorm on January 14, 1986. Also killed was the singer-songwriter Daniel Balavione, helicopter pilot Francois Xavier Bagnoud, and journalist Nathalie Odent. Sabine's ashes were later scattered at the Lost Tree in Niger, which the rally thereafter described as the "Arbre Thierry Sabine." Many Dakar racers go there to pay respects.

Sabine is by no means the only tragedy. Since 1979, 76 have died in the Dakar. Among the 31 competitor fatalities, 23 were motorcycle-related, five in cars, one in a truck crash, and two competitors have died as a result of local rebel conflict. The Dakar has received criticism because of its high mortality rate, with the *Vatican Paper*, of all the famous journals, describing the event as the "bloody race of irresponsibility." The event understandably received criticism in the 1988 race, when three Africans were killed in collisions with race vehicles.

Wind forward to 2008, where the rally was to start in Lisbon. The event was cancelled amid fears of terrorist attacks in Mauritania following the killing of four French tourists in 2007. There were also unsubstantiated reports of riders getting shot at in Mauritania. A bullet is not really a good thing for any motorcyclist's future. These rumours ended being properly substantiated, in the most horrific of ways.

On January 13, 1991, Charles Cabannes, a support truck driver for the Citroen-Factory Team was shot dead by rebels at the side of the road in the small village of Kadeouane. His co-driver, Joel Guyomarch, escaped with a superficial bullet wound. The killing was not claimed by any rebel organisation but was believed to be related to the conflict between the Malian Army and Tuareg Rebels. Organisers cancelled the following two rounds, and the Malian Army escorted the competitors through the country.

On January 3, 1996, while attempting to complete the Fifth Stage, Laurent Gueguen, driving the Mercedes support truck, got caught up in a conflict between the Moroccan Army and the Polisario Front rebels. Trying to escape, some 400 metres from the assigned route, the vehicle hit a Moroccan land mine, causing the truck to explode, overturn and catch on fire. Gueguen was killed instantly. Pascal Laudenot and Vincent Bauden were able to escape, just.

So, the rally was moved to South America and here we were. I have painted a picture of carnage and death up to that point. While there's no denying the tragedy, there is no shortage of incredibly inspiring stories of success over adversity, either. That's what I lap up. I am, and always have been, an extreme sports/adventure lover, but it was the Camel Trophy and the Paris-Dakar Rally that really ignited a little boy's imagination living in Kenya. So, I was not going to miss the likes of Toby Price, Sam Sunderland, Matthias Walkner and company rocketing through the desert. I was not going to miss the opportunity of filming it, either. Problem.

My beautiful camerawoman had been floored by the "San Juan Revenge" and I desperately needed a replacement. Enter, stage right, Slavic, a Polish fellow who made a fruitcake seem like the sanest of cakes. But what a nice cake he turned out to be... in the end. We had met him briefly outside our room the previous evening, where he was cleaning the chain and sprockets of his BMW 650 Dakar with a pink toothbrush dipped in petrol. Judging from his stunning white teeth, he evidently had another toothbrush.

That morning Slavic was sitting downstairs, in the communal kitchen, examining every single corn in his cornflakes with a grimy spoon. I greeted him, sat opposite and explained my dilemma. Slavic was about 65-plus and looked like Robert de Niro, except left in the oven a bit longer and with a more bulbous nose. It must have been his eyes that reminded me of De Niro because you could not really see much of him.

He had a huge grey beard, which spread across his BMW T-shirt like a sun dial, a similarly massive mop of grey hair, another sun dial, silhouetted against the blue sky. His face was garnished with thick-lensed and framed black glasses that seemed to be constantly steamed up and greasy, even when he was riding. Added to this he was bright red, so looked like a movie extra who had just stepped off *The Black Pearl* and was about to explode.

However, Pavel was quick to volunteer as cameraman. He had such a great face and beaming smile that I stupidly agreed. I did not know at that stage he had more personalities than the village I lived in in Mexico, most of them super nice (his personalities). Every time he spoke, he squinted for emphasis, his eyes watered and he leaned forward to share his words of wisdom and his rather aromatic garlic breath. Still, it was excellent of him to offer help, so I rushed upstairs, mopped the food poisoning victim's brow and whispered suitable kind words and we were off.

It turned out that the junction outside had become a meeting place for bikers who wanted to head to the Dakar. We left in a group of six bikes. I was quite pleased to be riding with a few others. It was a novelty for me.

There was a Dutch couple in their early 20s, suitably blonde and good looking. The husband was an ex-policeman who now worked as a bouncer in Rotterdam. He was quite keen on threatening imaginary people and very enthusiastic about telling us how he could kill six people simultaneously with his thumb. I steered clear. There was a German couple in their early 'hundreds', who spent most of their day huddled over a GPS. There was another German, with the clichéd round spectacles and unfeasible tallness, on a Honda 500 with a see-through tank. Dieter must have been six foot eight and, even on his tall bike, his knees were warming his ears. Then there was me, alone on my Tenere. Also, a novelty. Pavel had agreed to take a clean-cut, enthusiastic, teenage Dakar fan as pillion.

We headed off and all was good for about 200 metres. Then it all went odd. I saw Pavel pull up ahead of me and jump off the bike, redder than ever, with steam coming out of his ears and nose. He was gesticulating at the young Argentinian, obviously berating him for something.

"I cannot ride with you, you stay here, you make me crash. Fuck, shit, thank you, goodbye," said Pavel.

Apparently, the young lad had been squirming around in the saddle and making it difficult for Pavel. I could not blame the pillion because in this short distance I had noticed some worrying traits in Pavel's riding. He had already gone straight through a red light and his acceleration was erratic, to say the least. One moment he would be ambling along at a snail's pace, then he'd suddenly accelerate and be off like a ferret on coffee.

"You can't just dump him here Pavel. There is nobody around."

"This man is no good on the moto, no good on back, no good," he replied, gesticulating wildly in the air to some invisible god.

"Okay, but we are in the middle of nowhere," I pleaded. Slavic was having none of it and after some strange conversation about being let down by the world, I realised this situation was not going to be resolved. As I was wondering about the next course of action, a battered pickup kangarooed towards us. I flagged them down, asked if they could drop the traumatised pillion back in town and it was done. Then it got weirder.

As we were exiting the city it became glaringly clear that Slavic was stopping at every green light and going through every red one. After pulling up alongside and quizzing him with my arms and eyebrows, he just rocketed off. Then he would wait at a vital junction and rocket off again. As soon as we hit the dirt he turned into the most amazing rider, I must admit, and disappeared down an arrow-straight road, in a cloud of dust, up to the horizon, over a hill and gone. We continued and met up with Slavic at various splits in the track. At least he was waiting at strategic points, but were they strategic points? After 80 wrong turns and an extremely circular route, we tied Slavic up and left him by his bike, with a little bit of water and a mango. No, we didn't!

We eventually arrived at the river crossing. I am convinced to this day that Slavic found the river crossing by pure luck and would have continued for days, until he shrunk to nothing and died of thirst.

The location was superb, the atmosphere electric. The Argentinians had pulled out all the stops. If you have ever been to an English country fair, multiply the stalls by 1,000, add 5,000 screaming Argentinians and

Bolivians, a sprinkling of Germans, Dutch and the unhinged. Add smoke-billowing asados—an Argentinian barbecue of ludicrous proportions—picture three cows upside down being cooked next to each other. Add in thousands of litres of Quilmes beer, zillions of litres of Mendoza red wine from the nearby hills, international flags fluttering in the breeze, and the smell of fuel in the air and there you have it... not an English country fair at all.

The entire scene was divided in two by the river and road crossing it. On one side of the river were the 5,000 fans partying like there was a pandemic coming soon, as well as some high-powered vehicles, and on the other side was a cordoned-off section with Winnebagos and 4x4 trucks with tents, tarpaulins and barbecues. Important people were running around with radio mics and high-speed important walks. I was so excited.

We found a spot with a view of a sweeping bend on the approach to the bridge and water crossing. I had the stills camera and I showed Slavic how to use the handheld Panasonic HD camera and taught him the basics of how to film the riders, preferably not pointing the camera into the sun, and never zoom, etc. It was Neanderthal-basic instructions, but it was better than having no cameraman at all. Slavic seemed to concentrate and take it all in. But that was before he turned from hippie Robert de Niro into Captain Barbossa.

Picture this: You are set up with all the bigwigs of adventure filming, Fox Sports, Red Bull TV, etc., and the anticipation is palpable, the atmosphere electric. Everyone is making last-minute sound checks and radios are crackling, announcing the imminent arrival of the fastest men in the world on two and four wheels. The danger element is, of course, always there. Most fans are aware this is a difficult section and many have died trying to complete the Dakar. It is a strange, morbid attraction, the morals of which I will not go into now. I will always be an avid defender of extreme sports, whether it is solo climbing, ultra-distance running, free diving, whatever. Overcoming adversity and stretching the mind and body to its limit makes people, and me, feel truly alive. Let it flourish. Love it all.

As I was fighting off a desert wasp, which wanted to hurt me, I heard the crowd stirring, somewhat muted at first but then they started clapping and then screaming. The Dakar was on. The riders were coming first, followed by the four-wheelers. Right, my plan was to do a quick piece to camera, then swing round to the sweeping bend and follow the bikes through the water crossing. I would use the stills camera, Pavel would do his best on the Panasonic video camera.

"No panning bru, keep the camera still and let the subject pass."

I turned to Slavic to give him the thumbs-up about the plans that were in my head, and he was nowhere to be seen. I spun round and looked down the slope of the riverbank to where the epicentre of the crowd stirring was occurring. There was Slavic, on the river's edge, close to where cars and bikes would be hurtling through at 150 kilometres an hour. He was bent double performing a moonie to the opposite riverbank. For those of you who do not know what a moonie is, here's my definition: "When a Polish motorcyclist shows his lily-white bum to a crowd of 5,000 spectators at the Dakar Rally, causing untold distress and embarrassment to another unnamed motorcyclist, who probably wants to disappear into an abyss."

My cameraman and, therefore, in the sandy eyes of the Dakar organisers, my responsibility, was showing his worst side to the world via TV, not to mention the large well-alcohol-oiled crowd witnessing his revealing. I ran down the hill super-fast, shouting "Slavic, Jesus Christ man. What the hell are you doing! This is a conservative, non-bum exposing country."

Slavic pulled up his trousers, managed to look a bit sheepish, or llama-ish and said, "Sorry, I thought it was funny and get the crowd much happy."

"Yes, if you were 18, out at a party in a Polish university town. Come on man, pull it together."

I could just see the headline: "NAKED DESERT RUNNER FROM POLAND CAUSES DAKAR CRASH."

Okay. Those were not the headlines in *La Nación* newspaper the next day, but they could have been. Guess what Slavic did next? After following me a few steps up the hill, he turned and bolted back down the dune, removing his boots as he ran. He then sat/fell and simultaneously removed his motorcycle trousers and underwear, quickly and impressively, I must admit. He stood up in his white T-shirt and stained white socks, his proud belly sticking out from underneath his *BMW* shirt. He then gyrated his hips in a circular motion, displaying his Polish jewels to huge applause. Did I mention the 5,000 people witnessing this? Now it was 8,000.

By this stage, the organisers were livid, and Slavic had, unsurprisingly, caught the attention of security and the police, who were armed to the hilt, and rapidly approaching. Surrender was not an option in Slavic's head. Now he was William Wallace. Off he ran, at Dakar speed across the dunes, not before taking a quick detour over the road, crossing the route of the soon-to-arrive competitors. He ran down the line of spectators, arms in the air, like a World Cup winning striker, before peeling off across the desert with many uniforms after him.

Success and fame would be short lived, and he was rugby tackled by five men, much like a streaker at an English football match, except in a desert and with no football to be seen. The crowd were cheering him on hysterically and, when he was tackled, undoubtedly causing friction to his tackle, there was a collective *ahh* of disappointment that he had been caught. As he escaped for a final time from the clutches of the law, then it was a Champions League goal reaction from the crowd, followed by a red card. Pavel was finally taken down.

With all due respect, the police were remarkably civil and led Slavic off to a metal container in 42°C and locked him up to frazzle to death. We realised that our biker friend was struggling a bit and all the bikers sprang into action. After splitting up we eventually located the container more than a kilometre away. We managed to persuade the police to get our potty Pole out of the container. They agreed, but only to move him to the holding cells in town. They made it clear that he would be released the next morning.

Cathy spent the night worrying, phoning various dead ends and trying to find out on the net where Pavel could be. At 6am we were up, and after numerous phone calls and red herrings, we eventually located Slavic's whereabouts and got him released. When he arrived at the squat, evidently traumatised by his evening's accommodations courtesy of the Argentinian taxpayer, he turned into Jean Claude van Damme and just wanted to karate all of us.

"You leave me, you leave me to die, shit people bad, bad."

We tried to reason with him, but it did not work. He was too distressed and all over the place. "You left me with police, I kick you," as he swung at my shins. I jumped up and performed a Polish restraint manoeuvre that I'd learned in the Selous Scouts. I tried to explain to him that I was not the naked desert runner, he was, and it was his choice. I tried to reason with him, explaining that Cathy had been on the case since the minute he was rugby tackled.

"Foreigner shits," was his retort. That made me laugh. Difficult to be more foreign than a Polish dude in Argentina. He was not thinking straight, and we all made light of everything and cracked a few Quilmes to mark his freedom. Pavel was still extremely tense but after a few manly biker hugs, things eventually calmed down and we all headed off to bed with a modicum of tranquillity restored.

Let me now twist this story on its head and tell you why it is the feel-good factor story that Sam Manicom asked me to write. On the surface, this is a story of danger, death, tragedy, and obvious mental issues. What is it that links someone like Joey Evans to Pavel? The only obvious link is that both were in Argentina for their love of motorbikes. But that's a tenuous link.

The link that joins them is the tenacity to never give up, albeit for different reasons. I stayed in contact with Pavel, and he admitted freely that he was struggling from grief and some mental health issues. On top of that, and thank God, mental health issues are not such a dirty secret anymore; several well-known adventure riders have also admitted their struggles. Without wanting to be contentious, and forgive me if I offend, or you do not fit into that category, many seeking extreme adventures are often running away from something or trying to resolve issues or trying to find something meaningful about themselves and the world. I was so pleased to see the emergence of mental health issues in the motorbike world and the fact that The Overland Event, to name one example, is backing the Mental Health Motorbike Support Group U.K. (MHM). In the light of Covid and the way it has affected human interaction, this subject will only become more important to cope with.

Pavel not only returned home and pulled himself together, he also told me the support he got from bikers, not only with us but throughout South America, had literally saved his life. He said he was sorry to have caused us grief. Not a problem, I said. He went on to further surprise me.

Pavel had returned to Poland, controlled his issues and had also set up a Mental Health Support Group for Bikers. It had proved extremely successful and had saved Pavel, to boot. He was planning to bring a group of 20 bikers on a three-week tour culminating in watching the Dakar. During our many conversations, he once slipped that he had raised over €8,000 to support mental health schemes.

So, on the surface, you can see me as slightly taking the mickey out of someone, with my story of Pavel, but it is not the case. It was comedic at first, but then worrying (I cleared it with him before I submitted this chapter). We still celebrate our love of travel and bikes, and life, and adrenaline and hardship, the experience and stimulation, and friends. And small subjects like the complexity of the mind. Joey and Pavel made me realise that when you are worrying about yourself and your reactions to life, always think about what others are going through. A man with no feet cannot understand complaints about uncomfortable shoes.

Survivors and never-give-up people are my heroes. I am not one, but I do know that the difference between success and failure is to keep trying one more time and, if that is not enough, 100 more times. From these two men I learned to travel with a mind more open to the struggles of others and to be more accepting of those who stray from the norm. My life is easy. Complaints must stop and my love of fellow man and this beautiful planet must be multiplied. This Dakar Rally, on the surface, was amusing; deep down it was a Eureka Humanity moment for me.

Pavel's struggles were so different from Joey's almost self-inflicted ones but no less impressive. We all have our mountains to climb, some higher than others and some need to do the climb with a pebble in their shoe. These two men, during Dakar week, made me realise that we need to celebrate our differences and support and cherish each other, help each other succeed, acknowledging our strengths and weaknesses, but living life to the fullest. I had not been doing that. I was too cynical to trust others.

Those two also compounded my motto, "Day by day, border by border, nothing lasts forever". This is a maxim I have been living by since 2009. Luckily, the future comes a day at a time. Take life in little chunks and savour them. "Nothing lasts forever" is about the good and the bad, so suck up and overcome it. "Border-by-border" means keep moving forward in life.

I was learning all the time. Open mindedness to others is vital. As Stephen Fry, the English genius said in an interview, "I have no idea why people talk about dysfunctional families as though it is unusual, 80% are dysfunctional. How are their families going to be normal if we judge them by that standard, expected circumstance and behaviour?"

I concur. My mother's sister committed suicide, my wonderful grandmother had callipers on her legs and spent much of her life in a wheelchair due to polio. She never complained and was a ball of sunshine. Other family members were institutionalised. My Mum's Uncle Bert was run over by a steamroller. It's 100 percent true. He obviously was not quick off the mark, or it was a Dakar steamroller... do not be embarrassed to laugh. So, dysfunctionality, I have an inkling of what it's about.

This is what I believe the Biker Code is: "Try not to judge, and always help others, wherever possible." I try to live it, but fall short all the time.

It should be a life code.

About the author:

Spencer Conway was brought up in Kenya and moved to Swaziland (now Eswatini) at six. He went to the *United World College of the Atlantic* in Wales and then to *Edinburgh University*. He completed an MA Honors in Social Anthropology and then taught at *The Polytechnic School of Art and Design* in the Seychelles.

Spencer gave up the suit and tie in 2009 and became a full-time adventure motorcyclist and writer. He says, "I am also lucky enough to be sponsored, which helps the dream."

He has circumnavigated Africa solo and unsupported through 34 countries and 55,345 kilometres. This culminated in the TV series *African Motorcycle Diaries* on *Travel Channel* and the DVD and book, *The Japanese Speaking Curtain Maker.*

He then circumnavigated South and Central America and Mexico, with **Cathy Nel**, his girlfriend. They travelled through 22 countries and 106,000 kilometres. This culminated in the series *The South American Motorcycle Diaries,* which sold to airlines as well as the book *The Zimbabwean Psychiatrist's Hat.*

All these trips were done on a 2009 Yamaha Tenere 660Z. He has travelled to 132 countries, working his way around on motorbikes, yachts and cruise ships.

Spencer is a qualified cliff rescue instructor, lifeguard, diver, first aider and TEFL teacher. He is an ambassador for *Motorcycle Outreach,* an organisation that provides motorcycles, training and workshops for nurses and midwives to reach remote areas. He is also an ambassador for *Metal Mule Luggage Systems, KLIM* clothing and *Yamaha Japan*. Spencer is a regular contributor to motorcycle and adventure magazines and often presents at motorcycle festivals.

At the time of writing Spencer and Cathy are in Zicatela, Oaxaca, Mexico waiting for it to become possible and polite to travel again. Their aim is to circumnavigate every continent and write about each expedition. This includes a one-hour documentary attempting to cross the centre of the Darien Gap.

Spencer and Cathy are launching an adventure company called "The No 10 Spanner Company" and *YouTube* channel. He says, "My biggest loves are motorcycles, travelling and animals (above and below water)."

Peace, love and sardines rule.

Website: spencer-conway.com
Facebook: Spencer James Conway
Instagram: @spencer_james_conway
YouTube: Spencer James Conway
Spencer's books are published as paperbacks and on *Kindle*, and Spencer and Cathy's films can be bought from their website and from *Amazon*.

Iron Angels

by Shirley Hardy-Rix and Brian Rix

"Roads are made for journeys, not destinations."

—Confucius

When riding two-up around the world, glorious times come in all forms, shapes and sizes. The bad times can hit when least expected and pass within minutes. One of our brightest moments came in the shape of angels... Iron Angels, who came to our rescue when we least expected it. This is why we do it....

Russia

Brian: We've just spent a few days in Mongolia and are headed back into Russia for the final leg of our journey to Vladivostok. Leaving Mongolia is an easy border crossing. Getting back into Russia proves to be just as simple, especially when we have a document with assorted official stamps to prove our ownership of the bike. Within two hours we are back on the road to Ulan Ude, the home of the world's largest Lenin's head statue.

When we left Ulan Ude for Mongolia it was festival time. The square was festooned with lights, piped-in music, and children playing and eating ice cream in the sunshine.

In just a week, things have changed drastically. The festival feel about town is gone. There are no red, blue and white lights in the square and no lights in the fountain. There is a chill in the air. Winter is coming.

We enjoy our time in Ulan Ude and for our last night we dine at the Churchill Bar, on the side of the square. The irony isn't lost on us that Vladimir Lenin looks down on the face of the British leader over the door of the bar.

Shirley: The fun of a few drinks and a good old-fashioned meal of bangers and mash is behind us. We now have to hit the road. It is getting colder, down to about 11°C and we want to be in Vladivostok before it gets worse.

We wake to a cold, bleak morning. The sky is grey, with low clouds that threaten rain. We check the map to sort the best way to get to Chita, our planned stop for the night. The main road, the M55, is 700-plus kilometres, a long way on any day, but on a day like today seems to be shaping into, it will be even longer. We decide on the shorter route, a yellow road on the map. Even though we know it won't be the best ride it is about 70 kms shorter.

The road is typical of those we've ridden across Russia. It goes from high-quality tarmac to poor road surfaces to really rutted surfaces to road works. Their works go for kilometres, and with the intermittent rain, the brown mud surface is like riding on glass. I get the usual order to sit still. The bad stretches are too long for me to get off and walk, lightening the load for Brian. The trucks are churning up the mud, making it even more treacherous.

Brian: It's not their fault. Eastern Russia has its fair share of cold, miserable weather and the roads suffer accordingly. Russian truck drivers are, over all, pretty good. They may look like they're rough and tough, but they are also skilful. Just look at who wins the truck segment in the

Dakar. They're good, and have to be to negotiate the remote back blocks, rivers, mud and treacherous conditions out here. Mind you, most belch black smoke and are well overdue for a change of diesel injectors. Most are covered in dirt and mud and seem to be used 24/7. KAMAZ is the truck of choice out here. Tough, reliable, and rough looking just like their drivers, they are capable of taking on anything this rugged terrain can throw at them. You won't find big road trains out here like in Australia, but semi-trailers and tip trucks are plentiful. While the drivers are good, I go by the rule that might has right of way to ensure we stay alive mixing with these big boys of Siberian roads.

Most trucks and some cars use the huge earthen ramps in parking bays to change oil and for other repairs, so they're off the road as little as possible. The ground underneath the ramps is black with oil dumped directly onto the ground, with the occasional discarded oil filter littering the landscape.

Shirley: Brian does a great job getting us through these sections without coming off. It is a slow and torturous ride with a car right up our backside, but we make it.

We've been on the road for nearly six months, and I'm finding days like today a bit hard to deal with. Unlike here in eastern Russia, riding in western Russia, a break at one of the petrol stations offers a respite. They are modern and usually have clean toilets. The little shops where you pay for your fuel sell an assortment of tasty treats that we keep in the pannier for snacking along the way. My favourite is the slab of toffee and peanuts. I even convince myself they are healthy.

Brian: I know these days are hard on Shirl. It's cold. The thermometer on the bike says it's only 11°C. It's wet and the riding conditions are tough. We both need a break after the seemingly never-ending roadworks, so I pull into a fuel station. It only sells petrol, so we fuel up. We have to pay before we get the petrol and Shirl does a wonderful job managing that while dealing with a very unhappy woman who seems to live in a little box-like structure. Her role in life is to take the money. She shouts at Shirl in Russian and Shirl points out that no matter how much she shouts at her, she will still not understand Russian. With her very basic knowledge of Russian numbers and handing over more than enough cash, she gets the bill paid and our change.

Now, I can try and find somewhere to eat, or at least get out of the wind and have a snack from the dwindling stash in the pannier.

There is so little infrastructure on this road the only thing we find is another petrol station without either a café or shop. It does have a toilet of sorts. I bite the bullet and try it, and it is disgusting—a hole in the ground with shit everywhere. I can't believe the sanitation is so poor here. We have holes in the ground or, as we call them, "drop" toilets in Australia, but it is simple to keep them clean and hygienic. It's not quite so bad for me, but I have to tell Shirl she would be better off hanging on for a while. Squatting over the hole would be disgusting. Standing over it is bad enough.

Shirley: I take Brian's advice and decide against using the toilet. Squat toilets don't worry me but squatting over a quagmire of excrement is beyond the pale. I often get Brian to pull over when he finds a spot where we can get off the road and I can have a pee in relative cleanliness. Not today, though. It's too bloody cold. I can't think of taking my pants down in this howling wind and rain. At times like this I yearn for the servos of western Russia.

Our overnight stop is Chita, a city on the Trans-Siberian Railway route and 900 kilometres from Irkutsk. We are making progress, but it is hard going in the bad weather. Chita was closed to foreigners and most Russians during the Soviet era because of its proximity to China and military installations. When we ride in looking for our hotel, the communist past is easy to see—plenty of plain, Soviet-style buildings—just colourless concrete blocks. Our hotel is in the heart of this area. The staff speak mainly Russian and Chinese, but the man on the desk speaks a little English. He explains the hotel is undergoing renovations, but our room is complete, except for the hot water. I can't blame Brian for opting out of a shower after the cold ride. The upside is a good Chinese restaurant. Some decent tucker and a whisky or two and we put another hard day behind us.

Brian: The water is still cold this morning, not a good start. We want to get to Chemyshevsk or Mogocha, more than 200 kms further on. There is a hotel in Chemyshevsk without a shower and only a shared toilet, and there doesn't appear to be a food option.

I am finding every day a slog now. It's so close to the end but Vladivostok seems so far away. Communications with the shipping agent are problematic. We really need to know when we can lodge the bike with them so we can book flights home. But tying them down to dates is proving tricky and we can't even get a ballpark figure of the costs. To get home from Vladivostok means a ferry to South Korea, and then a freighter to Australia for the bike, but we'll fly home. I know it will all come together, but it is frustrating.

Chemyshevsk is a particularly uninviting city with grey concrete buildings and no welcoming signs of cafés or shops. It's only 1pm so we push on to Mogocha. We take a break but don't get fuel. I am sure we've got enough and will fuel up again when we reach Mogocha and also get a room for the night. According to Trip Advisor there are a couple of hotels, so getting a room shouldn't prove too difficult.

Like most of the towns in this area Mogocha is off the highway a way. When we get to the town I have about 80 kms range left and the GPS is directing us to a fuel station. The clouds gather and the rain comes down in buckets. I can't find the fuel station so a room is my next priority, but I can't find anything that looks remotely like a hotel.

It's raining. It's gloomy and Mogocha looks depressed and depressing.

I turn down a side street hoping to find a hotel or fuel. A dilapidated, dark grey Lada pulls alongside, and the driver's window comes down. A heavy wave of smoke billows out and a disembodied voice says simply, "Club House. Follow." I do as I am told and follow this clapped-out old remnant of the Soviet era through the streets of Mogocha.

Shirley: I ask Brian if I heard right. Did that voice say to follow them? Yep. And that is exactly what he is doing. They pull up outside a two-storey shed-like building and get out of the car to introduce themselves. Alexi is the vice-president of the local motorcycle club, wearing wire-rimmed glasses and sleeveless denim jacket over a tracksuit top. He doesn't look like a big, tough bikie. Sasha is a biker visiting from Vladivostok, with a massive, welcoming smile. They are our saviours on this cold and wet afternoon in the middle of Siberia. They are the Mogocha Iron Angels and this is their clubhouse.

We have heard about the Iron Angels but had no idea how to find them. It seems like we didn't need to—they found us.

Alexi and Sasha open the double doors and signal for Brian to ride on in. It seems like we have found a room for the night.

Brian: The Mogocha Iron Angels built their clubhouse after a friend was murdered while camping in the nearby forest. They decided camping in this area was way too dangerous and set up their clubhouse as part of a "Bike Post" network throughout Russia. Rather than wild camping or paying for an overpriced room, the Iron Angels open their clubhouse to bikers from across Russia and around the world.

With the bike tucked away safe and sound we climb the rickety stairs to the upper level. It's one large room with three couches, a coffee table, an empty fish tank and piles of stuff around the walls. It is pretty basic, but it is dry and warm, and the bike is safely out of sight.

When Sasha asks if there is anything we need, Shirl asks about a toilet.

Ah, well... there isn't actually a toilet. There isn't actually any running water. But he assures Shirl there is a toilet nearby and we pile into the Lada and head into town.

Shirley: No toilet? I am sure I can make do. Jammed into the Lada we head to a supermarket that has a café and toilets. After a comfort break, I join the boys at a table in the café. Of course, the conversation has turned to bikes and the Iron Angels. Sasha speaks very good English and acts as interpreter. Alexi wants us to try some of the local dumplings—a delicacy in this part of the world. They are very tasty and come with some soup and black bread. It is a meal fit for travellers. Alexi won't accept any money from us and has to get money from the ATM to pay. It's a gesture of friendship that he probably can't afford.

I excuse myself and hit the supermarket. Vodka, wine, coke, water and snacks to soak up the alcohol as a way to say, "Thank you". Thinking of everything, I get some yogurt for breakfast. Alexi and Sasha have local beer that comes in three-litre plastic bottles. It's going to be quite a night.

Brian: With a few drinks there is more talk of bikes and travel, and we discover Alexi can speak a little English. It just needed some lubrication. The beer goes down well, and everyone is pleased to toast everything from Australia to Russia and lots in between with shots of the very pleasing vodka.

As the night progresses Alexi's son arrives to take Dad home. The Lada will spend the night here. He speaks excellent English and explains more of the story behind the Bike Post network.

Their friend was murdered by someone living in the forest, a local who came across the bikers' camp and demanded they drink vodka together. When the biker refused, the crazy man killed him. The local police weren't all that interested in investigating the crime so it was up to the local bikers to see what they could find out. When they discovered someone wearing their friend's clothes, they took matters into their own hands. A business run by a man who protected the killer mysteriously burnt down.

More importantly they vowed no one would camp in the forest again. They pooled their funds and built the clubhouse. Travellers now have somewhere safe to stay without having to pitch a tent.

The story clearly upsets Alexi, who has tears in his eyes as he produces photos of a magnificent memorial to his murdered friend, built by the roadside where the killing took place. Each year bikers from across Russia come to this remote area in Siberia to remember their buddy.

Shirley: I hang on as long as I can but have to make the tricky journey down the stairs and into the back garden where I find a little corner to pee. I make sure I don't enjoy too many toasts to lessen the need for too many sojourns to the pitch-black garden.

After a couple of hours, we hear some bikes pull up outside. Some locals have found another traveller riding in town. Francisco is from Spain and very grateful to find some food and drink on offer as well as a warm room on such a cold night. When it is finally time for bed, the boys have toasted all their hometowns, travellers, bikes, Mother Russia and, most importantly, the Mogocha Iron Angels.

In deference to our age and marital status we are given the vinyl convertible night and day. I remember one of these in our loungeroom in the 1960s. It's surprisingly comfortable, and tucked up in our sleeping bags, I am forever grateful Alexi and Sasha found us by the side of the road.

Brian: We are packed and Shirl is ready for another trip to the supermarket toilets. When she comes out of the shed, she discovers there is virtually no fence, and the clubhouse is on the corner of two very popular streets. It seems the entire population of the town is walking past on their way to work!

Alexi arrives to collect his car and leads us back to the supermarket for breakfast and a much-needed toilet break.

Replenished, we follow him to the petrol station. No wonder we didn't find it last night. It's hidden behind a six-foot high nondescript tin fence, no sign to indicate it's a fuel station. Again, we encounter an unhappy woman living in a small shed selling the fuel. The battle to pay is much easier with Sasha helping.

Sasha is heading to his home in Vladivostok and Francisco decides he will ride with him to the next Bike Post club. We travel together as far as the memorial to their Russian biker friend. Made of black marble, the memorial sits alongside the roadway, near a clearing. It's covered in stickers from travellers who have visited to pay their respects, including some we have met along the way. It's a solemn moment, even though we didn't know this young man who left behind a wife and children.

Shirley: The memorial seems a fitting tribute. His friends still grieve his passing. Like all the bikers we've met in Russia, the Mogocha Iron Angels are incredibly friendly and more than happy to share whatever they have with strangers.

When we met Alexi and Sasha, we were wet, cold, hungry and low on fuel. We didn't know where we were going to sleep or eat. But that chance meeting in the wilds of Siberia restored our faith. They made us realise why we do what we do. It is about the roads. It is about the sites. It is about the food. But most importantly, it is about the people you meet.

Thank you, Mogocha Iron Angels, for looking after two Aussies a long way from home and in need of a helping hand. We will never forget you and hope our paths cross again.

Spasibo. (Russian for thank you.)

About the authors:

Brian Rix and Shirley Hardy-Rix have been riding two-up for decades. It's the way they like to travel.

Brian cut his teeth riding in his backyard, 145 kilometres of river frontage along the Murray River in southern Australia years before he was old enough to ride on the roads.

Shirley has always enjoyed the pillion seat, riding from beach to beach north of Sydney when she was in her teens.

When they met in Melbourne in the 1980s it was a match made in heaven. Brian was a dedicated police officer for 36 years, mainly in criminal investigation including heading the State of Victoria's Homicide Squad before becoming president of Victoria's police union. Shirley was as a highly respected television and radio journalist with stints in magazines, publicity, and film production. Their love of motorcycling relieved the stress of their working lives.

Riding around Australia offered plenty of travel experience and whetted their appetites for longer rides outside of Australia.

In 2003 they swapped their backpacks for a BMW R1150GS, shipped it to the UK and began a 12- month journey home via Europe, Greece, Turkey, Iran, Pakistan, India, Nepal and Southeast Asia, arriving back in Darwin for a quick 3,700-kilometre dash home to Melbourne.

The year on the road did nothing to stop their urge to explore the world. In 2011 the 1150 was upgraded to a BMW R1200GSA. They chucked their jobs and headed to South America. For the next 16 months they rode from the bottom of South America to Alaska (with a side trip without the bike to Antarctica). From Canada they flew with the bike to the UK, hoping to get to Egypt and ride through Africa. However, the Arab Spring worked against them, so they headed back to the UK and flew to Africa to explore the southern part of the continent. Back in Perth it was another 3,400 kilometres across the Nullarbor back home.

Still not done, in 2015 they rode from Greece to the top of Norway and then across Russia, the "Stans," and Mongolia, ending in Vladivostok. A short trip across France and then to the Isle of Man in 2018 was their last international ride.

Covid-19 put an end to their next trip. They hope to hit the road again when things return to normal.

Website: Aussiesoverland.com.au
Facebook : Aussies Overland
Instagram: aussiesoverland
They are the authors of *Two for the Road, Circle to Circle* and *The Long Way to Vladivostok,* and are co-hosts of the *Adventure Rider Radio "RAW"* show. All their books are published as paperbacks and on *Kindle* and are available direct and from *Amazon*.

Escaping the Net
The Priceless Gift of Perspective
by Ted Hely

"Not all those who wander are lost."

—*J.R.R. Tolkien*

"Africa! Tea towel-wearing terrorists in the north and spear throwing savages in the south. You'll either have your head severed by Muslims or be boiled alive for dinner by grass skirt-wearing cannibals. What the hell are you going there for? Have you lost your mind?"

These are just a sampling of the many things friends, family and colleagues told me when I shared my travel plans with them. There's no other continent that can conjure up as much fear and ignorance as Africa. But you don't hear much good news about Africa do you? Thinking back to when I was planning this trip, I'm not embarrassed to say that I also had similar presumptions. Civil war, lawless states, disease, poverty, droughts, genocide, etc. The list goes on and on.

It would be irresponsible to attempt to convince you that these things aren't a reality in too many parts of Africa. But I want to share with you the other side of this truly magical continent, the experiences and adventures that will change anyone who dives head first into these lands with an open mind.

There were many reasons why I shouldn't attempt to ride to Cape Town from the UK. When I decided to do this trip, I'd just returned from seven months riding South America. I was flat broke and over £7,000 in debt. I'd no job and needed to live with my mum and sister. A rough cost of a trip through Africa was going to cost another £8,000, at least. I didn't even have a bike, as I'd sold my trusted XT600 in Bogota to afford the flight home from Colombia. Finances aside, there were also many worrying developments in Africa. Terrorism was flaring in the west and civil war was raging in the east. Borders were opening and closing daily.

In contrast, South America had been relatively easy to travel. Visas are granted at the borders, you don't need a Carnet de Passage for a motorcycle, and I only really needed to learn the basics of a single language, Spanish. Africa is vastly more complicated. Visas must often be obtained in advance and there's no certainty they will be granted at all and, yes, you do need a Carnet, adding a significant cost. But the more I thought about it the more I wanted to go.

I set out a two-year action plan. I'd stay living at my family home to keep costs down and find a job as soon as possible. Before I left for South America, I'd been working in a motorcycle dealership, which I detested. The six-day week and the very long commute got to me. But I took a deep breath and fired off an email to the boss anyway, and he took me back immediately. It felt like a massive step backwards, but I justified it to myself that it was temporary. Living at home was also going to be joyless. However, I knew that I'd be immersing myself in preparations.

I focused on saving 80% of my salary. From my previous trip I gained experience at living cheaply. I could make my own wine and bake my own bread. I didn't go on holidays, and I didn't waste money on anything that wasn't going toward the trip. It sounds drastic but I actually enjoyed it. I learned a lot and it helped me realise how little I actually need. Our society is consumed with consumerism, and it really doesn't do much to make us happy, mostly shackling us with possessions and tying us down in debt.

It felt really good to step out of that life, and with this routine I paid off my debt within six months. By the end of the first year, I had enough to buy another bike, a seven-year-old, low-mileage Suzuki DRZ400S, for £1,800. I then hammered away on weekends making luggage racks, and spent evenings scouring the internet for second-hand parts, a long-range tank, touring seat, etc.

Those two years were a blur. I worked long hours and spent my evenings sipping home-made wine while researching Africa. Social life consisted of weekend camping trips, or Overland meetings. It was at one such meeting that I met Neil. We were the same age, both had DRZ400S and also intended to ride Africa. After a few weeks of emailing, we formed a plan to at least start the journey together. I think we were both apprehensive about the trip, so having a wingman for moral support made a lot of sense.

The hourglass was nearly empty. With only a week before leaving, everything was ready except my mind. Only when I was packed and ready to go did I have the time to sit down and absorb the reality of what I was about to do. And that's when anxiety and fear crept in. I imagined that these might be the last days I'd see my family or home. What if I got kidnapped by terrorists, eaten by savages or involved in a fatal accident on African roads? My stomach sank. I lay awake thinking that it wasn't too late to change my mind. I had all this money saved. I could go somewhere else. Australia, the US, Europe! But cancelling the trip would be letting Neil down and that would be a real arsehole thing to do. So that's what I focused on for the last couple of days—*not* being an arsehole.

It was a Saturday morning in late August, bright and sunny but unseasonably cold. I was shivering in the riding gear that I'd chosen for the African sun. My sister didn't even get out of bed to wave me off. My mum asked if I had enough underwear, before saying goodbye as if I was just going to work for the day. "Cheerio, don't do anything stupid!" she shouted. As I wobbled my overloaded enduro down the road, I realised that this trip was only a big deal for me. Everyone else has their own lives and adventures going on in their heads. Why was mine any more important than theirs? It wasn't. But to me, it was everything.

I wish I had adequate words to describe the feeling of finally being on the road during that first hour. It was such an incredible relief, like stepping through a door into another universe. With every mile, fears and doubt drifted away into nothing. My mind changed focus from the trivia of day-to-day life to the simplicity of the moment. All that lay ahead was potential. For the first time in two years, I felt happy—*really* happy.

I arrived at Neil's cold and tired. We had a couple of nights before the boat to make final preparations, which was just as well as Neil's brakes had problems and my second-hand airbed started leaking. In spite of the best planning there's always something unexpected at the last minute.

The ferry docked in Santander at 6am and we rode off bursting with enthusiasm. That was surprising considering how little we'd slept on the reclining chairs, surrounded as we were by merry Brits who'd been drinking throughout the night. But we were in Spain, the sun was shining, and our wheels were turning. We headed straight into the mountains to meander our way into the countryside and visit Neil's Spanish family. Rural northern Spain is stunning, with its sweeping mountain roads, small villages, and beautiful forests. We were greeted with enthusiasm and hospitality wherever we went; everyone was excited about our journey.

After enjoying a week being fattened up by Neil's family and friends we headed to Barcelona for the ferry to Italy. I presumed Africa was going to be very different from Europe, and that I should enjoy myself as much as possible while I could. We partied hard in Barcelona, and then fell onto the ferry early the following morning. Just six hours later we docked in Italy, with a ride from Livorno to Bologna, to Pisa and then finally to Venice for the next ferry to Africa in front of us. It had been a rapid tour through parts of Europe with some budget sightseeing along the way with no money to spare on too many frivolities. I was on a permanent high, enjoying each day, feeling injected with confidence and high on good vibes from the people I met. If I'd been on a two-week backpacking trip through Europe, I probably wouldn't have felt the same. I wouldn't have interacted with locals in the same way. Or been dragged over and introduced to complete strangers by others who had been strangers just minutes earlier. All this happened because we were travellers on motorcycles, doing something pretty cool, something many of them wanted to do, too.

One of the best things about overlanding in this way is meeting and spending time with other travellers with vehicles. It's a near guarantee you will become friends, as they're already in your club and team. They also understand exactly what you're going through and generally all are in great moods. We met New Zealanders Craig and Cameron at a dusty campsite opposite a Lidl supermarket near the port of Venice. They were on the same route as us but travelling much faster, we'd share some interesting times.

With our bags filled with pasta and wine, we were soon on the short road to the ferry terminal. Once there, we'd stamp ourselves out of our comfort zones and board the ferry to Alexandria on the north coast of Egypt. Ferries are dull, and the four-day ferry passage was a prison sentence. Neil, Cam, Craig and I were crammed in a small cabin and with the obscene cafeteria prices we were forced to eat our rations. And that required huddling into the en suite shower, putting a plastic bag over the smoke alarm, and firing up our Coleman petrol stoves. Pasta alla doccia! We took risks and were playing with fire, literally, but we saved ourselves about £800 over the voyage and it was a lot of fun avoiding being ripped off. I'm not sure how covert we were though. Our corridor smelled of petrol, basil and rosemary. Luckily the crew were Italian and our choice of seasoning probably saved us from a good telling off.

As is common on these transit bottlenecks we met a few other overlanders amongst the truckers. A few were bikers but most were Germans in overland trucks. Time was whittled away in the bar drinking smuggled booze and playing cards. It turned out that one of the guys had a hotel in Alexandria saved in his sat-nav and suggested we travel there together for the first night. Sure, why not.

Land ahoy! As the coast got bigger so did the butterflies in my stomach. It was around noon, and I presumed we would be on the road in an hour or so, with plenty of time to get our bearings in the daylight and find the way to this hotel. *Hah!* So naïve. This was Egypt and things were going to happen on their schedule. I was feeling on edge, as it was getting late, and I didn't want to start my African adventure in a busy city at night.

It took Egyptian officials four hours before I had a stamp in my passport and Carnet. At last we were given the green light to disembark. Finally... freedom. Africa here I come!

Not so fast, Ted. A soldier with a huge moustache directed all foreign vehicles to another shack dockside. Apparently, we needed Egyptian number plates, and they needed our engine and frame numbers, too. Our bikes were dressed in luggage and bash-plates and that meant all the numbers were hidden, so on the side of the docks in the fume-filled evening heat we stripped them down. It was absolute chaos and confusion on both sides. I'd been on African soil for but a few hours and was already sweating and frustrated. I hadn't even left the port.

Nine hours after the ship docked, and totally exhausted, we were allowed to leave. We'd had our first taste of Africa. Seven bikes stood on the side of the dock in the middle of the night and hiding on the other side of a five-metre-high wall, was Egypt. The rusted iron gate was dragged open and *wow*, an instant attack on the senses. It was like being thrown onto the set of an action film. From the tedium of a four-day ferry trip into a torrent of beeping cars, donkeys, bright lights and fast traffic. Exotic smells and toxic fumes fought for dominance and the noise was deafening. Our friend with the hotel booking couldn't get his sat-nav working. It hadn't been turned on since Italy, and now it was struggling to work out why it wasn't in Venice. Meanwhile, we were already being surrounded by merchants and puzzled locals. Luckily our new biker friend also spoke some Arabic and arranged for a local to take us to this hotel for $5. What we didn't know was this guy thought he was the Egyptian Louis Hamilton and wanted to show off how fast his old car could go. He led us on, without question, the most dangerous motorcycle ride of my life. Seven bikers were flying through the packed and chaotic streets of Alexandria desperately trying to follow a car through five or six lanes of traffic, with cars continuously chopping and changing direction. No one wanted to get left behind, so we had little choice but to run the gauntlet. A true baptism by fire.

We pulled up outside the hotel and I drew a deep breath. Everyone was high on adrenaline. Staggering off my bike I pulled my helmet off to catch my first proper look at this exotic strange land which should be filled with rogues, thieves and terrorists.

A smartly dressed man with a beaming smile approached. Nothing to do with the hotel, he introduced himself as Micky. Probably not his real name, but it turned out "Micky" was an F16 pilot for the Egyptian air force and insisted on taking us for a tour of the city that very night. *Errrr.* What? Who? Sure, why not! This day couldn't get stranger.

We threw our luggage into a room and just an hour after leaving the port were being led around Alexandria by an Egyptian F16 pilot. Even though I was desperately tired, I absolutely loved the randomness of it all. And especially the random act of kindness. I had Nile snapper for dinner; there might have been a shisha pipe and a few beers involved, too. My memories of my first day in Africa are still a blur. It could have been all a dream.

The Call to Prayer woke me up. *Wow,* it was hot. But it wasn't a dream, and I was in Egypt with my bike chained up under the window. I needed to ride to Cairo, so we ate breakfast and packed our bikes. From there, with Neil, Cam and Craig, we found the highway and set off on our first day of riding in Africa. As we didn't have a specific address to head to, it made navigating pretty easy—just follow the signs to the capital. I thought the traffic was chaotic in Alexandria until we got to Cairo, which remains the most insane and confusing city I have ever travelled in. Road signs made no sense, and we spent half the afternoon riding around in circles. But it was still fun to ride there. We were lost but so what. Eventually we tired of looking for the city centre and pulled over at the first hotel we saw with parking.

The next few days were spent zipping around in confused excitement chasing down a visa, permit and paperwork task list. I'd also received a letter of invitation from here to take to an embassy there, with instructions like, "Come back in three days, but not Wednesday."

There were many delays resulting in being stuck in Cairo for almost two weeks, but it wasn't wasted time. With delays come experiences. We met Matt and Kim, who were also heading to South Africa on motorcycles and became instant friends. One morning we got to chatting with Ali, a short, rounding but energetic local man. He insisted we follow him to his village and meet his family. He jumped on the back of Neil's bike and we all followed, zipping our way down small streets and over bridges before arriving at his smaller village just outside of the city.

It turned out Ali was the mayor's son, and far away from the tourist trail he took us to some lesser-known pyramids in the quiet desert. It was such a random and heart-warming day; exploring the backstreets of Cairo with real Egyptians and being treated as family by strangers. Ali's wife cooked an amazing dinner and we relaxed in his courtyard playing with the village children. You really don't get this with a package holiday.

With visas in hand, we were back on the road. Matt and Kim had joined our gang and together we visited all the Egyptian hotspots. We went scuba diving at Hurgharda, visited temples in Luxor, and then Aswan where we boarded the ferry across Lake Nasser to Sudan. With the freedom of our own vehicles, we could stay outside the cities.

Aswan gave us one such place at Adam's House, a simple but beautiful and tranquil home in the desert owned by a young Egyptian guy, Adam. He hosted overlanders and was incredibly hospitable and helpful. Not only did he take us to the local market to buy supplies but introduced us to the people of his village. Egypt is such a country of contrast. In the cities you are treated like a cash machine, but when you step just outside you'll experience a modest, welcoming, friendly and hospitable country.

After several days of office hopping in Aswan, we finally had our ferry tickets and most of the relevant paperwork to leave Egypt. Then, within just hours of the ferry's departure, we were told that we had to submit two number plates to get our Carnet stamped. But as we were riding motorcycles and not cars or trucks, we only had one each issued in Alexandria. No exceptions allowed. "Go back to Alexandria," we were told. Disaster!

Our Egyptian number plates were nothing more than painted Arabic numbers on scrap metal. Not difficult to make in a shed back home and so a plan was formed. I found a small fabricator and somehow explained our requirements. He couldn't help us but he jumped on the back of my bike and guided me into the traffic. In a convoy, he took us around Aswan until he found a small workshop that was happy to drop everything and make us replica number plates for pennies, in double quick time. Not only did they save our trip, but they gave us sweet tea and biscuits while we waited. It seemed we were not going to leave Egypt without a final act of hospitality.

We were herded onto the side of a jetty which could only be described as mayhem. Sudanese and Egyptians huddled and jumbled together. People, food, machinery, and everything else that goes to Sudan from the north seemed to make its way onto this ferry. And now we jumped on board, too. Our vehicles were to follow on a barge towed behind.

After a very uncomfortable night's sleep on the deck of the ancient and overcrowded ferry (with my valuables hidden in my underwear), we arrived in Wadi Halfa on the Sudanese side of Lake Nasser. Following the hordes through the various offices, we collected stamps and photocopies and then, without really knowing what just happened, we were ejected into the desert, and told to collect our bikes later. Wadi Halfa is a small settlement, and our first impression was that it was a shit-hole in the desert that only exists because of the ferry. We found a hostel where the ancient beds had mattresses you could have grown potatoes in, and a toilet odour which attacked our noses from 20 metres away. We were desperate to get our bikes from Customs and leave.

There's a new road heading south, built by the Chinese so they could exploit the country more efficiently. However, there is still the old sand road through the desert for those seeking adventure. We chose that route. Once we'd rescued our bikes from the Customs tent, we loaded up with fuel and water, and giving the middle finger to the Chinese road sign on our way past, we set off to cross the Nubian Desert. Six motorcycles, and now a Land Rover with Brits Dave and Steph.

We struggled to find the old road out of Wadi Halfa by following a wobbly line on an old GPS map. Road? Not anymore, just sand. Lots and lots of it! It was incredibly hard going. After a couple of hours, we had all crashed multiple times, but I was having fun. My bike was smaller and lighter, and the excitement of riding through the Sudanese desert helped me power through the sand, though with more enthusiasm than skill. I was so carried away in my own world that I didn't realise my companions were no longer in my rear view mirrors. Oh crap... I waited 10 minutes and nothing. Bollocks.

Disaster! Kim had crashed badly. Her bike was busted, she was concussed, and her wrist broken. We were barely hours into a two-day desert trip with a nightmare situation on our hands. This event was poignant to me and I still think about it a lot. Craig and Cameron, the two friendly New Zealanders who we'd spent the last weeks with and we classed as friends, said that they were sorry, but they were going to carry on. They didn't have the time for delays. They got on their bikes and left.

It turned out to be a blessing that Dave and Steph were following in their Land Rover. They scooped Kim up and headed back to Wadi Halfa in search of a medical centre. Matt stayed with their bikes in the desert, and Neil and I rode back to Wadi with them to find someone to help recover Kim's bike.

After an arduous journey back to Wadi Halfa, Kim was taken to the police station/clinic/truck station. We caused quite a commotion and, within minutes, people were trying to help. A businessman who could speak English translated and got Kim medical attention. Another guy grabbed a policeman, who mobilised their truck and headed out with Neil to recover the bike. Here we were in this poverty-stricken, war-broken Muslim country full of "terrorists," and the only ones who weren't helping were the two friendly westerners who rode off to enjoy their holiday. This was one of those *real Africa* moments, where those who have nothing and owed us nothing dropped everything to help total strangers.

With the help of the wonderful Sudanese people in Wadi Halfa, Kim's bike was dropped off at the famous Blue Nile Sailing Club in Khartoum; we would meet it there in a few days. No one knew the driver, but no one was concerned. "No one steals in Sudan," one man said.

After three very long, hot and thirsty days riding south through the middle of Sudan's desert, we arrived in Khartoum, and the GPS took us to the sailing club where Kim's bike was waiting. But just before we found it, and in the midst of stopped traffic, a local guy jumped upon us, enthralled by our foreign motorcycles and the Land Rover.

"Welcome to Sudan. What do you need? Hotel?" he inquired enthusiastically.

"We need a workshop for a crashed bike."

"No problem, follow me."

Again, saved by a total stranger, he took us a few blocks to Farbest Autos, a shop of full-on hustle and bustle of activity in an open courtyard. Banging, hammering, painting and repairs were going on to all sorts of vehicles, and in a little office in the corner sat Ali, a small rounded man with a huge beaming smile and excellent English.

"Welcome to Sudan. Welcome to Farbest Autos. How may I be of service?"

Within hours Kim's bike had been picked up and brought to his shop. He had arranged for us to rent a huge luxurious penthouse apartment at local prices, and that evening took everyone to dinner and introduced his friends. Over the next couple of days Ali showed amazing hospitality. One night he took us to his home to meet his family and more friends where we enjoyed a magnificent feast. I simply cannot imagine a scenario where a group of Sudanese travellers would be shown such help and hospitality in the UK.

Fully recharged with the warmth of our friends in Khartoum, it was time to head to the Ethiopian border. After another long hot day on the road, we pulled off the road and into the endless surrounding desert.

While pottering around camp, out of the haze I spotted something in the distance. Just like in the movies, the air shimmered above the horizon and slowly I could make out what was coming. It was a camel train, and leading the convoy were five men who looked like they could skin an infidel from 10 metres away. When they approached and surrounded our small group of tents there was an awkward silence. We checked each other out for a minute and then everyone smiled.

"Salaam alaikum!" I said.

"Wa-Alaikum-Salaam!" they replied.

They dismounted and sat with us. We shared snacks and water without saying a word. Twenty minutes later they got on back on their camels and left as mysteriously as they had arrived; how totally and utterly surreal.

That night in my tent the desert silence was only broken by the occasional howl of a desert fox, and the wind-carried sand pattering on my tent. I contemplated how completely vulnerable we were. But it didn't matter. In this country of war, famine and political turmoil, I felt safe. The real victim in Sudan was our ignorance and preconceptions of Africa.

* * *

Ethiopia. A length of old rope, two scruffy guards and hours of paperwork is all that separates Sudan and Ethiopia. No one is in a rush, nor do they understand ours. After seven hours at the border, we were let into Ethiopia with only a couple of hours of daylight remaining, and a long ride to the first town of Gondar.

Ethiopia is one of the most beautiful countries I've ever seen. In stark contrast to the deserts of Sudan and the TV portrayal of the country, the first 1,000 miles were a mountainous, green and lush country full of trees, wild nature and vegetation. The tight, sweeping mountain roads made it a motorcyclist's dream, but daylight was fading fast and our destination still hours away. As the sun finally dropped, it suddenly became so dark that we couldn't see our hands in front of our faces. There was no light pollution, no street lights, no cars or houses in the distance, just total darkness. With only our pathetic enduro headlights the ride was treacherous. The roads were dangerous enough in daylight, but the decision to stop for the night was made by fate.

I hit a massive rock that tore a huge gash in my tyre. Bollocks! Already exhausted, dehydrated and hungry from our delay at the border, we set up camp in a field. I was so hungry and worried about the tyre I hardly slept. I packed up early to change the tube and patch the tyre with some cardboard. It should hopefully get me to Gondar.

After a beautiful morning riding through the twisting mountain roads, we arrived in town where we were immediately jumped upon by smiling and energetic children. They wanted pens, coins, trinkets... anything tourists can provide.

"Hotel?" I asked.

A teenage boy jumped onto the back of my bike on top of the luggage and excitedly gave me instructions. A few minutes later we arrived at a small guest house with a secure compound where a few other overlanders were hanging out. These children are the local version of Google and know where people want to go before they know themselves. I thanked my guide with baked snacks from a local food stall. They were delicious and everyone was happy.

I woke up in a comfortable bed for the first time since Khartoum. The sun had found its way through a gap in the curtain and warmed my face. I felt elated. I was in Ethiopia and rode here on my own. I can still remember how that smile felt.

Wandering out of my room I took a look at the DRZ's tyre. Bugger. While the others lazed in the sunshine, with one of the helpful kids as my guide, I set out on the bike to the town centre looking for a tyre seller. I needed an 18-inch rear but the shops only had 17. Damn!

After a few more stops the lad took me to the local truck mechanic who made a perfect patch from an old truck tyre and vulcanised it into place. What a craftsman! This is how Africa keeps rolling.

I was really enjoying being in Africa but enjoying being in a group less. It had begun to feel claustrophobic and there was nothing to be frightened of in Africa. People are amazing. The "head-severing terrorists" were nowhere to be seen, and I didn't see a single white man stew on any menu. With a knee-jerk decision, I just let everyone leave without me the next morning. I needed it to be just me for a while.

As I waved off my new friends, with whom I'd shared so much with, I hesitated and worried that my safety net was also leaving. But a safety net is also a trap. After so many years saving and planning, it would be crazy to adhere to someone else's schedule.

There is something very special about travelling alone. I believe it's when you truly get to know yourself. Only when the familiarity and comfort of companions is stripped away do you have to look to yourself for inspiration and direction. However, my direction was easy. South. First to Addis Ababa to collect more visas, and then on to Kenya.

With my newfound freedom and solitude, I found a new me. I could now stop when I felt like it and interact with whoever I wanted without worrying about losing the others. It was another layer of normality and responsibility that was cast off and I felt lighter for it. I'm not sure I would have even done the trip if it wasn't for the reassurance that these people gifted me. But now I was here and immersed, realising I didn't need that safety net at all. It turned out that the hardest part of my adventure so far had been starting it.

I weaved and twisted my way through stunning Ethiopia. Children roamed the verges, most smiling and waving, and some throwing stones for fun. Out of the cities, it was almost medieval in places. Lost in time. Untouched. I loved it.

In Addis I stayed at a hostel run by an old Dutch guy, Wim, and met more amazing Africa travellers from all over the world. But a very different breed of traveller. If you're the kind who is drawn to Ethiopia, you're bound to be different. I met a guy who'd walked out of a high-flying job, got on his bicycle and had been cycling around the world for five years. I met an Israeli soldier who deserted and ran away because he couldn't live with the atrocities he committed. And a lone Japanese girl, who after years of abuse by her father, secretly applied for a passport and booked a ticket to the first city in her English dictionary. These were just some of the wonderful and inspiring travellers I met. Such insight into the lives of others changes you forever. And they give you that priceless gift of perspective.

In Addis I also met James, another Brit solo biker, and we agreed to ride the "Bandit Highway" to Kenya together for safety — a perilous 300-mile-long unpaved road through desolate bandit country.

I love how easily friendships are made overlanding:

"Got a bike?"

"Yeah."

"Going South?"

"Yeah."

"Wanna ride together for a while?"

"Sure."

We weaved our way through Ethiopia to the Kenyan border, and once across set out on the worst road I have ever known. At the border we bumped into three young Polish guys with a van full of junk food, beer and porn. It was a party bus. They were travelling around the world in style and joined us for the 300-mile, teeth-rattling journey. It was a torturous and difficult road. Bolts rattled loose and their Volkswagen camper lost its exhaust and bumpers. But we had a lot of fun picking each other up and finding parts that had fallen off the vehicles. In the evenings, the Polish guys shared their luxuries of booze and snacks. We camped in the desert and listened for the roar of lions and the crackle of gunfire we had been warned about. Luckily, we heard neither.

After days of battling the bandit highway, James and I said our goodbyes to our new friends and set off to explore the countries surrounding Lake Victoria. Uganda, Rwanda and Tanzania all seemed to drift into one as the borders were so easily crossed. We had such great times visiting the towns and camping in the abundance of nature. We camped on lakes filled with hippos, and dodged crocodiles when hunting for toilet spots. Monkeys stole our dinner and we played football with the local kids on the streets. We went white-water rafting on the White Nile, chased chickens with restaurant owners for dinner, danced with local girls at fuel stations and huddled under shelters with road workers making tea when it rained. I especially loved watching the children playing in the dust who'd stop and wave as we blasted past on our noisy machines. On stunning Lake Bunyonyi, where we were ferried between beautiful islands by small children in dugout canoes, I swapped a Liverpool football shirt with one for his paddling work, and he cried with joy.

At every shop, hotel or fuel stop we experienced nothing but hospitality, interest and warmth. Even the borders were fun. The guards tried to look professional and serious, but they couldn't help beam a smile at you if you dared to smile first. James and I sometimes rode together and sometimes our own routes, meeting up days later. It was a perfect system. We felt the freedom of solo travel but would catch up for a beer and laughs.

Days turned into weeks, then months, and the miles clocked up, but I didn't even check my speedo, or log distances anymore. This was just normal life. Wake up, make coffee, pack bike and wander off down another interesting road to somewhere else. Who will I meet today? Where will I stay tonight? Who knows? Who cares! Every day is guaranteed to be somehow different.

We arrived in Malawi, rightly famous for its spectacular lake, so big that it could be an ocean. We were having such a great time and now had beaches and warm, clear water to play in. We spent Christmas in a hostel on the beach in bamboo shacks, enjoying a hog roast and local spirits. There were more backpackers there and we partied hard. I would tell you more, but my mind is blank.

Around Lake Malawi I also witnessed the tremendous power of nature in Africa. One night I watched in awe a thunderstorm, where warm rain bucketed from the sky while hundreds of massive lightning bolts shot into the expanse of the lake.

New Year's Eve was spent at Cool Running camp. I won a fancy-dress competition in full drag because I let the local women at the market dress me up. The market women were in tears of laughter dressing up this Muzungu (white man) in women's clothing. It was so much fun, and for my prize the hostel owner took us fishing and snorkelling in his speed boat. Just brilliant.

After working our way down Lake Malawi, gorging ourselves on mangos, sunshine and laughter, we had different routes in mind. James wanted to see Botswana and I was keen on heading down the coast of Mozambique. We shook hands and agreed to keep in touch and meet again somewhere in South Africa. James had been a fantastic companion, but we both knew that travelling alone opened different doors.

The coast of Mozambique is simply stunning. A paradise. It felt a little like Brazil, with its climate, landscape and Portuguese language. It was untouched and wild in many places. The locals still fish with small nets and rods, dragging their catch onto the beach where the villagers come to barter. It was so peaceful and relaxing that I stayed for 10 days in just one place. One evening, I got chatting to a Belgian dive master at a bar and the next day learned how to scuba dive in the Indian Ocean amongst the turtles, manta rays and sharks. Just unreal.

As I travelled farther south in Mozambique, approaching South Africa, things started to change. Nature had been tamed and things became more modern. It wasn't bad, just different. Colonial Africa is incredibly interesting and diverse, and as I rolled into Maputo, the southern capital of Mozambique, my mind was blown. This ex-Portuguese colony was absolutely beautiful in its colonial grandeur, which has mostly been left to crumble. Huge palm trees line the streets, and Portuguese palaces and fortresses are hidden in the strangest of places. It's a photographer's dream. In the daytime you can explore the old buildings in the city, and in the evening relax in an African jazz bar; a true blend of cultures and history in one place.

Just a day's ride away was South Africa, and then Lesotho and Swaziland, which bordered inside of it. If I were to jump off a plane from England to land in South Africa it would have felt foreign, wild and maybe scary. But after riding the length of Africa, it was as if everything was getting easier and less exciting. Cash machines, supermarkets and funky hostels were everywhere. It's still a spectacular, huge country, though, and I had a fantastic time making my way down to Cape Town. Scuba diving, hostel parties, wine tours, safari parks, cage diving with sharks and numerous braais with the super fun South Africans I met along the way.

After seven months on the road, I was tired, broke and a big part of me was desperate to get to Cape Town. To say, "I've done it," to get there unscathed, without being robbed or cooked… but another part of me was dragging my heels. I didn't want the trip to end.

I took the beautiful coast road into Cape Town. I can't tell you how I felt. I didn't scream into my helmet or do a little dance by the sign. I just kept on riding as I always had.

At a hostel in the city centre James was waiting.

"You made it then," he said.

By then I had changed as a person. I'd seen and learned so much from the wonderful people I'd met, which again had contradicted so many of my own ideas and preconceptions. Not just about Africa, but about people, life, the world and everything that goes with it. My trip through Africa remains the most exciting, difficult, and diverse trip of my life. But most importantly, it was the most significant education of my life. I would recommend it to anyone, but with the warning, "You won't return home the same!"

About the author:

Ted Hely is a rider and traveller who refuses to grow up. He has been exploring the world by many means for nearly 20 years but feels most at home when exploring on two wheels.

He writes articles for magazines about his various journeys, which include a seven-month adventure through South America and a seven-month journey the length of Africa.

He is a motorcycle mechanic and founder of the *MotoReviveWorkshop*.

Ted lives in Liverpool in the UK.

Website: TouringTed.com
Facebook: Edd Hely | Moto Revive Workshop

The Final Frontier

After motorcycling from the bottom to the top of the planet, Alaska stole this rider's heart.

by Lisa Morris with Jason Spafford

"Travel is about the gorgeous feeling of teetering in the unknown."

—*Gaby Basora*

Skirting northeasterly around Denali National Park, I was hit with countless chevrons of snow-capped, glacier-studded mountains of interior Alaska—my hunger for wildlands was going to be well-nourished here. It was a sweet spot that seemed the very acme of Alaskan wilderness allure. For us, it was the final frontier—the beginning of the end of a four-and-a-half-year road trip that kick-started at the windswept southernmost tip of Argentina. Life alongside Jason, motorcycling the Americas, was an extraordinary adventure, packed with more highs than lows. Every time I rode with him, I seemed to appreciate him more—even on the days he maddened me to the core.

Along the way to the 49th state, the benefits of social media connected us with a gregarious biking group called the Fishhook Fatties from south central Alaska. Man alive, they loved their big adventure bikes. Their ethos was "work hard, play hard," at least during the short summer months when uninterrupted daylight is in high demand. Due to its far-reaching location, summer months see up to 24 hours' daylight, but winter stretches out over five months of the year. If inhabitants are lucky in winter, they grab a few riding hours where conditions dictate snowmobiles over motorcycles.

The Dust to Dawson motorcycle event was just around the corner in June so, upon invitation, we jumped at the chance of joining the Fishhook Fatties. Perfect timing before our final push to Prudhoe Bay, the northernmost place you can reach by navigable road in the US.

Like day one usually goes on any two-wheeled jaunt, my expectations comprised of no more than finding my stride in the saddle. Cue Pearl, my trusty BMW F650GS, who benefited from a bit of nursemaiding at certain junctures. Jason's F800GS looked more like a testosterone rocket to studliness than my darling, old dear. Little did I know what lay in store—an Alaskan's Alaska astride two wheels. I'd always wanted to explore the 49th state; to my mind, I knew if I met a good bunch of natives, they would show me the real Alaska off the tourist trail.

The Great One

When the clouds are not obscuring it, Mount Denali will do anything but disappoint astride one's moto on the George Parks Highway. As North America's highest peak located in Denali National Park, it's also known as "The Great One." Go figure. Jagged edges to razor-sharp points glowed blue with an endless supply of ruggedness. The centrepiece towered above us; an incredible natural fortress more than 20,000 feet high. Looking at it as the wind blew, the passing clouds revealed a panorama unsuspected only seconds before. It seemed like a phantasmagoria of something utterly new and unknown that shone under the beams of an Alaskan sun. Not a single wisp of cloud veiled the dramatic sight of Mount Denali—a gold-encrusted moment for sure.

I noticed the sheer beauty in the wonder of things both little and large: the pop of wildflowers that sprung up here and there or the grand sweep of a bluebird sky. Mind and cobwebs blown, it was a time when I stopped to pull over, stare out and mouth, "*Wow!*"

Ensconcing ourselves in the dirt-biking rapture that led us onto the Denali Highway, all the way from Cantwell to Paxson, going headlong across the tundra, we were free from the feeling of captivity you sometimes get in cities. As we continued scooting northwest up the Elliott Highway, it became our starting point for the 156-mile munch to Manley Hot Springs. Situated north of the Tanana River, the hot springs is one of numerous geothermal systems in Alaska. Fortunately, they're one of the few accessible by road and, in this instance, via an old Gold Rush route. The kind of route where the lush, dense undergrowth hemmed in the odd truck, taking back the road to what it once was.

These hot springs, in particular, took the form of a bathhouse tucked inside a greenhouse run at the time by Chuck and Gladys Dart on their property. Gladys' nephew, John Dart, has been operating a produce farm taking full advantage of the warm ground to utilise an extended growing season along with another expedited inside the greenhouse and across his fields.

Its origin began in 1902 when gold prospector, John Karshner, settled on a homestead and 278-acre vegetable farm. Four years in, Frank Manley financed a resort hotel while providing Karshner with financial backing, which saw the farm prosper beyond geothermal greenhouses; it flourished into a market garden and dairy along with poultry and hogs. A shame that the resort burned to the ground just six years later. Still, the village thrived during the gold discoveries, and the hot springs kept it on the map during stints of mining inactivity. Today, it's a quiet rural community of less than 50 residents who continue to subsidise their living by growing their own produce, fishing, and hunting.

Size Matters

The route to Manley Hot Springs bestowed magical views of the vast Minto Flats, a large wetland running along a northerly loop of the Tanana River, making us earn every sloppy mile. I looked up and gave the sinister sky a slit-eyed appraisal. Having fallen out of favour with Lady Luck, a backdrop of boiling, distended clouds loomed overhead as the weather cooled down. It turned a world of pleasurable dirt road into a rain-dark, raw and grey space. Ominous and tortured, the heavens opened, and rain lashed down on us in a crazy assault all the way to the springs.

Like riding on snot over marbles, we trudged our way through the pale grey calcium chloride with some artful slides thrown in for good measure. While I tried to accommodate its tactile presence and ingratiate my riding style to the soft mess, it coiled around me inescapably—a slick climb in places, and pure shambles in others. On high alert, with the backside muscles poised for a long cardio workout and my lips pursed, I felt the bottom dip temporarily out of my world.

Anyone who knows me well knows that the thought of riding in thick sludgy mud sends cold shivers down my spine. In the dark recesses of my mind, I wanted to think I'd left my muck-riding days safely behind in South America, buried like nuclear waste in airtight containers.

"Why, pray tell, can't I stay in first gear?" I enquired hopefully to Jason. "I *like* first gear, and I feel a lot more in control," I persisted, spitting out a pellet of possible explanation but conscious of hiding any princess-like tendencies.

Jason's eyebrows rose, and his expression told me he wasn't buying what I was selling. I persevered, not yet wishing to quit being an ostrich.

"Second gear is a tad too fast for me, and I *can't* give it handfuls of gas in first," I moaned, instantly regretting not having voiced the thoughts of my pity party in the safety of my head first. The thought of getting hurt always leaves me feeling soft-bellied and vulnerable.

Jason had countered this fruitless argument with knife-sharpened rationale dozens of times before. He did so again and extracted the nonsense from me as deftly as a prankster whipping a tablecloth from beneath a holiday feast. Namely, over-revving the engine in snatchy first gear would prevent me from going a notch faster in the slidey stuff when I needed to regain balance. He was right, of course, though I experienced a physical pang at the prospect.

Still, isn't that why I have thrived on adventure to this point; endlessly rugged and a little dangerous, sharing my failures and successes? An idea struck me that was so far out I had to repeat it to myself. After I did, it seemed even more outrageous. It stemmed from a Zen story about the villages of Khun Yuam, a small district in northern Thailand, where the locals occasionally ensnare monkeys, presumably for entertainment rather than dinner. The narrative delves into how the villagers chain a ewer—a bulbous-bottomed pitcher with a wide spout—to the bottom of a tree. They fill the container's base with nuts and other goodies appealing to the primates.

At some point, a monkey ventures over and slips his hand down the narrow neck, grabbing the loot with its hand while making a fist. That means the hand is now too big to withdraw from the slender neck, and he's trapped.

The moral of the story is: If you want to be free, all you have to do is let go. The tale struck a chord with me, partially because when let loose on wet, runny terrain, I tend to over-clench my handlebar grips, the left one being worn smooth. It was time to go, and if I could hold on to some enlightenment, it might just lead to *"Slowly, slowly, catchee monkey."* With any fears now ring-fenced, I threw my leg over Pearl and got going.

Astride luggage-laden Pearl, who weighed in at 240 kilograms, I scrabbled, lost control, and groused, watching my wheels fling manes of brown spray everywhere. I should have long ago embraced the concept "light and tight," where size *always* matters off road.

Having located a drier section, I shelved the dampened spirits and smiled like the sun was coming out. It wasn't, but I went for it with a handful of throttle. Failing to realise we had reunited with the squelchy malevolence of the mud, I scared myself silly at 60 mph as I squirmed mid-corner in a mire. "What the...!" I cussed, careening horribly towards a ditch, my brain unable to gauge the speed at which enthusiasm superseded skill. Language went away and, for a split second, I prayed in a soft, high-pitched lament any human listener would have termed a dizzy yelp: "Oh my *GAWD*, I forgot who I was!" I took a moment to stop my heart's wild drum solo. Thank goodness for adrenaline.

At the end of every rainbow....

Eventually, we cleared the sloppy passage. Determined to claim victory from the jaws of defeat, we struck gold at the end of the Elliott and entered a little green village known as Manley Hot Springs.

Just outside the hot springs we found the Manley Roadhouse, the oldest roadhouse still open for business in Alaska, and with mining equipment displays from its heyday. Wearily, we pegged out the Dome Sweet Dome at a tent site on the slough opposite. As we did, Alaska's unofficial welcoming committee descended as the summer-loving regiment of twin-engine mosquitoes. With the utmost dispatch, they rushed to meet and greet us like tiny stealth bombers: silent, painless and deadly.

Having ditched the riding gear, I found that the dirt had penetrated every part of my clothing. Our exposed skin must have looked like a banquet. Why is it that the bloodsuckers are drawn to some more than others?

Beaten by the will of my own mane, my hair had completed its final descent into disreputability. I scraped back a riot of unruly red tresses in a bun atop my head. A Garden of Eden experience awaited us. Cue an indoor tropical garden of paradise. Jumping straight into the spring-fed baths a short walk from where we had made camp, we kept the winged assailants at bay.

Gloriously, the spring-fed greenhouse is home to three concrete pools of varying allure. Slowly, we eased ourselves in to soak, unwind and relax the worked muscle groups I didn't know I had. Each bath differed in temperature, although I soon found my Goldilocks one that was *just right*. My skin tingled with awareness of the world around me as I struggled to kick-start my exhausted mind. It was a heavenly yang after the yin journey to get there, an unexpected oasis of Alaska's interior.

No one else was in attendance aside from our party that afternoon, so we bore no qualms in fully immersing ourselves in the setting, which hummed thick with colour. Namely, from the exotic fruits in bloom: hot pink hibiscus flowers, yellow Asian pears and clusters of hanging grapes. A tot of honey whiskey took the experience to an unprecedented level of wonderful. Moreover, a price of just $5 per person made losing oneself in this soothing comfort impossibly inexpensive to boot.

At dusk, my thoughts soon began to turn teaward. After sitting amid an assortment of edible plants and fruits, I became ravenous, and could have eaten a scabby donkey. Courtesy of the roadhouse, I chowed down as if I had lived through a famine. Local resident Doug, propping up the bar, talked the hind leg off me. He was one of those unforgettable drunk gold-miner chaps, giving it the biggun on his Klondike story. With a face full of years, his legs were thin, his socks sagged, and the grit of decades seemed settled in his face. Melancholy draped itself around this guy's shoulders like some invisible but almost tangible quilt. Rested and relaxed, I let him chew the fat while I nodded and smiled, nodded and smiled.

Camaraderie

The following dawn brought an unexpected win in the road surface lottery. It was a corker of a morning, accompanied by lovely swathes of afternoon sun as we rode the same route back on a mocha-coloured satin surface. Gratefully, it was free from squelchy ground all the way back to Fairbanks. From there, we wended over 180 paved miles on the adjoining Richardson Highway. This merged onto the Alaska Highway and deposited us in a sea of bikers at Thompson's Eagle's Claw Campground in Tok.

The campground is a popular choice for riders of any discipline, expressly favoured by bikers en route to Dust to Dawson. The place was a bottle green forest of intimate snuggeries, the tall protective trees aptly arranged to nestle in your bike and tent from any wandering beasts—bears have been known to roam there. *Ahem,* I carried a bicycle bell in lieu of a gun. Still, the green from the trees was luminous. Spokes of sunlight poured through, which backlit this cosy spot and set the tone splendidly. Sure enough, the day rapidly became an amphitheatre of motorcycle noise and unrestrained, spirited banter from all. It was filled with the unmistakable biking camaraderie that springs from the fellowship of the road.

Despite the intense midnight light, I rubbed callused palms into my sleep-heavy eyes. As sleep gathered around me and the light bathed us in its ageless peace, I crawled into bed under the weight of the sun and solid times happening outdoors, collapsing in a heap and closing my eyes. A gentle breeze caressed the tent. I surrendered to the happy fatigue sluicing through my body like water down rock and sank like a stone to the sounds of people laughing, a cathedral choir of laughter.

The following morning, Jason gently brought me to with a steaming mug of coffee. Awaking to a haze of green lichen mist, the forest at Tok was as enchanting as I'd remembered, its sorcery still holding me rapt. The huge spruce trees were shimmering kaleidoscopes, each needle a polygon of morning light.

Courtesy of a Fast Eddy's breakfast, I re-established cordial relations with my stomach. Wonderfully, the meal comprised all the trimmings of an English muffin, Canadian bacon, and a poached egg drizzled in the deliciously tangy goodness that is Hollandaise sauce, but with an addition of steamed spinach on top. I never did understand why Benedict and Florentine had to be mutually exclusive.

With no snot on marbles in sight, the day saw us scoot out of Tok to Tetlin Junction. Favourable conditions on our side, the connecting Taylor Highway saw us enjoy 60 paved miles before it turned to a good dirt road for the remainder of the way to the border. Magnificently, this saw us join the Top of the World Highway, open only through the summer months.

Built in 1955, the highway was named because between Dawson and the corresponding junction on the Taylor (Alaska Route 5), it wanders for 79 miles around the region's high points, including the hill crests and ridgelines above the tree line at an elevation that projects sharply down on the valleys. Further, it's one of the most northerly highways on the planet. Needless to say, it's a "top ride," especially if narrow, serpentine mountain roads are your bag of fun.

Crossing the border, the route becomes known as the Yukon Highway, which saw us negotiate partially paved but mostly reconstructed chip seal. Chip seal is a pavement surface treatment that sees asphalt combined with fine aggregate "chips." On occasion, the gravelly roads were a little challenging, although I cared little and less because of the light cast on the mountains along this fabled road, eventually linking us with Dawson in the Yukon. I studied the clouds that brushed the turquoise sky in long streamers sweeping southwards. Others were slender feathers of clouds that floated across the bleached belly of the sky. In a heartbeat, I fell head over heels for the landscape.

The City of Gold

At the heart of the world-famous Klondike Gold Rush, Dawson found its place on the map when it saw three Yukon "Sourdoughs," George Carmack, Dawson Charlie, and Skookum Jim, hit the jackpot on Rabbit Creek (now Bonanza Creek), a tributary of the Klondike River in 1896.

Before the big strike, two discerning Yukon traders, Joe Ladue and Arthur Harper, jumped at the opportunity to invest and establish the townsite of Dawson (named after Canadian Geologist George Mercer Dawson) about 12 miles from Discovery Claim. During three years, $29 million in gold was plucked from the ground around Dawson City. News reached the outside world in 1897 when two steamships reached San Francisco and Seattle with the triumphant miners from the previous season hauling the precious "Ton of Gold" cargo.

Word spread like wildfire of a place where "nuggets could be picked off the creek floor" to a recession-afflicted world, triggering an unparalleled bolt of 100,000 people to rush to the goldfields. Most knew little about the 3,000-mile trek ahead of them. Their perilous journeys involved uncharted backcountry, snow-choked mountain passes and icy rivers in staking their claim to fortune in the Klondike.

For many, it was more about escape from the humdrum, the adventure of a new frontier. Many of us can relate to that. The decadent town, bountiful in gold, soon became known as the "Paris of the North." Overnight millionaires roamed the streets, splurging their wealth. Today, the same spirit can still be found in Dawson. Although the rush is over, gold mining continues to thrive, as does the adventure it takes to get there, thanks to events like Dust to Dawson. Although it's infinitely less arduous—that is, when it doesn't rain!

Dust to Dawson

If you've never heard of Dust to Dawson (D2D), you're in for a treat. Just punch in your preferred sat-nav route to Dawson, hop on your bike in June, and get giddy at the prospect of what lies ahead. If your schedule permits, try not to go hell for leather in getting there, for a ride both rewarding and nurturing is likely to unfold. Oh, and when you rock up to Dawson, like us, you'll probably be told not to call it a "rally."

Whatever you think it is, you'll be in the thick of an atmosphere abuzz with the boundless joy that is D2D.

The backstory begins with three unassuming blokes: John "Cash" Register, Jim Coleman, and Mike "Fighter" Stein. Dating back to 1992, D2D was concocted over a few pints in Dawson's Midnight Sun, a hotel bar where the trio first met. In operation for the past three decades, the establishment was rebuilt in '84, congruent with the heritage character of the original Midnight Sun's cream and maroon wood frame construction.

As Fighter recounts, a 500-mile road trip between the three amigos up the Dempster Highway to Inuvik was set in motion, during which Coleman and Cash branched off to Eagle, Alaska. Awed by the place, a pact was made that the others would return to the North Country with the ashes of the departed when one of them kicked the bucket.

When Coleman was hit by a Chevrolet Suburban, a family-sized sports utility vehicle, on his BMW GS a couple of years later, Cash re-enacted their road trip in '95. Mile for mile, he kicked the side stand down and paid homage at the same pit stops, refuelled at the same cafés, and drank another cold one at the Midnight Sun, all the while carrying Coleman's ashes in the tank bag. Dawson's dusty route gained momentum, magnetising riders from all corners to make a pilgrimage: to pay their respects, come together, and celebrate.

D2D's 24th anniversary (2016) saw bikers sign in from 20 US states and six countries worldwide. Hosted by "Dawson Dick" and his wife at the Triple J Hotel, the 400-strong motorcycle event comprised three days of biker festivities, local charity fundraising, on-the-fly poker games and sausage-gnawing amusement. A gourmet steak dinner, real ale and a silent auction awaited on top. Awards were given for "Hard Luck" in the trials and tribulations getting there and the most spectacular crash to Dawson. Jason and I even received one, which took the guise of a small trophy adorned with a motorcycle and plaque: "Farthest Ride."

D2D wouldn't be D2D without the biker games. No less than 27 plucky if not willing motorcyclists took to the fun and frolics. Starting with the slow race, which as my nickname "Captain Slow" suggests, I aced! We progressed onto the next event: a slalom of increasingly tight cones, then riding while blindfolded, and climaxing the activities with the pillion contest. *Hah!* Folks who can normally ride to a reasonable standard turn into gibbering wrecks when 300 pairs of eyes are boring into them.

By folks, I mean me. Hungry to give it a go alongside the other female rider in the competition, I bit off more than I could chew. Certainly, in the game involving a "wiener" (hot dog sausage), strung at the end of a fishing line from an elevated height for the pillion to stand up and snap at. Duty-wracked as a pillion, I garnered all the sportsmanship I could muster while my oversize eyes bulged as the sausage hove into view from the start line.

Craven dread crept through me like a rat up a drainpipe as I held to Tanner, my rider, and spied the audience: all too knowing for my liking. Comically, it was a test of showmanship and humour far more than skill. I was with the Fishhook Fatties; by now, I shouldn't have been surprised. Through mouth-plastered hands, unruly giggles surfaced and accrued strength. Head at full tilt, I laughed so hard my sight went dark, struck by the audience's supporting hysterics and sidelong gawps that whirled and spilled my way.

The pulse of the free-form gathering at D2D seemed to work through my body until I recognised it as music. I heard the enlivened rhythm of engines starting, beer cans being popped open, and folks catching up on lost times with gusto. The ground was astir with a heady conviviality interspersed with animated interest as much as raucous entertainment. What a hoot!

After perhaps the liveliest "non-rally" experience to date, the return route to Tok beat backwards under us. Reluctantly peeling away from the Fishhook Fatties, I arose the next day muddy-eyed, having burned the candle to a nub. My head was cotton and my mouth gravel. Nothing would cut through the mossy feeling in my mouth. Wending out of Tok, we rode into a peevish wind via Fairbanks towards the Dalton Highway. As far as milestones go, it was the last leg for us on a route north. That is, until we ran out of road. The day passed a poor, sluggish thing that departed almost gratefully as night took its place.

You know that "right time, right place" magical thing... that happened.

Somehow, I had curried favour with Lady Luck again. An uncharacteristically dry Dalton Highway guided us on a glorious, incident-free 248-mile stint as we glided northward along an easy dirt road from Fairbanks. Dry, bright sunny conditions permitted us to ride over the calcium chloride and gravel with zero fuss. It was the perfect combination to allow my mind to wander as I traversed between the rolling, forested hills across the Yukon River and Arctic Circle. Into the Brooks Range and over the North Slope to the Arctic Ocean, a great place to dip your big toe in and mark the occasion!

Upon reaching Wiseman, 12 miles from Coldfoot and the halfway mark to Prudhoe Bay, we took full advantage of the last place to fuel up. Wiseman is also home to a fabulous little overnight stop, the Gold Rush Campground, situated amid lush greenery. I couldn't deny campground owner Jim's shaggy appeal as he grinned at me through his big white beard. He was undoubtedly a consummate ladies' man who exuded all the Alaskan playboy charm you could wish for.

It seemed a no-brainer to stay in Wiseman compared to Coldfoot. The latter purpose-built as a no-frills construction camp for the Trans-Alaska pipeline workers and long-haul truckers. And it was no surprise to learn that Coldfoot is the world's northernmost truck stop. However, I liked discovering that the town got its name in 1900 when travellers got chilly feet with the onset of Alaska's unforgiving winter. You may have even seen these truckies on *America's Toughest Jobs, Ice Road Truckers* or the BBC's *World's Most Dangerous Roads*.

Now and again, the landscape that followed took on a raw, peculiar beauty with a bleak *Wuthering Heights* quality—isolated, wild and windy moors but without the stormy weather, or moors. Every fibre in my being was gripped by such untamed surroundings, the solitude gulped me down whole. The only landmark vying for our attention was the light grey, low lying industrial pipeline that accompanied us from Fairbanks to the top. That, and Atigun Pass in the Brooks Range, where the Dalton crosses the Continental Divide. The area holds a strong resemblance to the prominent peaks of Patagonia, Scotland, or New Zealand. Take your pick, it's impressive.

Although Jason did let it slip that he felt vaguely cheated by Alaska's glorious skies and the optimum riding conditions that are typically unpredictable. "Really?" I asked, my eyes rolling to the top of my head in a visored facepalm moment. After which I received a short lecture about how weather is the defining quality of a landscape, which determines the two most pivotal landscape photographic features—lighting and mood—so the wilder it is, the more compelling the pictures. I get it: give the man drama in the skies!

Never so happy to be wrong, I carried on riding in a liquid-warm state. I rode gazing at Dall sheep nibbling on the green upper slopes, while bald eagles soared majestically overhead. A heard of reindeer crossed our path; an Alaskan rush hour, while a family of muskoxen grazed on the roadside grasses. It was the first time I'd ever laid eyes on a muskox, a stocky, hoofed beast with almost no neck, bearing a large head. They're made distinctive by their big, curved horns, presented in a Lego-lady's-wig-meets-Viking-warrior hairdo. The thickset goat-antelope creature stands on short, stout legs, and its body is draped in a thick, straight-haired coat of long, dark brown fur. It reminded me more of a woolly mammoth than your standard ox, and I didn't doubt their stoic ability to withstand the ice-cold winter.

It's true what they say. Alaska has two seasons: winter and construction. Inching closer toward Prudhoe Bay gifted me a white-knuckle ride on a loose section of road under construction. If I'm going to cruise beneath warm sunny skies to this point in the Frozen North, I've at least got to earn my spurs on the last smidgen of it.

"Lisa, please listen. Promise me you'll stay in second once we head down this loose section, and then give it the tiniest amount to stay positive when it feels twitchy," Jason begged as the focus of his gaze swallowed all of my thoughts. Knowing he was alluding to both the throttle as much as my temperament didn't take a lot to fathom. *Mmm*, I mused.

"You just need to suck it up. I can't ride your bike for you," was his pragmatic conclusion. Looking back, I think it's the reason you never hear the phrase "male intuition."

As I swallowed Jason's words, I wondered if they would take root. A stratagem came to me, like a god thundering in my head: just keep riding. I surmised that after 47,550 miles, my journey on Pearl was set to continue as a great enterprise of balance. She imparts to the gravel a generosity of spirit and, while urging me to relax and let go, Pearl frequently saves me from myself.

Aided on the Dalton's loose stuff by bumping into Lyndon Poskitt—a Brit who races the bike on which he travels—instilled a "cock of the walk" hubris in me that I didn't know I possessed. When it comes to riding, Lyndon Poskitt is incontestable; he's as certain as the sky. Pearl took heed and hesitated not a second in jolting my muscle memory, enabling me to slip back into a groove of sorts. She seemed certain of the first step in her lead as we embraced the lumps and bumps together. I felt alive by my motorcycle's flair for emboldening me to take the reins in wielding her with artful precision.

"Lisa, just keep doing what you're doing!"

"Okay, darlin', I will," to Jason's relief.

Partway to the top, Jason enquired, "Are you enjoying yourself?"

"Yep! Sure am," I blurted in a surge of glee.

"Super, because you're riding like a pro today. I'm impressed". There was a timbre to Jason's voice where he had said that to me only a handful of times in my riding career to date. I was ecstatic and fed off his compliment. I think I dined on it for a couple of days because, for once, my belief in my off-road riding ability remained intact.

The problem with Lady Luck is never knowing when your good fortune runs out at any hairy moment. A patch undergoing heavy construction comprised soil, earth, and loose stones. "Okay, here we go!" I cried as Pearl bobbled over rocks that ricocheted off her boulder basher, pummelling her relentlessly. Without even thinking about it, I got into a flow, throwing Pearl this way and that, slaloming through bundles of rocks, sending up clouds of fine dust, and closing fast on the finish line.

The afternoon passed triumphantly. Riding somewhere close to my technical limits, I was in a heady frame of mind. Buoyed by skimming the loose stuff as opposed to drowning below its surface, tingling with delight at every curve ball thrown my way. While the Dalton was a long, desolate road needing extra fuel and grit determination, it's one I'm glad I did. If you time your weather window right, you'll find your axis of bliss.

Cataclysmic endings.

Hurrah! We'd made it from the bottom of the planet to the top. Damn, it felt good. I admit it, I was amped.

Where there's a pinnacle of pleasure, there's Prudhoe Bay, and all told, a surprise in store. Out of nowhere, a hotel shuttle bus driver came hurtling towards us. At that very moment, we—a trio of elation—smiled for the birdie in front of Jason's tripod, standing a few feet away from us perched on the gravel road. That second, my pride was in full flower at how far we had come. Someone said something amusing. Oh, I loved that laugh of Jason's, the low, treacly joy of it. He should laugh more; it suits him, seeing how the furrows around his brow vanish, and his ears ease back.

We'd set up the camera in the road to capture the feat of having conquered a ride from the planet's bottom, Argentina, to the very top. Admittedly, we took a chance positioning the camera where we did. The odds looked agreeable: everyone was aware of the maximum speed limit of 5 mph when people are near the road system in Prudhoe Bay, the traffic was light from the oncoming direction, and nothing had appeared in the lane of Jason's equipment.

Without warning or apparent reason, an oncoming white 16-seater veered out of its lane into ours at around 20 mph. It clipped Jason's camera with its wing mirror, obliterating several thousand British pounds into the bargain as it toppled, and bounced hard down the road.

I stopped. I tried to bring order to my tumultuous thoughts while Jason saw red. To have our hopes of revelling in our little personal moment at the top raised, and then so monumentally dashed, was a blow.

Picking up the battered and broken remnants, dread fermented into a sickening brew in my guts. Jason's livelihood and creative outlet to connect with the world would be suspended for the foreseeable future.

Running at full pelt 100 feet down the road, I finally caught up with the shuttle bus. During a brief conversation with the driver, the roar of his indifference filled my ears to the brink. I had to hold my tongue and restrain every instinct of becoming a storm of accusation. Still reeling from what had just happened, I noticed a lack of emotion in his eyes looking out of a boxer's face, with a flat nose, a broad chin and close-set eyes. Together, his features were suffused with the naked apathy that made him who he was. I went for neutral with a willingness to listen, but incredulity and stress hijacked the message and delivered strained and upset.

It was time to rally—no fulsome expressions of regret and apology were headed Jason's way. I reached hungrily for his hand, our fingers interlocking. I squeezed his fingers, a Morse code to convey what was in my heart. He nodded. *You don't have to tell me anything* is what he was saying.

And this year's Oscar for services to the word "SH*T" goes to....

I recounted and catalogued the events, giving each their due, putting them in the most effective order. Propelled by a recognition and the sudden lightness that follows an unburdening, I couldn't deny the camera and tripod should not have been where we had planted them. Thoughts raced around in my head as I fought to stay calm. I succeeded in spite of myself but saw how grief imprinted its tracks on Jason's face, tightening around his mouth and eyes, ringed by worry lines. Jason was a world away. I studied him as I might examine some specimens set before me. I saw the smile that struggled for purchase on his face and failed, and then I saw the disappointment that came in its wake.

Meanwhile, Lyndon's modus operandi had been listening, comforting and caring. Assuming an impartial mediation role, he assertively led a group meeting with the hotel safety officer, local law enforcement, and us. Sometimes, you just have to draw a line, chalk it down to, "Stuff happens, right?" and write these things off. Apart from the haemorrhage to our budget, I acknowledged there had been no harm done to bodies or bikes.

While there were open wounds to lick, the hotel offered the three of us two complimentary rooms with full board. It's the gestures of goodwill like this and Lyndon's—when you've not been in a place or known someone for five minutes—that endear you to them.

Learn, evolve and be open to life.

Camera catastrophes dead and buried, reaching the oil production centre put a somewhat anticlimactic full stop on proceedings. Especially from the Americas' most southerly point, which had encompassed epic souls and scenery over a lifetime of firsts. Up to that point, we had taken in 21 countries from Antarctica to the Arctic Circle and about 300 miles beyond. While it took two-and-a-half years to reach Prudhoe Bay, Alaska, we weren't ready to quit the saddle, so we spent another two years in the States and Canada. Something rang in me like a bell: I couldn't revert back to my former life in Old Blighty for all the gold in the Klondike.

Riding the Americas changed us. During the journey, I decided against having a child, which shocked the heck out of Jason. We want to see where an unscripted future takes us. Although I did get tired after16 years of waiting for him to propose. So I took full advantage of it being a leap year while getting wide-eyed on the grey whales in Mexico, and I popped the question. He said yes. Our biographies are so intertwined that we share nearly every page. Gratefully, our partnership has gone the distance and is here to stay.

We live at large, and the thrill of motorcycling together has made our lives tender and raw, tough but euphoric, and absolutely, inextricably linked. There is nothing better than sharing your life with someone. For me, that someone is Jason. My voice of reason, my best friend, sometimes my opponent, but always the love of my life.

Alaska will make you express your joy, not seek it.

Just like the road to get there, your pleasure-drenched memories of Alaska will calcify, and you won't experience it without feeling you've blossomed many friendships and deposited days of gold in the Good Times Bank. I'll remember the summer days as cloudless, the air fresh and pumped with excitement. There was an undeniable sense that having made it this far, it was part of the way astride two wheels to something else, an elation. If "ecstasy" means the intrusion of the wonderful into the ordinary, then it had just happened to me.

There will always be under-the-radar pieces of our planet that have defied all attempts to tame them; many of them are wondrous. Alaska is one of those places. Overlanding the Final Frontier state sharpened the realisation that there is no time to sit around and overthink how life should go. It's a region that will leave you ready to stop trying to *matter*. It will make you ready to simply *live*.

About the authors:

British born, **Lisa Morris** and **Jason Spafford** are self-confessed thrill-seekers. The motivating force is adventure travel, enabling their passion as photographers and media professionals. Previously, they co-ran scuba diving trips around the watery globe as dive instructors and guides.

Having hung up the fins after a decade, they jumped on their saddles and *braap'ed* their way from Argentina to Alaska, taking in Antarctica to the Arctic Circle; spanning a total of four-and-a-half years.

Having remained location-independent since 2014, they next planned a 4WD cape-to-cape jaunt from Nordkapp to Cape Town. The Nordic countries did anything but disappoint, but the photographic expedition

91

was cut short after six months when Covid-19 hit, forcing them back to the UK.

Meanwhile, Lisa helps keep the wheels rolling by contributing their tales from the trails to publications worldwide, while Jason takes care of all things visual. Field testing outdoor products complements the brand ambassadorships, kit sponsorships, and paid collaborations.

As an advocate for female riders, Lisa has consulted with manufacturers of women's motorcycle gear. Not the most natural off-road rider, she says she's proof that you can pass your test and go. Near or far, it's empowering!

Pandemic permitting, their travels will continue to see them roam—wherever the next itch needs to be scratched.

Website: fourwheelednomad.com
Facebook: fourwheelednomad
Instagram: @fourwheelednomad
YouTube: FourWheelNomad
Vimeo: Jason Spafford

The True Value of Travel

by Mark Donham

"If you haven't learned the meaning of friendship, you really haven't learned anything."

—*Muhammad Ali*

You may know me by my ADVRider.com screen name of "Radioman." If you do, you'll know about my two-and-a-half-year motorcycle journey around the world. Two occurrences in particular stand out from this adventure. They opened up a new set of values and appreciations that are key to my life now. They underlined this thought: *If a traveler embraces the opportunities of a transcontinental journey, and does so with an open mind, travel magic is sure to follow.* I'd like to share what's on my mind.

I was riding and exploring the dusty gravel roads of six countries as I traveled south along the length of the Andes from Colombia, aiming eventually for the dramatic landscapes of Patagonia.

Staying off the beaten path as much as possible was full of the surprises and fascinations I'd hoped to find on my journey. The backroads were a brilliant mix of challenges and the unexpected, and the people along the way were always interesting, usually kind and often funny. I stayed in places I couldn't have imagined and ate foods and fruits that I'd never heard of. I'd hurt myself, but never more than a sprained knee, cuts, bruises and a little scuffed pride. I had surprised myself with the realizations of just how much I could achieve. But South America isn't where this story begins. First, I need to take you back to my pre-trip home in Portland, Oregon.

Living a suburban life in the United States was very good. My wife and I had good careers and a home life we loved. Our days were full of work, lots of my stepsons' school activities, socializing with friends and family, and many annual holiday trips. But then life changed forever. Chris started developing the hallmark signs of early onset Alzheimer's disease. With that diagnosis our lives were forced to change. She was in her mid-40s, and with family history we knew how this disease was going to progress. I left my job to care for her full time; this was going to be a journey we'd make together. After eight years of the best and worst parts of life, Chris, with a steady and heartbreaking decline, died of this awful disease. The process of losing her was heart wrenching, a painful journey for everyone that knew and loved her.

My passion for motorcycling had started many years prior but, as is the way for so many, other parts of life had taken over and I'd let riding ease into the background for a while. Once Chris had been diagnosed, the decision to spend all our time together meant that we were able to share some amazing two-up rides to see family and friends around the US. I'm forever grateful for the fun of those adventures. We put more than 40,000 miles across the States together. After a while she was no longer able to join me, but getting out for a ride was healthy for me mentally, and Chris understood this. Riding was my way of getting a much-needed break from caregiving. It gave me the chance to clear my head and renew my body, mind and soul.

Alzheimer's disease, as it devastated Chris's abilities, meant that I'd been losing much of her way before her actual death. I had been processing, reading and attending a grief support group along the way, and during the final months of her life, I started to dream of riding a motorcycle around the world. I'd traveled with a backpack throughout Europe, Australia and New Zealand in my late teens and early 20s and loved exploring other places. These trips had taught me not to travel for travel's sake, nor for just beautiful scenery or vistas, but very much for the people, culture, and foods, too.

You'll imagine that the six months after Chris passed away was a period in life that I'd never want to repeat. But the dream niggled at me and the thought of it gave a vital streak of positive to hang on to. I knew I had to make this vision come alive. I was on the roller coaster of grief from the loss of my wife and reeling from the huge changes that lay in front of me, but it was a *wake up* moment; life is very short sometimes. The plan was not to try to run away from what had happened. I was going out into the world to visit the places I'd not been but wanted to see.

I clearly remember telling others of my plans, and that so many had boldly told me all the reasons that I should not do it. Obstacles such as, "What about your house?" "... your career?" or warnings like, "You are going to die in Mexico, it's too dangerous." These comments always made me smile. My mind was made up, I was going, and I knew that the journey would unfold as it was supposed to. It was crystal clear that I wasn't running from death but embracing the life ahead of me. I knew that the hurtling ups and downs of grief were something that would be with me at times forever, but now it was important to reset my life.

Fast forwarding to the dusty roads of Chile and the far south of South America, it was month 16 of my travels and I'd just reached the famous Carretera Austral, the road into the rugged beauty of Patagonia. The Patagonia region is a sparsely populated area known for majestic mountains, beautiful lakes and fjords along with glaciers and national parks. This appealed to my sense of outdoor adventure, the hiking and mountaineering, as it did in my youth.

My stop for a few nights was the town of Puyuhuapi, a peaceful settlement on the edge of a Pacific Ocean inlet. The town was founded in 1935 by German immigrants. It's said that the climate and mountainous landscapes made them think of home, and many of the towns of the region still have a distinctive German look, even feel, to them. The town was located on the edge of the inlet, with fishing boats pulled up on the shore and more moored on the water. I stayed at Casa Ludwig, which is a colorfully painted guesthouse that faced the water and reminded me of places I'd stayed in Europe. That night I found a very tasty steak and vegetable dinner in town. Good food is always a highlight on a long trip and so worth a mention.

My timing was impeccable; I'd arrived on the day of a town celebration to honor its founding. This included folk dancing in the streets, which I really enjoyed watching. One of the joys of a motorcycle journey is the luxury of time and the flexibility that having your own transport gives you to take advantage of such opportunities. With those in mind, I was very much in the moment of enjoying the beautiful little town, the people, the food, and the celebrations.

Solo motorcycling around the world has its times of riding completely free of the compromises of traveling with others, and at times being on your own in the world feels like exactly the right place to be. There are times of aloneness and loneliness, which are part of the realities of solo travel. These emotions would be strong at times, but they passed and changed during the course of the time on the road. At other times, riding with others met along the way is one of the best possible things you can ever have the opportunity to do. You never know who you are going to meet next, and for me as a solo rider, meeting travelers and others along the way is a significant part of the magic of travel.

The day after the celebrations I rode south along the waterside towards the next scenic stop, the Cascada de Ventisquero Colgante Park. This is home to the viewpoint for a "hanging" glacier. Little did I know what this day would bring, and how it would influence future travel plans. I rode into the park to pay a 2,500 CLP (Chilean peso, approx. $5 USD) entrance fee to the attendant. He was a friendly guy in his 40s who spoke no English and was perched in the small ticket booth. As he handed over my ticket and change, he indicated there were some motos just ahead of me in the park. Our conversation was in Spanish, which I'd been working on for the past few months. I was improving over those months and was now able to speak comfortably about daily needs, but still short on vocabulary. I was never able to have deep conversations.

As I rode into the park, I could indeed see two loaded bikes. They were parked next to the pathway out to the hanging glacier viewpoint. Just as I got off my BMW F800GS along came three fully geared-up riders. Greeting others on the road usually brings big smiles, as did this random meeting, but before I could actually say anything one of them said, "Hey, I know you, you're 'Radioman.'"

I'll never forget how it felt to get this greeting from a stranger in the middle of Chile. I have the video I took of this exact moment, and it still brings me great joy. I'd been posting ride reports using Radioman as my screen name on ADVRider.com. The report, which I'd been sharing since the start of my journey, was daily writing about the ride, my experiences and thoughts. Dick told me, "I've been following your report through Central America and South America. In particular I was looking for your information about border crossings."

Border crossings are always such an unknown process for overlanders and there's a kind of information underground that shares hints and tips of information. From them, riders can get a sense of what to expect and what they might need to cross the various borders. This was one of the reasons I talked about it in my blog and shared photos on ADVRider. I'd had the same concerns and learned from others before my trip. One of the things I like so much about overlanding is how people naturally share.

As a side note, my main advice for border crossings is to have patience, and a smile. Some crossings can be very confusing or complicated and can take several hours to navigate. Crossing into Mexico was easy, with fairly straightforward paperwork and fees. Going into Central American border crossings like Honduras felt much more hectic. Lots of "helpers" harass you for a fee to assist with navigating the system within the inevitably crowded Customs buildings with little or no signage, or logical process to get all your paperwork completed. The extra hot days of the region didn't help.

Don't worry, you'll get across. Smile and have a good time; this attitude helps at all border crossings anywhere in the world. There's no need to be upset if the process is not smooth or simple. If you're patient, you will work out how to do it. My other tips are to be well rested, and to have some water and snacks available; sometimes progress is very slow.

With hindsight, this chance meeting with the trio in a national park in Chile really was even more of a magical moment that I realized at the time. This crossing of paths was about to change the course of the rest of my journey around the world.

After striding down the gravel path to look at the glacier, I headed back to the bikes where the Kiwis were waiting for me. We decided that, as we were going the same direction, we would travel together. We were all aiming to head south along Ruta 7 (the Carretera Austral) and then were planning to drop into Argentina. Once there we'd link up with and ride along the fabled Ruta 40. The last section of the route we were looking at would take us toward Ushuaia and "Fin del Mundo" ("End of the World"). Not far from the town was the southernmost point of the South American continent that anyone could ride to. To the south of that point there was little more than a scattering of islands, craggy roadless headlands and the freezing seas that led to the snow and ice of the Antarctic.

I'd been riding on my own for quite a while, so it was fun to have others to enjoy this beautiful and stunningly visual part of the world with. We rode our way south, enjoying the amazing mountain views. The snow-covered peaks, contrasting with the lush vegetation and blue water lakes, took my breath away. We stopped at the beautiful Capillas de Mármol on Lake General Carrera. These are stunning marble caves with swirls of color and patterns that are quite unique. And as we experienced the beauty of the area, we also developed our friendships. Dick and Diana, and Ken were on the final leg of their five-month journey from Alaska to Ushuaia. As we rode, we started to get to know one another and about our individual travels.

They were an "older" trio from New Zealand. There had been four of them; just a week earlier Ken's better half, Shirley, had needed to return to New Zealand. The four of us got on well and, with lots of time in the evenings, we shared our stories and life experiences. Dick and Diana had a very interesting history, as they owned the Hubbard Foods Ltd in NZ, and Dick had been the mayor of Auckland. They had wonderful stories and were very proud of New Zealand. Ken kept me on my toes with his dry sense of humor. They were riding big BMW GSes for their travels.

One day we came across a section of road being graded. As a result, there was lots of loose, deep gravel. The driver of the grader had stopped right in the middle of the narrow road. Having to move right to the side, I ended up sliding down the bank and tipping my bike over. Fortunately,

Dick and Ken helped get it back up the deep, loose gravel while Diana documented the event with photographs. Diana was also admirably skilled at engaging locals in conversation with her bright smile and big heart.

We stopped for a few days at El Calafate in Argentina, where we headed out from to get a view of the Puerto Moreno glacier. This glacier is huge. It's over 19 miles long and is 240 feet high in the section that faces the lake. Giant chunks of ice calve off, plunging into the water to the cheers of tourists and with a booming sound that echoes around the lake. Together with a guide, and geared up with crampons, we hiked up onto and into the glacier. What an amazing sensation to be surrounded by this mass of almost turquoise blue ice. The tour included a glass of whiskey topped with thousand-year-old glacial ice. Who can say they have shared that experience! From there, we continued down into the stark, stunning beauty of the Torres de Paine National Park and then headed over to ride the southern section of the famously windy Ruta 40.

This definitely lived up to its reputation for being a rough gravel road and for the extremely high winds that batter it, as evidenced by road signs that show a bending tree. These winds are an experience for anyone attempting to traverse them. They make you ride with constant tension as you're blasted from one side of the road to the other. Full days of riding were tiring but gave us a true sense of accomplishment.

Our final destination together rolled ever closer; every day giving me the sensation of time very well spent. As we traveled towards Fin del Mundo it was clear to all that our paths would cross again. This would not be our last ride together.

Reaching Ushuaia in mid-summer, the December sunshine welcomed us to the town. Extreme weather conditions make this region a place where only the rugged live year-round. In the open season, fishing and tourism are the main industries. Cruise liners call into the small port on their way to Antarctica and elsewhere around the rest of the world. Curious tourists and adventure-sport addicts fly in or travel down by car or bus to experience the End of the World.

We were celebrating the completion of Dick, Diana, and Ken's journey from Alaska. Our celebrations sparked many discussions about whether travel was about the goal being the journey itself or the destinations. In the end we decided it really is about both, but in different ways.

Before we parted in Ushuaia, the guys asked about my plans for the next section of my journey. I was going to ride north to Buenos Aires, the capital city of Argentina, and then ship to southern Africa and continue from there.

In a very New Zealander way, over dinner and drinks one night they suggested that I should simply head the other way around the globe and come to New Zealand next. They enticed me with an offer to pick me up at the airport, have a place to stay and told me that they'd gladly show me around their islands. The more they enthused the more it became obvious that this was exactly what I should do. New plans started to take shape.

Several months later I'd made it up the east coast of Argentina, and north into Uruguay and Brazil, before dropping south to Buenos Aires. After a couple of weeks exploring this intriguing city of extremes, during which I'd worked out all the shipping details with Sandra at Dakar Motors, I packed the bike and put it on an Emirates air cargo plane to Auckland, New Zealand. Having been traveling in South America for a year, heading to the Buenos Aires airport was a very satisfying journey.

It's an exciting time for a traveler as a big trip unfolds into new chapters. These stages are a mix of excitement and healthy "fear" of the next unknown. These emotions are a great part of the journey; pressing on, not knowing what the journey will bring next and embracing that.

But knowing that I'd soon be in New Zealand and would be able to speak my native language was comforting.

I spent the next months exploring both North and South Islands; sometimes on my own, at times with the guys, or with a couple other riders. Though relatively small, these islands are packed with beauty, quirky geography, a unique history, and unusual plants and birds. New Zealand is diverse in that the North Island gets tropical at the very top end, and the South Island feels much more like my home in the Pacific Northwest. Lots of gravel roads, lakes and mountains to explore. What a great decision to shift my plans around the serendipitous meeting of such wonderful and hospitable people. Knowing that was a good change of plans makes me smile to this day. It was confirmed as soon as I stepped off the plane and greeted Dick at the baggage claim area. Big smiles and big hug. This set the tone for the entire time in NZ, getting to visit Dick and Diana at their home and staying with Ken and Shirley when I got to Wellington.

Our chance meeting on motorbikes in Chile and the friendship that grew now carried around the other side of the globe. The time we spent together in New Zealand included riding to Cape Reinga in the far north and being introduced to their friends and families. Diana had set up a meeting at Alzheimer's Auckland, where I shared my journey with Alzheimer's. It was good to connect with and support a community helping families cope with the disease. Our friendship continues as we still share texts and emails about this time and also current politics and experiences from the Covid-19 pandemic.

My eyes were set on Australia next. Saying goodbye to these kindred spirits was even harder than it had been when we parted ways in South America, but my instincts were that we'd meet again. Every so often in life, relationships like this build and when they are seeded in travel they can become incredibly strong.

As I explored Australia, Dick and Diana got in touch with the news they were planning to ride there; it seemed that our paths could possibly cross again. A new plan was made. I had plenty of time to ride across the middle of Australia, and then head north to Katherine in the Northern Territories for what was going to be a wonderful reunion. We rode together for the next weeks and it was as if no time had passed since

South America, or New Zealand. We explored the Bungle Bungle range in Purnululu National Park in northwestern Australia and then I continued south to Perth. That was my hopping off point for South Africa. Now we had ridden in four countries on two continents together. Who would have guessed that a chance meeting would lead to that?

One of the key beauties of travel for me had turned out to be the connections; the meetings and sharing of friendships between both the local people along the way, and fellow travelers. I'd been traveling for more than two years by that time, and meeting so many amazing people taught me how valuable those relationships are in the scope of one's trip. I've only shared this one chance meeting and friendship, but there were so many more.

I arrived in Cape Town in time to enjoy the summer months in the southern parts of Africa and was lucky enough to link up with a South African guy and his wife. Jorg and Lily had been following my journey and invited me to not only stay with them in Cape Town but also added something quite wonderful: "Jorg is going to take six weeks off work and he's available to travel with you." All of a sudden it felt as if I had personal tour guides in these two. What an incredible sign of friendship; a phenomenal opportunity and a very humbling thing to have happened.

I could write more description of the superb experiences, the challenges and the discoveries of my ride through South Africa and on up into Botswana, Zimbabwe, Zambia, Malawi, and Namibia, but that's a separate story. That one has yet another twist in the tale.

I'd been keeping in email contact with Dick and Diana, and they'd mentioned that they were going to be in Africa to attend a wedding. They'd be flying to Maun, Botswana for a safari beforehand. I'd casually asked when they were arriving. Jorg and I were more than likely to be in Maun at that very time. In fact, we could *make* it happen. Fate was conspiring. I figured out their flight details without them knowing, and Jorg and I decided to surprise them at the airport.

Sure enough, they walked out of the arrival gate and were greeted with a loud, "Welcome to Botswana!" Big smiles and greetings as we gave them hugs and wished them well on their safari. Now we'd seen each other in five countries on three continents. Super fun.

I wrapped up my delightful ride around the world in Africa. I knew that after two and a half years on the road, I needed to get "home." It was time to determine what was ahead in my life and career. Fortunately, another meeting with Dick and Diana was in store. Upon returning home, I learned they were planning to ride across the US, and I intended to share the same hospitality. I met them in McCall, Idaho where they were staying with some good American friends. It was an absolute pleasure to ride with them again, and to have the chance to show them some of the beautiful roads and scenery of Washington and Oregon, before sending them off on their continued travels. Our friendship has now spanned six countries and four continents.

Chance meetings can turn into lifetime friendships. I am eternally grateful for this and all the others the road has brought into my life. It's almost as if the connections between kindred spirits are made so much more possible by being on journeys such as ours. We were all out there to experience and to learn, yet perhaps the most important thing travelers learn is the value of all that's involved with friendships.

As I write this, I'm still in contact with Dick, Diana, Ken, and Shirley; the miles and time do not matter. They have brought so much joy to my life, and hopefully I have brought a little to theirs. My life's journey has been improved greatly by travel; the motorcycle trip was due to the ending of one chapter of my life, but it was the beginning of a new one. All I experienced over the years traveling on my trusty motorcycle made me grow, and in so many ways it brought new horizons and possibilities into my world.

About the author:

Mark Donham has been a curious traveler since his late teens, backpacking around the globe in his early 20s and living in Austria for a year. For him, travel is about the people he meets and interacts with along the journey, as much as any sights he has seen.

For 30 years he worked in sales and customer service in electronic prepress and printing. His company printed a wide range of products including annual reports, catalogs, and all kinds of packaging. He says that he was fortunate to be in the middle of the change from old world craft to fully electronic techniques and equipment.

In 2011, after the loss of his wife, Chris, he jumped on his motorcycle and rode around the world for two and a half years. At that time, he was not sure how long he would travel; his original plan was roughly a year.

Mark documented his journey on *ADVRider.com* as a ride report and his own blog, which had over three million views. That was never a goal, but the friendships and interactions with readers around the globe changed his travels and life. The personal connections and experiences he had through his travels continue to make his life better.

He now works in sales of flexo printing corrugated boxes, but is looking forward to his next chance for longer travel, somewhere in the world.

Mark currently lives on Whidbey Island, Washington State, USA.

Facebook: Mark Donham
Website: RadiomanRidesTheWorld.com

Finding the Rhythm of the Road

by Graham Field

"Freedom is something that dies unless it's used."

—Hunter S. Thompson

I wasn't aiming my bike in the direction of adventure; this was escapism. Escaping an English winter, escaping a mortgage and heading down Mexico way, a journey I'd done before. However, as is often the case, the road had other plans. Crossing the Atlantic to begin my overland journey didn't change the season, only the side of the road I was riding on. I spent a week camping alone in the desert on the edge of the Rio Grande acclimatising to my hurry-up-and-wait journey. Progress is what happens on the road; the journey occurs when you get off the bike. This is a journey of timing, finding the rhythm that feels right to ride by. A stonking freeze to get here, solitude and tranquillity whilst I regenerate for the final leg.

A week of pastel desert sunrises and crimson dusty dusks. Take a breath, slow the pace. Now I've reached a warmer place to repack my stupid soft panniers with fingers I can feel after the desperate strapping on of luggage in a Denver December winter chill.

My Marmite has solidified; spreading it rips stale bread. All the wrong things are hard. More southness is needed. It's almost time to cross the river into Mexico.

105

I gather my debris from the desert floor to have a trial pack, a new system, but I'm not leaving today. This is a dry run; there's more preparation to be done. Time for some essential laundry and a half-hearted wash with some half-boiled water. In the past I've taken with me the three pairs of underwear mantra: clean, unseen and obscene. But this time I bought a fourth and the ratio has changed the routine.

The moon has steadily been getting brighter, showing by night how little there is out here and tempting me to make a sacrifice: it's time to heat the emergency ravioli. There is a gnawing craving for a taco and cerveza. It's been a very dry Christmas.

* * *

My water bottle doesn't rattle with frozen fragments this morning. With dawn's first light, I can see that's because it's solid ice.

This is not a drill. I pack the bike with numb fingers and when the sun shines on me it's with a warmth I wasn't expecting, making it hard to decide what to wear. Stupid bloody soft panniers. Even without the ravioli, there's still no room. At 9.30am, I'm ready to leave.

At the visitors' centre I throw out my rubbish and have a brief KLR conversation only to have rubbish thrown back at me. "You're going to Mexico? They kill babies and fill them full of drugs to get them across the border. Take a gun. No, take two."

Of course, this is armchair advice, he's never been there, but I have. Be afraid little mother fucker, live in fear, listen to your TV, trust us. It's pissing me off because I'm listening. I know the score. I know, I know, but I'm on my own. I have no one to help me defuse this negative bomb I've just been given.

Deep breath: out with anger, in with calm, tranquillity now. After six days of positive solitude, I ride out of the park. I've ridden 400 miles around it and all I've seen is how much more there is to see, but the place slowed my pace appropriately.

Now I want some momentum, 1,260 miles away is where I'll stay, I know the room I'll sleep in and restaurant I'll eat in. I know the supermarket I'll shop in, watching palms sway from the checkout queue; this is a commute to my semi-secret paradise.

The road to the border follows the Rio Grande. There are canyons, hoodoos and extreme undulations; crest a hill, stay on the throttle as the road drops into a corkscrew bend and a heart in my mouth humpback. It's not unlike the Laguna Seca Raceway circuit at times. I can feel the limitations of my cheap Kenda tyres. If only I had a fork brace. If only I didn't have a loaded bike, if only it was a Ducati. An exhilarating ride to a shitty destination. Presidio is perhaps designed to encourage you to keep going into Mexico; not that I need any encouragement.

For a country that's world renowned for being so difficult to enter, it's remarkably easy to leave. No goodbye. No "submit your visa." No exit stamp. No "have a nice holiday." I disappear out of the country like truth in a news report and ride into Mexico, stopping in an inspection bay for a brief check of my documents.

"¿De dónde eres?"

Okay, *¿De dónde eres? ¿De dónde eres?* I know these words. On the spot Spanish has never really been a talent I've possessed. Comprehension is slow; however, my response, although delayed, is enthusiastic... and wrong. My reply isn't understood. I have an arsenal of Spanish words and that alone makes it my second language. I revert to my first.

"England."

"Ah, hooligan!" comes the reply. That says a lot. That's your one-word response that sums up my nationality, or was it the way I rode here? It's true the names of certain countries can conjure up instant preconceptions: Kazakhstan—Borat, Iraq—Gulf War, Guatemala—Earthquake. We Brits know as a nation there's more to us than hooligans, but one-word generalisations are easy inaccuracies. It doesn't offend me though. It's not said in a way that is meant to. Listen, amigo. You should hear what they're saying about you just north of here.

It's a rare border crossing that is at a comfortable temperature: no traffic, no queues, no touts, no confusion, no shouting, no corruption and no delays. And contrary to the forums of fear, I'm not gunned down by an infighting drug cartel.

I'm waved out of the Customs compound and onto the street of food stalls. The air is filled with the aroma of tacos, meat and fish cooking over coals and wooden embers, but no dead babies full of drugs. I can't find a bank. I have no local currency, but that's my only concern. Less than a mile from the border and less than five minutes into Mexico, there's a screech of tyres and a crunch of metal at the lights as a car drives into the back of the truck waiting beside me. I've seen a dropped ice cream get a more hysterical reaction. I love Mexico!

The border town's boundaries blur into barren land so flat I can see the near future. I'll be on this road for a while; it's probably safe to stop for a wee. I'm back in the country where I began the year. It's all coming back to me now. Somewhere beyond my active memory is a force that recalls how much I like it here, how good it is for my soul, and it is this force that pushed me into renting out my house and breaking free from the British winter. It drove me to buy a bike and ride back to a land that takes away the tension.

The road to Chihuahua is bleak and brown, sparsely populated by both the permanent and transitory. It's a little daunting, more from what I've read and been told than from what I see or experience. On the plus side, it adds to the exhilaration and butterflies. My tank is full, my bike is running well, and it's less than three hours to the big city. There's a checkpoint and, unlike the border patrols in Texas, this one has smiles, no alarm or suspicion, no paranoia or fear-inducing authority, just a little inquisitiveness, a genuine welcome, and a blasé "¡Buen viaje!" That's all the contact I have until I'm waved through the next checkpoint, where the only negative experience is my annoyance that once again I'd had my judgment swayed by the nay-saying keyboard warrior. Still it keeps the tourist count low.

I remember "libre" means "free" and avoid the toll road all the way into Centro de Chihuahua, where I find a bank that spews pesos into my fingerless-gloved hand before my unattended bike can become a victim of the opportunist. In fact, it appears to go unnoticed by the early evening city shoppers. I can't find the recommended hotel and the low sun is in my eyes. I see a sign that implies there are rooms for rent, a homeless hombre sways outside with mental instability. Although he's minding his own business, I can't imagine he's generating any. After three laps of the one-way system, I give up on the guidebook and hit the side streets. I find a hotel; in a few more blocks I find a more appealing one. The bike isn't off the road, but the 24-hour reception will keep an eye on it for me. And the day is done. That's how you change countries: with wide eyed basic awareness, lots of smiles and a relaxed and gracious attitude. I knew that. I don't know why I doubted myself.

* * *

Travelling towards the equator from the north at this time of the year means the days get longer, but daylight is still limited, so I keep my desert habits and get up at first light to put my little plan into action. A long ride round the one-way system, but a short push across a vacant plot is a car wash with high pressure promise. So without warming the engine, I push the KLR along the pavement across a derelict lot to a place where I can remove the corrosive credibility collected whilst riding a frozen highway for two days, a coating that was then baked on in a week of desert riding. The cold engine doesn't crackle and steam as I soak it.

Wow, what a transformation! It looks gorgeous when it's all clean. While it drip dries, for the first time in a week I'll let someone else make breakfast. It's not so tricky, when I see the Desayuno sign, I confidently order huevos rancheros. The restaurant owner, a tall thin man with a permanent smile, has lived in the US and travelled all over Mexico too. He speaks English to me. He's an electrician by trade, though I'm not quite sure how that led him to own a one-table breakfast diner in a northern city backstreet. He didn't say. He wants to talk about women he's encountered and the beaches he found them on. I'm not about to interrupt. I tell him I'm going to Oaxaca; I took an indirect route the last time and I'm doing it again this time, Copper Canyon is too good to miss. I get a smile that says, I know you know the dangers and have heard the warnings about that place, I'll not say more. "Radio Gaga" is playing from the corner of the room, the door is open, and the sun is shining down on the dirty street. My eggs are perfect, my coffee instant and I've got that exciting foreign feeling, but it comes with the comfort of vague familiarity. I'm fed with the breakfast I craved, and it comes with a side of well-being. The next song to play is "D.I.S.C.O." I say goodbye before it sticks.

The other side of an impossible junction, my gleaming bike catches my eye. It just adds to the feel-good factor. It is D-Delightful. It is I-Irresistible. It is S-Shit, it's stuck.

So has my Marmite. With the warmer weather, it's liquefied and leaked, and the handle has broken off my saucepan. I blame all this on the soft panniers. The bike may look better, but the luggage is a disability. It doesn't just affect the aesthetics; anyway, sleek and desirable is not necessarily a favourable look, not that I have to worry about portraying that image, the bike's just cumbersome. The tank saddle bags keep shifting and pressing against my knees. It's an invasion of my personal space. It's like sharing a bus seat with some alpha male athlete whose giant steroid-filled testicles keep his legs splayed. I resent the intrusion and think perhaps the savings made on tyres and panniers were a false economy.

Until my rental money comes in, I'm on a very tight budget. That's why I haven't had a drink so far on this trip. No point pleading poverty whilst standing at the bar pouring beer down my neck.

Associated symbols of Mexico often include the sombrero and poncho-wearing, guitar-playing, tequila-drinking hombre sitting with his back to a cactus, the very effigy of lethargy. The reality, however, is that much of the country is high-altitude snow and ice, especially in December. Mexico is like a chili that has been taken out of the freezer and put in the oven for a minute. It's hot on the outside, but cold in the middle and, as for the seedy bits, if they exist, I don't see them. For some stupid reason, I ride up to Creel at 7,000 feet. Why? Because I sort of promised to revisit the place I stayed last time. They don't even know I'm here, so it's an unnecessary ride, but I don't make promises lightly and do everything in my power to honour them. There's little in life that feels better than integrity. I take the high road through pine forests and frozen puddles, and past pickups with huddled hoodies in the bed.

I've come into town from the other end and can't grasp it at all, until I cross a bridge over a railway and rotate my mental map. At the complex, I'm greeted by someone I don't recall. He informs me the guy I made the promise to isn't around. The restaurant is closed, the supermarket empty, there's no hot water, and the heater doesn't do the basic fundamental action that gives it its name. Cold and hungry, I question my decision to return, and how much more comfortable riding past would have felt knowing I'd broken a promise. Generally, I know better than to go back. I only go forward.

* * *

I can see my breath in the room and frost on the bike seat when I wipe the moisture from the window. Time to turn this trip around. On an empty stomach, I go forward into the cold on deserted roads that skirt Copper Canyon. I make sure to stay on the paved bit, I could drop 6,000 feet into the warm and humid canyon, but it would only be a brief respite as what goes down must come up and I know the road out is horrendous.

I'm wearing the four layers, both top and bottom, that I left Denver in. It's a high-altitude, low-temperature ride: 160 kilometres of twisting, uninhabited out-of-season road. In Guachochi, I have the same breakfast as yesterday. I've stayed here before. I remember the fuel station opposite the hotel. I make a stop in hope of a nostalgic view—the beautiful, voluptuous receptionist. As my tank is filled for me, I look across the road, but don't see her. She wouldn't remember me anyway. Or maybe she would; the one who drained his oil in her backyard and didn't promise to return.

I have no confidence in my tyres. They grip like condensation on a window and can run off unpredictably. 320 kilometres of scenic roads I've ridden before, I'm sure I have, but not a single thing is familiar. Wait a minute: yes, it is. The military checkpoint at the T-junction, I remember that. The soldier has his face covered with a mask and sunglasses. He's impossible to read; it's intimidating. That's why I always flip up my helmet and smile to officialdom. It stops the guessing. I'm waved through. They're preoccupied with a bus they've just pulled over. It's going to be one of those ride-until-dusk days—a mileage eater, a destination achiever.

I squeeze past an artic that has tried to reverse up an embankment. The trailer has dropped onto the rear driving wheels of the unit and the truck's stuck like a malicious slur. I can feel his fatigue, humiliation, and frustration. The best thing about being a truck driver is when you're not one anymore.

111

The road straightens, the clouds get higher and expose a token blue patch, but the sun won't shine through it. Cars wave when I stop and pedestrians wave when I ride. And if I leave a heated grip to return it, all hands go up. I think I've stayed in that town back there, but I'm not sure. I consider the storyline of *Zen and the Art of Motorcycle Maintenance*. Isn't it about a return? I couldn't bloody write that, could I? I wouldn't know if I'd got there.

The sun decides to reveal itself just as it's going down, which happens to be when the road turns to face it. It's the best scenery of the day and coincides its descent with mist rising from the valleys. That's the last view through my visor before my helmet is placed on the concrete floor of a perfectly reasonably priced cell for the night.

I walk the street and stop at a stall with the enticing smells of the freshly cooked, where I point and nod enthusiastically at the thing I want to take home. An elderly couple already have their order and they help me with mine. It feels like it's a special treat. Well, it is Saturday night. I scurry back to my concrete box; the aroma of grilled meat and melted cheese distract me from the four walls of chosen accommodation. Through my amber tint window is the shadow of my bike mirror so I know it's still there. Well, the mirror is at least, possibly taped to a plastic chair. But it provides enough comfort to induce good sleep.

* * *

It's hard to tell if the light is natural, but the echoes in the hallway and the banging doors are definitely real. I'll assume it's morning. Due to there being no restaurant, nothing delays my leaving. And due to a change in time zone, it's still later than I thought.

Last night's burrito doesn't look so appealing this morning: limp, leftover, uneaten, unloved, lying there unrefrigerated and congealed. I think it's best just left alone. I feel a bit alone too. I'd like some sunshine and some *wow* in my day.

So back on go the layers, minus one as I'm sure I'll be dropping in altitude today. I pay a quid to miss Durango—missing the capital of the state that is, not giving a local beauty queen a pound—and use the toll road. A pound well spent, as the highway crosses ravines and cuts through mountains. Best of all, it's smooth and new and there isn't a single red light. Nor, unfortunately, is there a fuel station. I ride 120 miles before breakfast. Perhaps that's why I'm feeling a little down. I try and think where else I'd rather be. I can't come up with anything. This is due to lack of imagination rather than contentment, and it doesn't make me feel any better. I pull over for a protein bar that's over a year old and has more crumbs than crunch, but I need to put something into my gnawing stomach.

Going onto reserve takes me off the toll road and I indulge in El Espinazo del Diablo Highway ("The Devil's Backbone"), one of those prestigious, twisting mountain roads that will provide adrenalin all the way to the coast. I really need to eat something though, if I'm going to enjoy this. I stop at Fanny Restaurant, a place of infinite joke possibilities and limited menu. Annoyingly, it's one of those places that questions your presence in their establishment and all I can get is coffee. Strangely they all come out to wave me off. My stomach keeps on churning and my tyres continue to handle with as little confidence as this hungry gringo with inadequate Spanish. Maybe a fork brace would sort it out.

The descent is steady, and soon I drop through the Tropic of Capricorn. Hairpin debris changes from pine needles to petals, butterflies fill the air and bug splats obscure my vision. It's time for a change of clothing. I've made the transition from the dry, brown death of winter to the green, humid jungle, alive with chirping and swarming, flying and crawling. I get bitten just taking off my thermals. Do I care? It's better than frostbite. Warmth at last. My clothes are strapped on all over the bike, with a little gap between the tank bag and dry bag I can just squeeze my arse in. I can see I'm going to have to either cut down on burritos or luggage. Smells once more fill the moist air: flowers and food, kids run beside me in shorts, not inhibited by clothing or the cold. Why would you live at altitude when this climate is so close?

A new highway is being constructed. Concrete stilts cross valleys, and tunnels have been bored through cliff faces with reckless extravagance. The road I'm on will be all the better if the new one takes the lumbering, lane-hogging vehicles away. I make a few dangerous overtakes, as do the oncoming trucks I come wheel to grille with. I have some impure Ducati

113

thoughts; I've got to sort this KLR out. I've never been dissatisfied with one before.

I wallow round the last of the Devil's Backbone Highway and into the last of the light. Then in Spanish, I manage to find and book a place to call "home" tonight.

* * *

Feeling smug is far better than feeling hung over. The noise of last night's New Year's Eve festivities faded with the darkness and I leave my room into a peaceful, but messy dawn.

The morning is damp, tropical birds screech and the sticky, thick moist air is reminiscent of something I can't quite recall. I settle for the memory of riding on the back of a moped after an all-nighter in a Goan jungle, secret saucer pupils accustoming to an India dawn after some tribal trance experience. It's a good memory, even if it's not the right one.

The first ride of the year is inevitably significant. I've got warmth at last. It may be induced by cloud and humidity, but warmth it remains. My clothes don't restrict me, my bike is willing, and no one is about. I ride into a new year. The smells are so lush and thick, I can chew on them: fruit trees and flowers, cacti and creepers, life, and growth. Not like that dormant winter that lurks above the cloud-covered hills.

I take the toll road to Tepic. Nothing very inspiring is occurring inside or outside my helmet. The bike has a noticeable increase in power at sea level. I use the throttle more and the gears less. Overtaking is effortless and the momentum gets me to the rain all the faster, so I extend with my toll road decision. I hand over peso notes at every toll booth and fill my already bulging pockets with more and more change: licensed highway robbery. I see a Spanish-registered Triumph, so I pull up for a chat. He's quite arrogant and is clearly fully sponsored. I should know better, but I ask him how come. He's a writer—yeah mate, we all are—got a book out in Spain, round-the-world motorcyclist, blah, blah, blah! It starts to rain again, but it doesn't stop his bragging. I put my helmet back on, and still he continues. Now he's moaning about it being an uneventful trip; nothing significant to write about. Well, you just met me, didn't you? His dreary monologue could never be anything but the blandest paragraph in my day.

I ride through flooded streets toward the coast, stop under a tree where rain is gathered on leaves, drips concentrated, and enlarged drops fall onto the bread I'm trying to make a sandwich with. It's such a pathetic sight it makes me smile. No one has ever enthused about soggy bread. There is a procession of oncoming traffic, the New Year exodus: hung over and homeward bound. My boots and gloves have leaked. The only distraction from dampness is blinding headlights and brake lights.

* * *

When the darkness turns to grey, I see palm trees lurching violently from a wind that has finished whipping up the sea. The skyline is poured concrete and rusty steel, pylons outnumber the palm trees and satellite dishes distort what little authenticity there is.

None of my damp clothing dried in the night, but the fact that I think they must have makes putting them back on less miserable. Pushing warm feet into wet boots is not as bad as I imagined, it's better than staying here. I'm on the road by 7:30am and don't glance back. No sunset, no sunrise, no second chance.

With an open jacket, what festered in the night is beginning to dry in the morning breeze, but the road takes me inland and into torrential rain. British conditioned, I assume a speed camera got me but it's only lightning. When I'm dripping by the fuel pump, I hear the thunder. The road is flooded, the fields are flooded, and the rivers are flooded. There are rockfalls on the road. I let a car pass just before I aquaplane across the washed-out surface. Oncoming vehicles project puddles at me with the force of a fire hose. I can't get any wetter; I'm even breathing in water from the scarf across my face. Another rock to avoid, but this one has legs and a shell—a turtle crossing. It's too wet for photos, but a turtle crossing says it all, it's wet, and that's all there is to it.

In these situations, I have to have optimism. I have to assume I'll ride out the other side despite no end being in sight. It can't rain this hard for this long, it's too extreme. After three hours, through the dirty distortion of my visor, I see dry road ahead. I must be moving faster than the storm and eventually leave it behind, as the road leads back to the coast and takes me into a sunny, warm, windy, jacket-flapping evening. This is better, much more enjoyable. So enjoyable I go onto reserve, just after I've left all opportunities behind me. "I'll fill up at the next one" should no longer be a part of my vocabulary. There are no excuses. Actually, I do have one. I've been driven by the hope of sunshine all day and haven't wanted to stop. In fact, I'll use that excuse twice. I've run out of water and haven't bothered to replace it. So now even a wild camp is out of the question. How can I constantly manage to do this to myself? It's the most annoying aspect of my own company. I have a firm talk to myself, but I'm not really listening. I'm watching the sun setting and, anyway, I can justify anything.

In a one-horse town, there's no need for a fuel station. I find a man with the hose, who leads me to his stable. Inside he has some big drums, they are symbols of relief, and he also has a clever syphoning technique. He sells me five litres of mileage and I get some water too, and with that come more options. Two miles later is a camping sign. No more options are needed. I ride onto the beach and under a cabaña. For the price of a litre of begged fuel I have a legitimate place to pitch my tent and somewhere to hang my clothes in a sea breeze. I watch the last of the sunset eating fish quesadillas in the open-air, palm-thatched restaurant.

In the space of 10 minutes, a nightmare situation can become a dream scenario. It's the perfect example of a day on the road. Leave a shitty place, find a worse one, get lost, get soaked, believe, endure, persevere, make a stupid mistake, get help, and finally fall asleep on a beach with a full tummy and the sound of crashing waves. This is how a hard road rewards the persistent.

* * *

Sleep by the ocean, woken by the sunrise. My panniers are drier, my maps more brittle and the mozzie coils less droopy. Only the boots remain moist.

This is the best time of the day to be riding. It's going to get hot, I can just tell. But for now the day still has a freshness about it. A lizard crosses the road in front of me: weather prediction by wildlife. Next is a tarantula. And there are also many dead and bloated dogs along the roadside. I'm not sure what this says about the weather; perhaps they went out in the midday sun, madness. The air is full of little bugs, they get into my ears and are really itchy, but I can't dislodge them. Some futile instinct has me hitting the outside of my helmet, unsurprisingly this makes not the slightest difference.

The ocean-hugging road has plenty of sweeping, swooping corners and the best ones are reserved by vultures sitting on posts doing what vultures do: lying in wait. Quite possibly for an Englishman with bad judgment and dodgy tyres to add a touch of variety to their accustomed mad dog diet.

Riding with my cuffs open to catch the breeze, I've basically made a net out of my jacket, and eventually something gets caught. It's a bee, he gets to my elbow and, upon discovering there's nowhere else to go, stings me. I'm lucky I don't react to such things, well, not in a profuse sweating, difficulty in breathing, violent convulsions and finally death kind of way. My reaction is far less dramatic, just repetitive swearing, which stops me from screaming like a little girl. I find a pharmacy.

"Do you speak English?"

"More or less."

"In that case, I've been stung."

He gives me some cream.

In the evening I get stung again, by a seemingly sweet little old lady who fucks me on the price of a nasty room.

* * *

I love this bit; another early start, sunbeams streak through the misty-morning fire smoke that hangs under the palms. I have scratched Oakleys, ripped gloves and, although my boots are nearly dry, my feet are uncomfortable. Even my Smartwool socks can't solve this problem. You'd think I'd been on the road for ages. I do feel a part of it all.

I get stung again, this one flies through my visor and when I stick my hand in to find where it's got to, it leaves its calling card on my cheek. Out with the cream again. I'm getting used to it now.

Today seems to be about the destination, not the journey. I ride erratically. Everyone is driving badly; there just seems to be a madness in the air today. Inevitably, it ends in crumpled metal and bloodshed. Not mine, but sobering to see all the same. Not that I've had a drink this trip, 16 days on the road and no alcohol, mainly because, well now I just want to see what refraining would be like. I want that delayed gratification feeling of the first beer when I reach the beach.

A bridge takes me over a wide, clear, fast-running river. It's too attractive to ignore, and the track beckons me down to the sandy bank for a bathe. This, for me, defines overland independent motorcycle travel. Some call it adventure. I'm not sure how adventurous it is, but this is definitely something you wouldn't do on your commute to work. Stopping by a river and having a wash, then spinning out on the sand, standing on the pegs, up the track back to the road. That's what you do when you go away on your bike. I think this defines the freedom of the trip, self-contained, independent and taking the opportunities that come my way. Not preconceived or researched, just an in-the-moment impulse that needs no explanation.

I know I'm getting close when I start to see the moped-riding, short-wearing, surfboard-carrying, semi-permanent locals who have made this paradise their home. Now I've become one of the many, no acknowledgement is needed. I'm feeling a little anxious; what if the place is fully booked? Perhaps I should have thought about that earlier.

It's taken two weeks to ride 3,800 miles through snowy, barren, frozen lands, through storms, humidity and heat to my beach of choice. I'm recognised. I'm remembered.

"There's one room left."

"I'll take it."

"The lock doesn't work, amigo."

"I'll fix it."

The price for a month's residency has me questioning my calculations. Is it really that cheap?

I'm here. I'm back. In the evening, I wander without knowing to the place where ribs are barbecued. The toilet block has changed since my last visit. I pop my head inside a new thatched hut and I'm handed a joint.

I sit at a table, sip beer and listen to Led Zeppelin, which is followed by Boston. I push my toes into the sand, lean back on the chair, so my hair falls away from my neck. Looking up at the canopy of palms above me, I feel the feeling, this is where I'm meant to be. I remember now. This is a return I only promised to myself, I'm very grateful I kept it.

* * *

I live on muesli and avocado, with a treat of street tacos for dinner. If I avoid the posh and tempting seafront, I can live in appropriate poverty. On the beach one evening, pointing my attention-seeking lens at the orange sky, a surfer dude interrupts, and I jump out of my moonrise daydream.

"You're clearly a professional photographer. Could you take some photos of me surfing? I'll pay you."

I'm not professional, but if he pays me then technically, I suppose I am, so I agree. I soon discover that they're a vain bunch, surfers. They say they want the photos so they can check their posture, their technique, their position, and so on. But actually what they really want, much like us bikers, is the perfect picture of them being confronted by and overcoming the most challenging and beautiful of environments. I photograph him, he buys me a big fat burrito and the next morning comes to my room to see the results. The images are transferred from laptop to memory stick as he gushes ecstatic gratitude and brings me some beer. Then he goes off and tells his surfing buddies.

Within a week, I become Mr Surf Photographer. I'm "in" with the beautiful people: the super fit and über cool. I point my lens in exchange for beer and burritos. I have a trail of pretty surf chicks and cool dudes coming to my door, flash drives in hand and high-fiving me with pure delight when they see what I've captured. My Facebook friends are all becoming younger and better looking, and their profile photos are the ones I've taken.

Opportunities are everywhere, but they rarely knock; they are not found on the road, they happen in the spaces in between. The journey occurs when you stop riding. Interaction happens when you put your phone down. Stories are what you experience first-hand. Memories are best sparked by smells and sounds, not social media reminders. Ride in the real world. I'll see you on the road.

About the author:

Graham Field was travelling to foreign lands before he was eligible to have his own passport, rode motorbikes before he was old enough to have a licence, and has kept a daily diary for over 30 years. He was born to tell tales of motorcycle travel; it just took him a long time to realise it.

The first 20 years of his working life was spent behind the wheel of a truck, thinking and not fitting in, then under a sink, fitting kitchens. One day he decided to ride his motorcycle to Mongolia, then told his story.

Now the author of five books, he has become a recognised name in certain niche circles and veers away from mainstream potential. His articles have appeared in publications around most of the English-speaking planet, and along with TV, column and podcast residencies, as well as presentations, his face, voice and words have reached the global receptive. Often outspoken, always opinionated, but rarely offensive, his ridicule is disarmed with a cheeky smile and cogent observations come with a cutting wit.

Graham dabbles in social media where he has a small but loyal following. Some might call him a cult, but not to his face. In 2015 Graham gave up his native Essex, UK to live in Bulgaria, where he remains misunderstood, but this is mainly due to his inadequate but enthusiastic attempts at speaking the language.

Bikes, travel and writing remain constants in his life, along with periods of solitude and introspection. He has an infectious way of sharing life-learned wisdom conceived inside the helmet, found on the road and gifted to him in those precious encounters that have always made travel harder to put down than a half-finished bottle.

Let Graham tell you about his return journey as a free audio download direct from his website.

Website: grahamfield.co.uk
Facebook: Graham Field Motorcycle Travel Author
YouTube: Graham Field
Twitter: @GrahamFieldRTW
Instagram: @Megaflid
Graham is the author of *In Search of Greener Grass, Eureka, Different Natures, Near Varna* and *Not Working*. His books are released as paperbacks and *Kindle*, and as *Audiobooks*. All are available direct or from *Amazon*.

Kyrgyzstan Eagle Hunter

by Tiffany Coates

"Tell me, what is it you plan to do with your one wild and precious life?"

—*Mary Oliver*

Death, when it comes, is swift, silent and shadowy. Hurtling at 90 mph, the impact creating a dense cloud of dust which, as it slowly settles, transforms into a shroud, swathing a dark shape now motionless on the ground. For a moment everything is silent and then the raptor stretches her head back, screeches in triumph and looks round hungrily for her reward, her eyes missing nothing.

Having been warned not to move, I remained frozen; stunned and breathless as I witness the reality of life for an eagle hunter.

Murder seems out of place in this idyllic setting in Kyrgyzstan. We are on a lake shore with gentle waves lapping on the sandy beach and snow-capped mountains in the distance. The victim this time was nothing more than some scraps of pelt and fur bundled up, fastened with twine, and dragged along using a length of string. If it had been a live creature, it would now have been dead.

Central Asia is home to some of the most fascinating cultures on the planet and none more so than the Kyrgyz people. These equestrian nomads, whose lifestyle has changed very little over thousands of years, are proud of their traditions and culture. They live in yurts and in harmony with the lands around them. I had just encountered a particularly brutal example of how they survive.

In my part of the world, we measure our prowess with pasty-making contests and rowing races. Things are somewhat different on the steppes and mountains of Central Asia. Here, the competitions are fierce and decidedly warlike, including wrestling on horseback, archery and buzkashi, the never-to-be-forgotten spectacle of polo played with a goat carcass in place of a ball. The main features of regional events are the demonstrations of the majesty and power of the golden eagle. But demonstration is too inadequate a word to describe the actions of this winged killing machine. And I have just arrived on my bike in time to discover why.

The lake I'm riding around is Issy Kul, the jewel in Kyrgyzstan's twinkling natural crown, and Central Asia's largest lake. Despite being surrounded by vertiginous mountains and situated at an elevation of 1,600 metres in a country where the average winter temperatures plunge to -15°C, the lake never freezes over. Its name translates as "Hot Lake". This is due to its extreme depth (670m) and geothermal activity where the boiling heat at the planet's core escapes towards the surface. I've seen many lakes on my world travels and Issy Kul is one of the most picturesque. It's on a par with Wakatipu on New Zealand's South Island, and Titicaca in Bolivia. Like them, its crystal-clear blue waters are overlooked by snow-topped mountains; in this case the aptly named Tian Shen, "Heavenly Mountains."

Kyrgyzstan is my favourite "'Stan," the 'Stans being the former Soviet Republics that make up Central Asia. Think of Uzbekistan, Turkmenistan and perhaps the most famous, Kazakhstan, and you'll get the idea why travellers nickname this region the 'Stans. It's a biking utopia, particularly if you're not afraid of a bit of dirt and gravel; roads are rough, with unexpected encounters around every corner. The 8,000 kilometre ride from the UK across Europe to get here is a fantastic adventure in itself and one that I've done twice. I've also flown in a couple of times and rented bikes; this is how I ended up sitting on a Honda XR600, mesmerised by the bloodthirsty eagle.

I am completing a reconnaissance route in preparation for a private group that are coming out to join me. They had requested an adventure somewhere, anywhere in the world, with the only proviso being it had to be on two wheels. I promised them something out of the ordinary and had set about achieving this.

I'd headed straight to Central Asia, travelling light for this scouting phase of the trip, just bike gear, basic camping equipment and Giant Loop soft luggage to pack stuff on the bike. In this case I had the versatile Great Basin Saddlebag, as I wouldn't know what bike I'd be riding until I arrived. Skimming over the mountains on the flight into Bishkek, Kyrgyzstan's sleepy capital, I enjoyed the familiar feeling of anticipation I get upon arriving somewhere that feels so different, especially to the greyness of my departure point in London. The sights, sounds and smells from home are replaced by something cooler and crisper in the mountain air, and people who approach me do so hesitantly. I look confident but it's obvious I'm not a local.

I spend a couple of days in the capital, talking to my support crew, briefing them, and going through the list of equipment for the support vehicle and ensuring they are ready for the trip we'll be doing. I'm also ensuring they're ready to be led by a woman, something that is as foreign to them as the sound of the Kyrgyz words tentatively issuing from my mouth. I soon revert to my rusty Russian. As this was once a part of the Soviet Union, many speak Russian as a first or second language. English lags behind at a poor third.

Everything is ready, and off I head for the reconnaissance phase. I'm relieved that the talking is over and it's all about the riding now. An early start sees me beating the morning rush hour as I ride out of town towards the rising sun.

Kyrgyzstan has numerous highlights, but no ride in this part of the world should miss out on Issy Kul, just a day's ride from Bishkek. It's a place that looks like the Mediterranean. It is also an area where Russian is widely spoken. The rouble goes a long way in Kyrgyzstan and it's just a few hours' flight from Moscow. No wonder Issy Kul has become a haven for beach-starved wealthy and middle-class Russians.

The northern shoreline is quite built-up by Kyrgyz standards; in fact, this nomadic culture considers anything that's not a yurt to be built-up. Grey concrete buildings, housing the remnants of Soviet-era sanatoriums, line the lakeshore. Nowadays they are interspersed with flashy four-star resorts. This is the Issy Kul that most travellers first encounter after leaving Bishkek. It's not my idea of fun, and I accelerate on past the sandy beaches with their sun-loving, overweight Muscovites in their Speedos and bikinis. The road is lined with small shops selling beach towels and inflatables, but these soon peter out.

They are replaced by poplar trees that provide much-needed shade for travellers. Also for the farmers who, with cheeks rosy from the high elevation living, have come down from the mountains and set up stands to sell their produce. Many wear their traditional clothing, the women in long dresses and headscarves while the men are in thick woollen trousers and jackets, and always with kalpak felt hats.

On display are jars of delicious mountain honey, fresh tomatoes, fruit, melons, and fur hats, apparently a must-have for the Russian tourists. Local hunters make them from the pelts of martens and foxes. There are chuckles at my efforts to bargain in Kyrgyz whilst buying some plums. Later I pause by a quiet spot by the lake for a quick swim and to eat some of the fruit. It feels so good to have escaped the diesel fumes in the city and swapped them for the clean air of the lake. I don't linger long, as the southern shore is calling to me. The shoreline in total is 700 kilometres, so to get all the way around I've some distance to go.

A day later and I'm far to the south, away from the bright lights and electricity. The lake is a different place here, hard to get to, remote and quiet. The riding is challenging as I try to pick a route on sand-filled tracks. There are very few vehicles, but I see the occasional pickup truck or a marshrutka, the local minivans. These are carrying people and their shopping. Market produce and other bulky items, including animals, are strapped on the roofs. This is the type of place I love. I can wild camp and spend my days swimming, beachcombing, and building fires from driftwood to cook dinner.

This trip does not give me the luxury of the time to do much of that, and I head to a yurt camp that a friend in Bishkek has recommended, to check out the facilities for my group. I knew I was onto a winner with its quiet location and beach setting. The yurt camp is a family-run place not far from the small town of Bokonbayevo, hardly a name that trips off the tongue. I manage to find the correct track amongst the sandy trails after a couple of U-turns and a re-direction by a passing horseman. Lakeside yurt camps are peaceful and a great alternative to hotels and resorts.

I'm warmly greeted at the camp, dinner is just being served and, after washing my hands, I sit cross-legged in the open-sided dining yurt to enjoy some plov, this being Central Asia's most ubiquitous dish, a type of fried rice usually made with mutton.

I'm pleased to find they serve a vegetarian version and even more pleased to be handed a beer, a local Steinbrau. It's not quite cold but it tastes like nectar. I sip the beer and relax, reflecting on the long day of riding and the progress I've made. I sit calculating times and distances and how I'll prepare the group for the sandy conditions.

Things are quiet at the moment, and I chat to Aiperi, who is clearing the low tables. In her halfway world between traditional life and tourism, she's wearing a combination of modern western clothing, with a long belted dress over the top. She's lived here all her life and dreams of travelling to far-off places. Her dark eyes take on a wistful look as she mentions New York and London. She then tells me that Nurbek will be around the next day, training his eagles. I sit up and take notice. There has been a tradition of using eagles for hunting in Kyrgyzstan for many hundreds of years, and it sounds as if I might be able to see one in action. I am fascinated by the planet's larger predators, those animals not afraid of people and which confidently go about their lives ignoring the two-legged creatures that are humans.

I make the most of the opportunities my travels give me to get closer, from diving with barracudas and sharks in the world's oceans, to riding past the big cats of Africa and hiking amongst the bears of North America.

Animals that are disdainful of our presence and deadly dangerous enthral me.

I decide to change my morning plans, which had been to head off to the local markets and mud baths, in favour of staking out the hills in the hopes of spotting Nurbek and his eagle. I ask a couple more questions as I savour another beer and write my journal. The sun has set, it's time to sleep. I share the yurt with a couple of travellers from Germany. Wishing them good night as we get ready for bed, I tie the sacking across the door more securely for the night in case the wind gets up. Each of us has a mat on the floor and we're in sleeping bags. We have head torches at the ready, as the electricity is switched off soon after we retire for the night. All is silent as I lie there listening to the waves lapping on the shore just feet from where I'm sleeping. My bike is parked outside alongside the yurt.

Up early with the sunrise, I take a dip and then go in search of Aiperi. She directs me west along the lake's trails a short distance, pointing out some hills. I take my bike and head in that direction for several kilometres. Parking it in the shade, I look around.

On a hilltop I spot someone, a silhouette that appears to be holding something. *Yes!* Using the camera's zoom, I can clearly see that it's a large bird perched on a man's forearm; it must be the eagle hunter. He signals down the hill and I see that further along on the trail is a boy. He's standing, waiting patiently with his eyes fixed on the hillside. Seeing me, he motions that I should stay still. And then, at a signal from the figure on the hill, the boy starts to run. He has a length of thin rope in his hand and, at the end of it is something furry. It turns out to be a bundle of fur and pelt. He runs at a steady pace twitching the rope as he goes, causing the decoy to move jaggedly.

Meanwhile, up on the hill the man holds his arm high, and I can see the eagle. Spreading its wings as it takes off, at first gliding around and then swooping lower, it finally goes into a dive heading for the ground, and that is when it "kills" the fur bundle.

As soon as he has released the eagle, the man on the hill rushes down the steep slope. He approaches, calls it to him, and holds out some meat for it. It flies over and settles on his forearm, which is protected by a

127

thick leather gauntlet. He feeds the eagle some meat and slips a small leather hood over its head, covering its eyes.

I approach the boy and talk to him. He proudly speaks some English and introduces himself; he is Damir, Nurbek's son. He tells me he is 12 years old, and yes, he still attends school but now it is the long summer holidays, and he is helping his father. He tells me to stay where I am as we watch his father take the eagle to a nearby tree where he offloads it onto a branch. Attaching the long leather leash (jess) to the branch to ensure the eagle stays there, he then comes over to introduce himself.

Nurbek is medium height with a stocky build, and his arms are powerful—they must be, as he has to hold an eagle for long periods, sometimes for hours on end. Upon his head is a kalpak. Kalpaks are designed to keep the head cool in summer and warm in winter and his is white, with black embroidery that depicts the mountains of Kyrgyzstan. He is wearing a high collared, deep blue embroidered tunic with matching trousers, and tall black leather boots. A leather belt with a large ornate buckle completes his outfit; attached to it is a bag containing the scraps of meat he uses to reward the eagles.

His English is as limited as my Russian and my even more limited Kyrgyz, but with Damir's help I find out a bit more. He is intensely proud of his eagles and his eyes glitter when he speaks of his hunters. Today, Nurbek has two eagles with him, the youngster Asman, who I have just seen in action, and Karrachin, a senior eagle, who is still in her cage nearby. They are extremely aggressive with one another and are not permitted close contact.

In total he has three eagles, and they share his house with him, his wife and their two children. I know from experience that Kyrgyz houses are small, and I try to picture it as he describes how the eagles are kept in the heart of the home, the kitchen. They need to be close to the humans and around them as much as possible in the early years. There are three cages in the kitchen; sheets of wood separate the cages. Without them the eagles would be tearing at each other through the wire.

Hunting eagles are always female, he announces. This is because they are much bigger than the males and, more importantly, much more aggressive. I feel pleased that eagles appear to be proponents of women's lib. Apparently, a male eagle will not attack anything larger than a ground squirrel, whilst the females will see off quite large animals and predators, including, I am amazed to discover, wolves and mountain lions.

They are the planet's ultimate apex predators, using their phenomenally sharp eyesight to feed their young and to keep their nests and fledglings safe. Apparently, eagles are able to spot a moving animal from up to three miles away. I'm not sure how scientists have managed to determine a bird's eyesight, for vision like that they would need to stand quite far away with the eye chart! I make a note to myself to check how animal vision is measured.

Meanwhile, Nurbek continues to talk. I do feel uneasy about birds being kept in captivity, especially magnificent birds such as these. It doesn't seem right. However, he explains that the birds have a long lifespan, around 50 years. He will work with an eagle for just 10 years and then it's time to release it. He went on to explain how he does it. First, he must collect a fledgling, which sounds simple enough until he describes the life of an eagle.

They mate for life and build large nests in towering cliffs and other inaccessible high places, to which they return every year. Females lay several eggs in the spring while the snow is still on the ground. Then, both parents take turns sitting on the nest, incubating the eggs for the next six weeks. The female, being larger, has the task of keeping the nest warm through the colder nights and the spring storms when they are at their most threatening. Both eagles protect the nest from marauders. It takes around three months for the chicks to fledge and only one or two make it to the summer period when game is plentiful. These juvenile golden eagles usually gain full independence in the autumn, after which they leave their home nest to wander. They roam for significant distances over the next four to five years until establishing a territory for themselves.

It is during the early stage that the eagle hunter will take them, around one to two years old, checking carefully to ensure they have selected only females. The capture, training and keeping of eagles has remained the same for hundreds, possibly thousands of years, with the skills and knowledge being handed down through generations of hunter families.

Training an eagle takes around three years and requires constant daily attention from just one person—the eagle will recognise and respond only to the voice of the hunter. Every hunter makes the eagles' hoods themselves, custom crafting each from small pieces of leather that are stitched together. It needs to fit perfectly; each has a distinctive finish with a decorative note or curl of leather on the top. This helps the hunter to distinguish which hood is for which bird as no two have the same shape and size head. The process takes hours. Each hood must be comfortable, slide on smoothly and encase the eagle's head in darkness.

As the eagle approaches maturity, the hunter shows it the hides, pelts and furs of the animals it must hunt so that it becomes accustomed to the smell. They also go to places where he knows those animals frequent so that she can learn the characteristics of the prey. They then start to hunt in earnest with regular practice, starting with the smaller animals and working their way up. Every time she makes a kill, he calls her back and she is rewarded with praise and with a small piece of rabbit meat from the bag on his shoulder. Even if she has killed a rabbit and could easily tear it up to eat it herself, she leaves the prey and returns to him for the praise, the stroking of her feathers and her reward.

Many tribal groups have eagle hunters, from Siberia in the east all the way to the very edge of Europe. Once trained, the hunters use their eagles to help feed their families by contributing rabbits, ground squirrels and other prey to the stew pot. They also have an important role for the livelihood of the village, by protecting its flocks of sheep and goats in the mountains. When there are new meadows being sought or there are predators in the area, the shepherd will send for the eagle hunter. The eagle is set to work. Her hood removed, she is sent into the air to locate and hunt the predators. Once she has spotted a threat to the flock, it may be a fox, a wolf or even a mountain lion, she goes into a stoop, diving down hard and fast, snapping the prey's spine upon impact and leaving the animal incapacitated. I'm impressed with this description of their incredible hunting skills.

At this point Nurbek fetches Karrachin from her cage. She stands tall and proud upon his arm, feathers ruffling a little in the wind but looking incredibly smooth and slick. She is in her prime. Her hood is firmly in place and, with her eyes covered, she is calm. He handles her a lot, stroking her feathers and talking quietly to her, a routine that he follows every time he carries her.

I have encountered golden eagles while crossing high mountain passes, remote places where it's just me and my bike, at times feeling like I'm on top of the world. On my first visit to the 'Stans I spied a distant speck flying closer and closer. Then, as it wheeled above me, I could see it was a golden eagle, with its massive wingspan and distinctive brown plumage. It was regarding me in my black plumage and white head with great interest. The eagle swooped around me, watching, working out whether I was prey or a threat. Luckily deciding I was neither, it wheeled off to check another mountain. Since then, I've come across them many times and sometimes they follow me for a while as I ride through the mountains on sinuous roads. Effortlessly gliding along, even coming so close that I can see their eyes, a beautiful, mystical and fearless bird.

Nurbek explains that when it's time to put one of his birds back into the wild he puts the eagle in her travel cage one last time, and they drive off in a borrowed car, one that is unfamiliar to her. Once in a mountain range far away he says goodbye and quietly slips the jess off her leg. He sends her up, high amongst the peaks and clouds, and then quietly gets in the car and drives away, never calling her back. Leaving her to find a new life, seek a mate, build nests and raise chicks; living the rest of her life in the wild.

It is time for Karrachin to demonstrate her power. Nurbek heads off to the top of the hill. Meanwhile Damir walks down the trail, grabs a hessian bag, and returns with it. Upending the bag, out drops a rabbit, which although startled, stays still, twitching its nose, looking around warily. A signal is passed up the hill and Nurbek releases Karrachin. She soars high, gliding across the valley, stretching her wings, and easily reaching the hilltop on the other side. Once there she perches on a rock surveying the landscape below her, and beyond across the lake. To my great surprise, other birds arrive and gather around her, a couple of crows and smaller birds. It's as if a celebrity has arrived in the neighbourhood and they're flocking around in admiration. They seem to know that, although she is the planet's deadliest killing machine, she poses no threat to them at the moment. Even when she takes off with a steady flap of her wings, they follow along like groupies chasing an autograph. In fact, she seems to be enjoying the attention a bit too much as she ignores us mere humans, and the motorbike on the valley floor. Her 2.3-metre (eight-foot) wingspan dwarfing the crows, she easily outpaces them. Finally, Nurbek's calls make her turn and look, and the rabbit moves off. Karrachin wheels round in the sky and silently swoops across, leaving the groupies far behind as she executes a perfect turn, speeding towards us.

Her stoop is beautiful to watch as she plunges towards the ground and smashes into the rabbit, deadly talons extended to crush the life out of it. Once more there is a cloud of dust. And then she looks around for her reward. Nurbek approaches and she hops onto his arm. She tears aggressively into her meat reward and then calms at the sound of some words of praise as he strokes her before he places the hood back on her head.

I am breathless and awed by her power. Nurbek then describes the tournaments they attend where Karrachin holds the stage and demonstrates her prowess to a much wider audience competing against other eagles. She is the supreme champion eagle for this region. He proudly relates how she once killed three wolves in one day at a tournament, a rare achievement.

I am getting ready to leave on my bike when Nurbek asks if I want to hold Karrachin. Amazed at the offer and wide-eyed, I nod my head. Sitting on the Honda, I'm handed the long gauntlet which I pull over my hand and up my arm. Nurbek then approaches with Karrachin and places her on my arm. I can only stare at her, this massive, beautiful bird. I feel as if my life has stopped. Aware that many tribes regard the golden eagle with a mystical reverence, I can sense that magic and mysticism. Photos are taken, I savour this precious experience and then my arm starts to ache; she weighs five kilograms. Even so I am regretful when Nurbek lifts her off my arm. This has been one of the most incredible moments I've ever had on my motorcycle travels. I feel humbled to have met them and to have seen and heard their story.

As a motorcyclist on a big (by local standards) bike, I offer the best way I can of showing my thanks, a ride on the back of the bike. Nurbek was a bit uncertain, but Damir loved it, and although he would like to be a motorcyclist, he assures me in just a few years he too will be an eagle hunter like his father.

I finish putting my gear on, thanking them for their time, all the explanations and the magical moments of seeing a golden eagle so close up. I'm also relieved to see the rabbit get back to its feet and that it's bundled away into the hessian bag. Apparently, he too is acting a part, as a fierce wolf, afraid of nothing.

We say our farewells, "Jakshy kalyngydzar," and set off in our opposite directions. As I pick up speed through the sand, I glimpse peaks in the distance and my heart soars. I'll be reaching the mountains today and look forward to the opportunity of once more being among peaks. Hopefully I'll see more eagles and, armed with my newfound knowledge, will be viewing them with even more awe. I feel a sense of fellowship with these incredible, solitary winged hunters as they roam the skies.

These sorts of unexpected opportunities are some of the reasons why I am a passionate traveller. Simply, they are addictive and are a big part of why I take people exploring.

About the author:

Tiffany Coates is without a doubt one of the world's foremost female motorcycle adventurers. She has ridden more than 300,000 miles and crossed every continent, some several times.

Her most remote trailblazing exploits are also her favourite journeys—Timbuctoo, Outer Mongolia, Tibet, Madagascar and Borneo.

Tiffany's travels on two wheels started with a decision to motorbike to India with her best friend. Neither of them had a bike, a licence, or any experience of riding. After five days of intensive training they bought a second-hand BMW R80GS and after two months of dropping and picking it up, they set off. Incredible adventures (including some eyebrow raisers in Iran), spurred them on past India, through Southeast Asia and on to Australia… and then the long ride home up the length of Africa.

After two and a half years on the road Tiffany was hooked by the bike travel bug and she has been photographing and writing about her exploits (usually on "Thelma," that same BMW GS) ever since.

Remote riding adventures are Tiffany's passion, and she enjoys sharing them as one of the world's leading freelance motorcycle guides. Pick a spot on the map and Tiffany has probably been there, and can advise and guide on two-wheeled travel to any destination.

Website: tiffanystravels.co.uk
FaceBook: Tiffany Coates
Twitter: @Tiffany'sTravels
Instagram: @Tiffanys_Motorcycle_Travels

CHAPTER 1: THE UNTHINKABLE HAPPENS

CHAPTER 2: FAR FROM HOME

JOEY EVANS

CHAPTER 3: THE BI-POLAR POLE
AND JOEY THE CAMEL COLLIDER

CHAPTER 4: IRON ANGELS

CHAPTER 5: ESCAPING THE NET

CHAPTER 7: THE TRUE VALUE OF TRAVEL

CHAPTER 8: FINDING THE RHYTHM OF THE ROAD

CHAPTER 9: THE KYRGYZSTAN EAGLE HUNTER

CHAPTER 10: A RETURN TO SINAI

CHAPTER 11: HOOKED ON A FEELING

CHAPTER 12: THE ROAD TO MYSELF

CHAPTER 13: THE AFRICA I LOVE

CHAPTER 14: THE KINDNESS OF STRANGERS

CHAPTER 15: I STILL HAVEN'T FOUND
WHAT I'M LOOKING FOR

CHAPTER 16: THE ROUGH SIDE OF SILK

CHAPTER 17: CYCLE SOUTH

CHAPTER 18: ALONE WITH THE GRASS AND THE SKY

CHAPTER 19: THE ROAD IN THE SKY

CHAPTER 20: WHEN LIFE IS FULL OF FIRSTS

A Return to Sinai

by EmmaLucy Cole

"We stand upon the shore and collect such
oddments as we find floating in chaos—
her customs, religions, her clothes and trinkets
and some, *alas!* of her virtues. We snatch them as
they drift forever out of sight and encase them
in an armour of words—and by so doing, not
unhopeful of the future, yet wage our little
losing battle against the fragilities of Time."

—*Freya Stark, Baghdad Sketches, 1937*

With relief I lean the ancient motorcycle on its side stand. It rests
sputtering on a patch of gravel and sand. The edge of the road is strewn
with litter thrown out of passing cars and blown by gusts of wind to this
dramatic bend in the valley. It is caught in a vortex until a truck hurtles
past and the sudden airflow launches the litter up into its wake, settling

145

it further down the hill towards the coast. I dismount from the battered machine, shaking in spite of the heat and too terrified to switch off the ignition in case I can't kick-start it again. Crouching next to it I catch my breath and gulp down some tepid water. There is no traffic, so the valley is silent apart from the irregular chugging of the engine beside me. Warm air drifts inland from the beach and I imagine I can smell diesel from the port, dust from the town, and the bay's salt tang passing over the desert towards me. Bracing my hands on my knee armour, I groan to my feet. The red earth of the Sinai Mountains spreads out on either side of the route ahead revealing a glimpse of my destination.

* * *

Ten years before, I arrived in Nuweiba' under a full moon. It peered over the barren crags and lit up the sand beside the empty mountain road as the minibus climbed. I was alone in the back, the only passenger to be collected from the airport that night by Saeed. Employed as a driver for the tourist camp, he was dressed in a Bedouin *gallabiyah* and red-and white-checked *shmagh* circled by a black cord. He told me he wasn't from the local tribe. I listened and nodded, too tired by now to ask questions. We reached a plateau, and I was a little concerned when Saeed then left the tarmac, driving off-road towards an empty shack. He pulled up outside as lights flicked on, and a man appeared in the glow of a doorway. Dismounting from the vehicle I was directed to some mattresses on the sand, then a minute later from a back room I heard a gas stove begin to hiss. This was a service station, opened only when passing customers pull in for a break. I relaxed and sat scribbling in my journal while we waited for the tea to brew.

It was past midnight when we got back on the road and the camp was deserted by the time we arrived. Saeed stopped the minibus on a track behind some wooden huts and carried my bags to my room. I followed, stumbling half asleep over the uneven ground. Disoriented by the sound of the waves that seemed to lap at the door, I slept fitfully, roused only a few hours later by the intensifying heat. Outside, a palm-leaf porch rustled above in the breeze and the stone veranda was cool under my feet. The sweep of the Red Sea filled my view. All its colour was bleached away by the sharp winter sunlight reflecting off the water. I'm usually dubious when people claim that an experience has been life-changing, but the impact of my first two weeks in Sinai was so profound that everything shifted.

Nuweiba' means "many wells" in the local dialect and was originally the location of a summer encampment for both the Mzeina and Tarrabin tribes. Their territories align along an area of fresh water, date palms and coral reef. A settlement grew as a vast tourism influx in the 1970s brought people, money and, inevitably, drugs. Camps were thrown up on the beach to cater to the visitors and the white sands were obscured by bamboo huts that over time were replaced by concrete hotels and restaurants. The town expanded and the flood plain sweeping down the centre from Wadi Watir was designated as the boundary between the tribes. On the far side of the Tarrabin-owned half of the town is the eponymous village. Tarrabin is a cluster of a few hundred concrete homes, some plain, others carved and curved and painted in terracotta and gold. There are carefully tended gardens with guava trees, flowers, and even grass, but then there are also piles of rubbish in the streets and trees with more plastic bags than leaves hanging from the branches. Practical and cultural infrastructures failed to keep up with the speed of expansion, creating social and environmental challenges that leading members of the community are still fighting hard to resolve. The camp I first stayed in sits a few miles north of the village and after enquiring about meeting local people I was invited to spend an afternoon with a lady called Um Abdul. Over the coming years she often shared her home and her culture with me, cooking Bedouin dishes, and teaching me the dialect. It was this generosity that changed my life completely.

Eighteen months after that moonlit arrival, I sold everything I owned in the UK to return and spend two years living and researching in Sinai. Since the Tarrabin tribe is no longer nomadic, I moved not into a goat hair tent as people like to imagine, but into one of the single-story concrete houses in the village. Situated in the heart of the community, amongst Um Abdul's family, it had been uninhabited for a long time. The windows were frameless, floors were bare concrete, there was no air-conditioning, running water or locks on the doors. There was, however, one ceiling fan that I learned to switch on by inserting the bare wires into a socket, resting them on the contacts until it began to spin. When the heat was heading towards a peak of 48°C I moved my bed underneath the fan and slept, ate, and wrote under its fly-splattered blades. Herds of goats would tap dance past the front door, spitting noisily, as geckos slid ninja-like up the smooth concrete and disappeared deep into the cracks in the walls. Palm trees grew through the windows and ants took over my kitchen, and at one point, my bed. In the evenings there might be a concert of cicadas singing in the garden accompanied by the blast of Egyptian music from a wedding tent on the beach. The volume was always turned up high enough to distort the sound as it echoed back from the mountains. Through my friendship with Um Abdul, I was invited to take part in family events, from weddings and funerals to desert trips and quiet evening meals. We would recline with the older women on blankets in someone's yard and I would learn words, mislearn words, listen to half-understood stories and gossip, and drink sweet tea until my tongue was furry and thick.

The heat became unbearable by early summer, but even with the coastline nearby I respected local values and wouldn't swim there in a bikini. There is no public transport in the area, and I was having to spend a lot on taxis to take me to the beach camps to cool off in the sea. After six months I was becoming irritated by not having my own vehicle. A small motorcycle or moped would've been ideal, but sometime around the millennium the Egyptian government tried to crack down on illegal activity in the peninsula by banning the import of motorcycles. They seem to have overestimated the capacity for two-wheeled vehicles to easily cross huge expanses of sand and rock, but nevertheless the ban still stands today. Car prices are exorbitant, matching those in the UK although average Egyptian wages are a tenth by comparison. Wealthier families have a shared pot of money which can be borrowed and repaid, like a cooperative among relatives. Those with a stable income might save for years and still only be able to afford the oldest vehicles, usually scarred by salt, sand, potholes, or careless driving. Jeeps and trucks can be more affordable second-hand, and they are generously shared so that those without a vehicle can still earn a living. If one person fails or struggles, it becomes a shared struggle.

I had no savings, and all my earnings were in local currency which mostly went on rent and food. Consequently, I couldn't afford my own vehicle and, with regret, moved away from village life. I settled in a camp called "Moon Island" a few miles further up the coast. My solid wood and bamboo *husha* had been built on a grey stone base, 20 metres from the water and perfect for catching the relief of a sea breeze. There is a natural sandy-bottomed lido in the shallows leading to a narrow entrance through the coral reef into the deep sea. If I swam before anyone else woke up, I sometimes met the resident manta ray, and watched her sweep away over the reef.

Life continued as before, with my research, visits to friends, desert hikes, and camel races between the tribes. I nested in my new hut, creating a wardrobe from a broken broom, shelving from a vegetable delivery box, a hanging system from string so I could draw back the mosquito net during the day, and I was adopted by a feral ginger kitten named Bryan who returned with me to England when it was time to leave.

Tourists were scarce in the uncertain years following the Arab Spring, and Egyptian Revolution. Most locals were circumspect about this change because life was slow and peaceful, but there was little work available. I had been collaborating with local companies on cultural events to earn a living, but this began to falter, and I needed to make a decision. All through the 2011 revolution (which barely touched us in the desert), the dramatic 2012 election (which mostly just prompted celebratory gunfire), and the various petrol, water, or food shortages, it was never an option for me to 'give up'. It wasn't fear of what I would do next that made me leave, and neither was it pressure from friends or family to remove myself from what was being widely portrayed as a dangerous part of the world. I felt safer alone in Sinai than I ever have in London, Edinburgh, or Toronto and was never once scared in the quiet goat-crowded alleys of Tarrabin. After two years of listening, learning, and documenting life in a village on the edge of the Red Sea, I had simply reached a point where I needed to recover my independence and mobility.

* * *

Settling back in was harder than I could have imagined. What had felt like a dynamic move revealed itself to be only one part of a process I hadn't fully thought through. Having made it back to England I found myself facing the same challenges as in Egypt: no money, no income, no transport. As familiar as the way of life in Sinai had become, I fell back into British culture, albeit with a thud, finding myself serving coffee, saving pennies, and trudging for an hour through cold, wet, muddy country lanes to catch the bus to and from work. I resented the relative ease with which we all functioned and, now more accustomed to tiny family-run shops with seasonal and often limited stock, I recoiled from the excesses of supermarkets. There was no silence. No hours spent quietly conversing under the stars, no more sea or shooting stars, and no more hot, empty days languorously stretching out ahead of me.

In 2018 I heard that Um Abdul's older brother was booked to give a talk at the Adventure Travel Film Festival just outside London. His visa application failed, but I went anyway, eager to meet anyone interested in travel and culture. When I arrived on site, I was shocked to discover that there were *hundreds* of motorcycles, with hordes of bikers swaggering past (now I know that was just due to the armoured gear of course). On the first evening, I sat in a hall crammed with other field-grubby adventurers, listening to a woman tell a tale of traversing the world on a motorcycle. Steph Jeavons' story was not so much laid out for us as it was spread-eagled on the lecture slides and in her words, dropped with a brutal and refreshing honesty. And that was the moment I decided to become a biker.

I spent a few weeks researching options for learning to ride. I wanted time to get used to the practical skills required to stay upright, but also to come to terms with what still seemed like a crazy idea. Outside a shipping container in a car park, I began Compulsory Basic Training (CBT), wearing my film fest t-shirt for luck. I discovered a few things that day. Firstly (and fortunately), I have great clutch control. Secondly, I struggle with turning right. But most importantly, I discovered that I'm capable of managing overwhelming fear. After a couple of hours pootling around cones in the car park it was time for road riding. I couldn't believe that anyone in their right mind would let me out in the traffic and was convinced that I was going to die. I was shaking so much I was in danger of dropping the bike. I ticked off small victories in my mind: "I managed not to stall!" "I turned a corner!" "I rode through college grounds without hitting any students!" I hesitated, held up traffic, and nearly got off at a junction wailing, "I can't do this!!!" but each little achievement kept me going, and we made it back in one piece. I was presented with a piece of paper to say that I could legally conquer the roads on two (small) wheels. It was almost more terrifying now that I had passed.

A week later, wearing all the safety gear I could afford, I went to collect a shiny silver Yamaha custom YBR 125cc. I signed the paperwork, asked how to switch it on, then the salesman tactfully left me alone. In my head I ran through the basics. Gloves on. Visor down. Key in. Start bike. Put in gear. Check blind spot. Check again. Once more for luck. It can't hurt to check one last time. And off I went, entirely the wrong way. Even given the slight detour a journey that would usually take 45 minutes took nearly two hours. I must have been going extremely slowly, but of course at the time it felt like I was roaring down those country lanes, narrowly avoiding the pheasants. I had never felt such exhilaration and joy as during that first solo ride.

Within months I was taking lessons towards a full licence and had exchanged the Yamaha for a big, bold, and beautiful Triumph Street Scrambler in cranberry red. She sat in my local dealership all through the winter as my tests were postponed because of fog, gale force winds, and even snow. Finally on a cold February morning, I wobbled my way through the test. "Well, you're never going to get caught for speeding," said the examiner, but passed me, and I rushed to collect my bike from the store. At 8am the next morning I loaded my tent onto a frost-covered "Beatrix," as she was now named, and set off for the Overland Event 130 miles away. I met one of the organisers on the way who kindly offered to wingman that first journey. It should have taken two and a half hours but since I hadn't previously been above 56 mph it took six. He was extremely patient. At the event I was surrounded by others who had already spent many years exploring the world on two wheels and over the course of the weekend they inspired an idea. I would fly to Sinai, rent a trail bike, and ride over the mountains to Tarrabin. I had secured funding for a research trip in two months' time, so that became my deadline.

One of the biggest challenges to the process was finding out whether there were even motorcycles to rent, and how much it was going to cost. Websites were vague and companies didn't return my emails. There was one rental shop in Dahab, a small town about an hour south of Tarrabin, and I hoped that if I turned up, drank tea, and discussed the options, something would be possible. From the outset, this was an adventure. Never known for packing light, I had to consider how I would get my bags on the back of a trail bike of completely unknown dimensions. I wore my gear to travel but needed to take gifts for the women in the village plus practical things like a water bladder, cable ties and a first aid kit. I squeezed everything into hand luggage, including a helmet, but once I was on the plane, found that it didn't fit in the overhead locker. I spent the flight with my feet tentatively resting on a Shoei lid.

* * *

A midnight landing into an eerily empty Sharm el Sheikh airport. Each step, each smell is familiar, from the moment the door of the plane opens and the warm air rushes in. Although it's dark as we shuffle out onto the tarmac, my feet move with the confidence of being on known ground, carrying me onto the shuttle bus. I sway expertly among the other travellers who sag from the ceiling loops. Clearing the unnecessarily big gap between the bus and the pavement, I bounce through the doors and up three flights of stairs while my companions from the plane slide up on a stuttering escalator. I grasp a £20 note ready in my hand as I weave through the tour operators at the top of the stairs poised to catch their allocation of tired tourists, eager to whisk them away to a sanitised, tiled, and gated resort.

First in the queue, in seconds I have Egyptian guineas as change from my English note and a fresh visa in my passport. A few dozen travellers are already forming unwieldy lines to get through security. I join them, watching with amusement as people argue at the border and are summarily removed to wait until last. I muse to myself that they would never behave like that in Heathrow, but I'm through the security check before I can pursue that thought any further. There's no luggage to collect as it's all in my hand so I stride through customs, avoiding the security officers' eyes, and out through the glass doors where I pass along a line of taxi drivers waiting for their fares. There is no sign for me. I make a beeline for the outer door and step with ease into Sinai.

Warm air envelops me and hugs me home. A balmy 25°C seeps through my heavy gear and I'm sweating before I even begin the negotiations with the taxi drivers outside. These men are the locals, Bedouin from the Mzeina tribe who own the land that Sharm and Dahab occupy, although generations of governments have seemed to think otherwise. Rarely granted official taxi licences because of their ethnicity, they must stand outside the exit and hope for a fare. A small group responds to my greeting in Arabic, and they laugh when I begin to negotiate in dialect. "*Inti min wen?*" one asks with glee, and I explain that I am from England but that I lived in Tarrabin previously, and there are murmurs as they acknowledge the association with respect. Without a second glance at my helmet (because Bedouin would be too polite to ask questions), I am led to a truck, and we head towards the hotel an hour away in Dahab.

Every place in the world has its own distinct smell and when you have lived somewhere for a length of time that smell somehow finds you even thousands of miles away. It drifts over your garden reminding you of warm roads through red mountains, it joins you in the morning with a breeze through the window that confuses you on waking. And it greets you as a friend when you land in its heart once again. I inhale deeply through the truck window as we pull away. The highway stretches ahead, punctuated with streetlights until we turn onto the mountain route where only the headlights and the stars remain.

* * *

Whilst living in Tarrabin was in many ways a dream come true, occasionally it would reach a point where I needed to get away on my own. I would beg a lift to Dahab when possible and the Paradise Hotel kindly extended the locals' rate to me, in part I think because I made an effort to speak Arabic. I'm not a fan of hotels in general, but this is an exceptionally lovely place. A double layer of rooms wraps around the circular pool, wooden balconies trailing with jasmine and honeysuckle. Palm trees mark the far edge of the grounds, reaching straight up towards a usually cloudless blue. I breakfasted outside under a canopy with mango juice and *shakshouka*.

Like Nuweiba', Dahab was a summer encampment for Bedouin, but is now known for its diving centres, laid back attitude, and trendy cafés lining the sea front. From these you can climb straight into the water to snorkel and re-emerge to recline on their seats with plates of fish *mechoui,* chips, and Arabic coffee. Leading back from the shoreline are narrow streets often charged down by marauding gangs of goats, who are otherwise found chewing on rubbish in the gutters. The residents are international; a mix of Egyptians who have come to work or start businesses, Russian women in search of Egyptian husbands, European scuba-diving instructors and ex-pats, and Bedouin mostly from the Mzeina tribe.

Strolling through the streets and avoiding the feral dogs that scare me, I made my way to the only motorcycle rental shop in Dahab. Outside were a dozen Honda CRF 250cc bikes, propped on side stands and mostly held together by stickers and tape. The tiny shop opened onto the street under a ramshackle awning and inside the walls were lined floor to ceiling with parts and accessories. The owner, an Egyptian in his late 20s, lolled on a plastic chair with a pale brown dog at his feet. Everything, including the dog, was coated with the fine layer of dust that is a constant in Sinai, and which I still find in pockets, around unopened zips, and at the bottom of bags. I'm fond of it now because in an instant it can transport me back to Sinai adventures faster than any photo.

The owner made little effort to hide his contempt when I explained what I wanted. He was a bully, shouting or laughing at his workers and the dog, who took the opportunity to move away from him and ease all her weight onto my feet. He claimed the rate I'd seen online was per hour, not per day. Tea was brought, time crawled past, and we eventually reached an agreement. My plan had been to rent for two weeks and then have a couple of days to recover before leaving, but after bartering in my most aggressive Arabic all he would concede for my price was four days. As it turned out that wasn't such a bad thing, because being more than 20 years old the bike was well past its best. Four days later the gear lever snapped off, leaving me to ride five miles back to the shop in 1st gear, in 40°C.

* * *

As early as was reasonable I returned to the shop, and the owner made a fuss of readying a trail bike from the assortment on the street. It had no electric start but was at least low enough for me to be able to touch the ground. They tried to teach me how to kick-start in flip-flops, and after half an hour I just hoped it would get easier with practice, and in boots. The oil and filter were changed, and every bolt tightened. Then I was asked, rather ominously, "You won't need the light, right?"Too many times in the pitch black of Sinai nights I had held my breath when a camel appeared in the car headlights, forcing the driver to swerve onto patches of sand or gravel. I had looked away when dogs shot out of the dark and were killed under the wheels of oncoming trucks. I had cried when they were still alive, hearing them scream until someone fetched a gun. There were no vets close by and certainly no one had money to spend on street animals. These were the most distressing moments for me in Sinai and I had no intention now of risking either my own life, or those of more animals, by riding at night. The mechanics sealed the smashed headlight together with tape, and then did the same to the side stand, which worried me slightly. No one uses helmets in Sinai, but on went my lid and I zipped up my armoured jacket despite the heat. Climbing onto the bike it occurred to me to check whether it was a standard one-down, four-up gear box. The owner seemed disturbed by this question. I thought it best to leave quickly. As I pulled away, I heard a groan of "Oh-woah-woah-woah" from someone, but I was on the road and heading away from their contempt and their judgment. I had only been riding for two months and may not have looked particularly confident, but to be fair I was more at danger from the scattering goats than I was from my limited riding skills. I was grinning behind the visor before I even made it around the corner. I have no memory of the journey back to the hotel but next morning there was the bike, safely parked behind reception.

* * *

The wind had picked up overnight, so I procrastinated for as long as possible. Days are short in Sinai where the sun dips behind the mountains by mid-afternoon even in the summer, meaning that I couldn't leave it too late. Armed with bungee cords, straps, and a cargo net, I secured the bag as best I could, filled my water bladder and tucked the hose into my mouth under the helmet. I was nauseous with fear, but also excited to start a new adventure. Feeling doubtful, I guided the bike to the end of the driveway. I stopped, gripping the brake hard, my fingers swollen and sweaty inside the gloves. Balancing on my left toes with a deep rut on my right under the kickstart, I looked at the traffic. The driveway is a sharp turn off a corner of the main highway along the shore and small white minibuses shoot back and forth between the hotels and the town, paying no heed to the speed bumps. The bike cut out. Perhaps because of the heat. Perhaps because of the angle. But due to the luggage and the tilt of the bike, dismounting was not an option. I perched on the silent machine, nose pointing out into a busy main road, the kickstart inaccessible. After a few minutes of wondering what to do, I checked the oncoming traffic as best I could, released the brake, and coasted down off the slope, across the lanes, and over to the far side. Miraculously, nothing hit me.

Restarting the bike, I sat looking ahead. I thought about giving up, telling myself that this was absolutely the most stupid thing I had ever considered doing. I barely knew how to ride, the bike was decrepit, and it was far hotter than I'd anticipated. Something was bound to go wrong. The bike shuddered and chugged forward as I released the clutch, but when I reached the next junction, I found myself turning towards the mountains. I focused purely on the surface of the tarmac, the gears, the patches of sand that materialised around corners, and the 10-inch-deep potholes that loomed as dark shadows on the path ahead.

The wind dropped and the bike and I moved slowly, manoeuvring between the lethal fissures and segments of road that had been swept away in recent floods. When I moved to Tarrabin I was told by an elderly Bedouin man that it hadn't rained for 25 years. In Spring 2012, I sat with friends at a camp when we smelled something odd. It was sweet yet rotten. Water falling on earth that hadn't been drenched for decades. The rain cloud reached us and as the drops fell we rushed around trying to get cushions and rugs under cover, called friends, laughed, whooped, and celebrated. The yellow sand turned dark purple. A member of staff slipped away to stand alone on a tree stump at the back of the camp, gazing towards the storm over the mountains.

After that the floods returned each year. Parched earth gave way under the weight of the water and churned down the mountainsides through *wadis* to the shore. In the dry decades, Egyptian businessmen had bought cheap land on the flood plains and built expensive hotels that were now carried into the sea by the torrents of black water. A body was found on the reef down the coast. Where the street crossed the *wadis,* vehicles would have to drive through a sudden deep river, and we would all pile into cars and rush to the edges to watch the deluge and help those who got stuck to safety. Coaches were swept sideways onto rocks, cars were abandoned, and it was common for entire sections of road to break off and wash away. Access to Nuweiba' now meant driving on the unstable ground left behind, and there were times when fresh water, petrol, and food simply couldn't reach us safely.

I didn't relax and enjoy the journey, or any buzz of achievement, until I left the second army checkpoint where the route forks either towards Mount Sinai or Nuweiba'. The checkpoints are tough places. Young army recruits are sent from mainland Egypt and spend months living in a small concrete box with no running water, the only shade coming from wooden canopies thrown together on the scrub behind the roadblock. There is always a small mosque and *Allahu Akbar* written in Arabic script formed by small white stones on a prominent slope of the red earth. Tempers can become fraught under these harsh conditions, but locals maintain a good relationship with these frustrated and overheated soldiers, dropping off food and bottles of water when they pass. It seemed to me not bribery but more a complex interchange of pity, power, and respect, from both sides.

I made sure to lift my visor so they could see my face before I reached a checkpoint, especially given the ban on motorcycles. I answered the usual questions about who I was, where I was staying, and what I was riding, which I think was more from amusement and curiosity than formal enquiry. I replied vaguely with the name of a tourist camp. Although I was unofficially staying with Um Abdul in the village, the staff at the camp would confirm they knew me. While the officers inside checked my passport, I asked one of them for permission to rest in the shade. He brought me a bottle of water from his own rations.

* * *

Every bend of the Nuweiba' road and each mountain's shape and colours are etched into my mind from before. As long as I travel slowly, there is no fear as I potter along the scarred tarmac. Trucks rush past with a hoot, simultaneously greeting and checking I'm okay. I pass the ever-so-cool camels that don't even glance up from grazing on thorn bushes. They appear to be wandering wild but are owned by Bedouin families settled in the clusters of rundown houses in the distance. I climb the final hill, the steepest section of the journey, and beg the bike not to stop, willing it forward to the peak where I come to a hesitant stop on the patch of gravel and litter. Down below is the port of Nuweiba', a band of concrete hosting the ferries to Jordan. The Red Sea stretches out ahead and Saudi Arabia appears in a pastel haze on the other side where, on a clear day, you can see the windows in high-rise buildings on the far shore.

I know what it will feel like to travel down the mountain and sweep into the long curve that leads towards Tarrabin. I know that half an hour more along the coast, past abandoned resorts, will bring me to the far side of the village and to a right-hand turn. I do not know that it is now marked by a loaded tank pointed towards the Israeli border 40 miles away. I will turn past the alert soldiers and navigate down the hill to my friend's home with the sea before me. I know the sound the tyres will make on the stony earth of her land and that she will be out in the courtyard of her house feeding the goats, perhaps with a few children helping because she is always fun to be around. I know how her headscarf will smell when we hug, and that she will be entirely unimpressed that I have arrived on a motorcycle. Climbing back onto the sputtering machine, I flip the visor down, check over my shoulder, and start the descent.

About the author:

EmmaLucy Cole is based in the UK as a researcher, writer, explorer, and speaker. She is a fellow of the *Royal Geographical Society* and is studying towards a PhD. at the *University of Bristol*, researching the representation of Bedouin cultures in travel writing.

After more than two decades spent studying and representing North African and Middle Eastern cultures, in 2011 EmmaLucy decided to sell everything she owned to spend six weeks with a Bedouin tribe in Sinai, learning Arabic and researching local culture. Two years later she finally left, not only having gained a ginger Bedouin cat and a myriad of stories, but also witnessing first-hand some of the ways in which marginalised groups can be misrepresented.

EmmaLucy is developing her theory of "Downward Exploration": rather than travelling long distances and seeing many places superficially, this type of exploration allows us to focus in-depth on communities and local environments, learning about the cultures, habits, food, and history. Riding a motorcycle is part of this process, allowing her to be more mobile and independent, yet also allowing for connection, deeper understanding and ultimately, ethical representations.

Website: emmalucycole.com
Facebook: emmalucy.cole
Instagram: emmalucycole
Twitter: emmalucycole

Hooked on a Feeling

by Tim and Marisa Notier

> "I am convinced that life is 10% what happens
> to me and 90% of how I react to it."
>
> —*Charles Swindoll*

Adventure motorcycling can have just as many ups and downs as there are passes through the Peruvian Andes. There are moments of pure bliss, when I've found myself looking around 360 degrees in complete wonder, asking how did I get here? And others when it seems like the entire world is against me as I struggle to gain traction through a muddy mountain pass, painfully grinding my way fighting for every mile gained, my energy draining faster than a AAA battery attempting to power a Las Vegas casino.

But the rewards have always outweighed the struggles. The emotional gains have always peaked higher than the deepest valleys of frustration.

My fiancée, Marisa, and I had one such roller coaster ride while in central Peru.

It was a sunny day in late 2018, and as we bounced along a remote dirt backroad we began a climb of steep switchbacks through the Andes. With every pothole, I hoped that the pair of crutches I'd fastened to the front of our KTM 1190's crash bars wouldn't shake loose. The crutches made the bike look more like an M4 Sherman tank than the average adventure motorcycle. In addition to our oversized bags were a patchwork of "badge of honor" stickers on the plastic fairings, and our shaggy sheepskin seat cover. The crutches completed the unique look of our motorcycle that often left people asking, "What in the world have they been up to?"

A few weeks prior, we had an unfortunate power slide on a gravel backroad that left Marisa with a torn ligament in her right foot (I say *we* only to relieve some of the guilt since she was my passenger, and the slide was my fault). After three immobile weeks of rehabilitation, Marisa was able to get back on the bike, and we were on the road again. I was relieved that there was no trust lost, and no regrets as she remounted the bull that had bucked and injured her.

A silver lining to the unfortunate event that paused our progress was that another two-up couple on a KTM 1290 caught up to us after months of stalking each other on Facebook. We were finally able to meet with Brendon and Kira Hak, aka 'The Adventure Haks', and were now nervously riding alongside them through some of the most difficult terrain Marisa and I had encountered to date.

With Brendon and Kira in the lead, I followed behind trying to dodge sizable rocks, while hitting medium potholes in an effort to avoid the larger ones. This was all standard procedure by now for backcountry Peruvian roads but, on this particular incline, a small creek flowed down the center of the road. I was a little more anxious than usual since the fall that had left Marisa's foot as fragile as glass, so I focused solely on the rough terrain in front of me, gripping the handlebars tightly as we made our way up the mountain.

The runoff had taken the path of least resistance and cut a deep ditch that wove from one side of the road to the other. Brendon and I had to maneuver through the creek in order to avoid getting caught in its rut, all while going up steep inclines that made 180° turns as the road continued its climb. All I could do was proceed with all the confidence I could muster. That was, until my confidence began to grind against my riding skills.

After guiding the bike up a particularly long stretch of uneven terrain that finally leveled out, I said to Marisa over our intercoms, "That was kinda intense."

"Yes, it was. But you did great," she replied, in an effort to boost my morale. She knew that confidence was half the battle in just keeping the bike upright.

For a moment, I had foolishly believed that the worst was behind us, until we once again began to climb the surrounding hills. The tight zig-zag pattern was made even more challenging by being two-up and overloaded. We twisted along the mountainside while weaving around water-filled potholes in the road. It was difficult to judge how deep any of the puddles actually were, so I played Russian roulette while trying to avoid the deepest craters. Sometimes I lost, as the front suspension fully compressed into the seemingly bottomless depressions, but I mostly chose wisely.

The main road had smaller branches that forked from it like bolts of lightning. As we rode the lightning, we found ourselves in a lost paradise landscape. Large, jagged, mountain peaks surrounded us while streams trickled down between them to crystal blue lakes. Lakes that had settled at higher elevations overflowed into more streams and small waterfalls that cascaded into other turquoise lakes further below. I could see that rain was coming down in sheets in the distance, but it didn't concern me, at least yet. All I could think of was that I had never been anywhere on Earth as picturesque.

This was what it was all about—good people and fantastic riding. We were somewhere we'd most likely never find ourselves again, and that feeling could never be replicated. I knew there would be equally fantastic memories to come, but each one was a memento in its own purity.

As we took a moment to eat lunch, I sat there smiling, admiring our surroundings.

"I don't want to sound like a broken record, but man, this may be the most beautiful spot I have ever been," I said as I breathed in the fresh, crisp air.

"Yeah, this place is pretty special," Kira agreed. "It's stunning."

We all nodded silently in agreement as we ate hard-boiled eggs and oranges.

I noticed a livestock pen in the valley below, built with stone walls. It looked like it could have been the foundations of an old, stone castle. The framework spread out in a square where a courtyard would have been. And long elliptical sections hinted at where a market may have sold fruits and vegetables long ago. Now it was just a giant livestock pen, where the sheep, cows, and llamas could have had their own society in a medieval version of *Animal Farm*.

After lunch, we packed and headed south, excited to discover what was around the next bend in the road.

Continuing down the gravel path brought new visual stimulation, to the point where Marisa had to keep reminding me to keep my eyes on the road, or being "gently" reminded to do so by a sudden jolt from an unseen pothole. It was just so incredible to be riding down a winding gravel road above fields dotted with hundred-year-old stone corrals and waterfalls cascading from the mountainside. I lost count of the number of lakes tucked into every pocket between the mountains.

The four of us were slowly catching up to the rain as we entered a new set of switchbacks. It now gently drizzled as we rode beside the bluest lakes I've ever seen. Marisa videoed nearly the entire ride as neither of us could believe how surreal the landscape was.

Twenty minutes later, we stopped on the side of the road at what might have been my favorite spot to have ever gazed out from. We were halfway up the side of a mountain that overlooked Laguna Tinquicocha with granite peaks that stuck out of a mossy green-colored landscape. Thick dark clouds hovered above, but for the moment they withheld from unleashing their torrents of rain, allowing us to appreciate the wonders around, free from the onslaught of the heavens.

"I don't want to sound like a broken record...," I started to say.

"No, this definitely surpasses the last unimaginably beautiful spot," Kira remarked.

We took our time to once again soak in the scenery. I snapped as many pictures as I could while Marisa filmed the surreal ambience around us. I wanted documented proof that this place existed, even though the landscape before us would forever be burned into my memory.

After another hour of riding from one spectacular view to another, we reached the town of Oyón. Our ride through the eastern side of the Cordillera Huayhuash Reserve and the surrounding area in central Peru had all of the elements of adventure riding—the good, the tough, and the insanely beautiful.

At the end of the day, we settled in a cheap hotel and ate a hot meal as we discussed the out-of-this-world movie set we'd just ridden through. The day had provided everything we could have asked for and we were eager to find out what the following day would offer. Little did we know at the time, the next day had hell in store.

We awoke early the next morning in order to get back on the road and into more blissful scenery. After a quick breakfast, Brendon and I marked the day's route on our phones. It consisted of a series of bullet points that followed a little, squiggly white line that headed south from Oyón. The first segment of the day would get us to the village of Rapaz, but from there it was difficult to determine what our exact route would be because the line on Google Maps didn't connect in some sections.

We took off knowing that we might have to backtrack, but crossed our fingers and hoped for the best.

Along the way, there were more rivers and small waterfalls lining the road. Donkeys freely roamed and *hee-hawed* at us in their funny two-toned call. The livestock were free-range, and it seemed the only way to differentiate between who owned the llamas, donkeys, and cattle was by the pom-pom earrings they wore. Colorful tassels hung from their ears like they'd just graduated from cow college (cow-llege).

At the end of one of the small villages we passed was an old, empty bullfighting arena. The girls dismounted to take pictures as Brendon and I entered with our bikes. We rode to opposite sides of the arena and revved our engines at each other like snorting bulls preparing to charge.

"Two men enter, one man leaves!" I shouted to Brendon.

Brendon pulled in his clutch, locked his front brake, and twisted his throttle while releasing the clutch. His back tire spun madly as it kicked a rooster-tail of dirt behind him.

"Yeah, I can't do that," I said.

As intimidating as Brendon was, I was the one who had a pair of lances protruding from the front of my motorcycle, Marisa's crutches arming me with an advantage in our mock jousting battle. I revved my engine back at him and scraped the ground with my left foot to create smaller, more pathetic clouds of dust.

"It seems we are equals," Brendon shouted back at me. "How about we call this battle a draw?"

"Agreed. No one has to die this day," I replied, releasing the gas.

The women cheered from the sidelines, as both men would be returning to them safely. Brendon and I did a couple of victory laps and exited the "battlefield" without any blood being drawn, though neither of us was aware of the actual battle ahead.

Half an hour later, we turned onto a smaller unmarked road and followed a gravel path that sliced through the terraced hills towards the town of Rapaz. We were now far above the rivers that we'd previously been riding next to and were just below a ceiling of dark storm clouds. And we were riding unmarked roads, this being the section of the day's journey I'd earlier been most concerned about.

The road became even less maintained as traffic rarely came this way. It was full of loose gravel, large stones, sand, and deep, water-filled depressions we had to avoid.

To the left, a sharp stone peak rose from the scenery. The mountainside was terraced with small houses nestled into peaceful nooks where the land flattened. From afar, it looked like a mini-Machu Picchu. Barely visible dots of white, that must have been llamas or sheep, were scattered across the grassy pastures towering high above a deep gorge where a stream ran through it. The riverbed was nearly dry, exposing the thousands of boulders that had once come from miles away to where they rested now. Once, those mighty stones had crowned some of the highest mountains, but over the course of time, they had found their way to the lowest point of the valley.

"Eventually, all things merge into one, and a river runs through it." I smiled, remembering the Norman Maclean quote that made more sense to me now than ever.

The narrow mountain pass we traveled continued to rise over 14,000 feet. We pushed on as we rounded tight corners climbing farther into the clouds.

"How is it possible we're still going up?" Marisa asked me over the comm.

"I know, right?" I said with a noticeable twinge of concern to my voice.

As we entered the fog and into the clouds, the scenery that had previously surrounded us completely disappeared. The only other soul we saw on this isolated path after hours of riding was a local man walking his cow back to some remote home.

"What the heck is he doing way up here?" I asked as we slowly passed him.

"I'm sure he's thinking the exact same thing about us," Marisa replied.

We finally made it to the intersection of the "main" highway marked on our map. I was relieved we were back on a more predominant path, but everything went downhill from there, figuratively. Literally, however, we were still going up.

The rain had turned the road into a mud pit that progressively got worse with each passing minute. Our rear tires were sliding around in the muck, and progress was diminishing to a snail's pace. It was cold, foggy, and raining, and all we wanted was the road to start descending towards some remote village.

I pulled up to Brendon as we stopped for a break to collect ourselves while it poured down on us.

"This was supposed to be the easy part," I said.

"Yep. This is getting pretty sketchy," he stated.

"There aren't many options at this point except to keep going," I said. "I don't think I have enough gas to get all the way back to Oyón."

"Onwards and upwards then," he replied as he turned and rode slowly off.

The road transformed from a thin layer of mud into a full-on mud stew that the tires could no longer sink their teeth into. Their treads filled with slime, making them slick. But we slowly trudged on, only progressing about 100 yards every 10 minutes or so. Eventually, the muddy road got so bad that Marisa and Kira had to dismount to help push the bikes through the muck. I kept dropping mine from one side to the other as if it were a fish flopping around out of water. With Marisa's hurt foot, we had to wait for Brendon or Kira to come rescue and help lift the bike.

We all had the equivalent of moon boots on, as the soles of our boots were elevated three inches by the sticky, slimy goo caked on them.

Kira and Marisa pushed us through the soupy mess as Brendon and I did our best to keep the motorcycles vertical. But it was slow going, and we were laboring to breathe. I was dropping my bike more frequently due to exhaustion, but the urgency to get down the pass before dusk kept us pushing ahead. At that point, my front fender was so clogged with mud the wheel would not spin, and acted like a dead limb on the front of the bike.

Even with Marisa pushing with all of her strength, I struggled to keep in the middle of the road. The rear of the bike pulled left, dangerously close to the five-foot drop-off into a watery bog.

"This is absolutely killing me," I stated to Brendon as we both stopped to gather our strength.

"I know, brother, this is no fun at all," he replied.

"Says the guy who hasn't dropped his bike once." I tried to laugh, but it just came out as a series of whiny exhales.

"These are the challenges that excite me!" Kira chimed in. "True struggles that test and push us to the limits, earning our place here!"

Marisa and I looked at each other. Neither of us was anywhere near as optimistic.

As Kira spoke with enviable positivity, I surveyed the landscape. I was at the point of completely giving up and was looking for the best plot of land I might be able to purchase from a local llama herder.

"Do you think we could raise llamas?" I asked Marisa.

"I think we should try to press forward," she replied.

I was beaten, spent, and drained from trying to fight the bike to do what I wanted. But in my despair, I noticed that there was a small single-track running parallel to the road just below the five-foot drop off.

"Can you go check that out?" I asked Marisa as I pointed to what was basically a trail the width of a bicycle tire. "That might be easier than riding through this sludge."

Marisa walked to the small path as I caught my breath for the tenth time. When she returned, she reported that a small 250cc bike would have been able to navigate down it without problems. But my huge, cumbersome, overloaded KTM without a rotating front tire would surely not find it as easy.

But it had to be easier than what I was currently up against.

The dilemma was that once I chose to take the small path, if it turned out to be just as difficult or worse, and there was no way of getting back onto the main road.

It was a risky option, but the track below seemed a little more solid than the slime we were on, and the bike was desperately trying to force me onto it anyway. I just had to allow it to get there.

Brendon looked at me as if I was half crazy, half genius. "That's either a brilliant plan, or a really bad idea," he said. "And you won't know until you're down there."

"I can't handle this road anymore," I replied. "I have to at least try something else."

"All right, then. Let's get you down there."

The four of us, as gracefully as possible, dropped the bike on its right side and pulled it down the muddy ditch as far as we could. Halfway there, we lifted it onto center as I got back on and wiggled the front tire back and forth to get the bike facing downwards. It was a skill called "the failed hill climb" I'd learned back in Oklahoma in Bill Dragoo's off-roading class. I was thankful that I'd paid attention and remembered that lesson as it successfully got the bike facing the correct direction.

Once on the narrow trail, I knew I'd made the correct choice. It was still a pain in the butt, but on a level that I could deal with. That small path was my saving grace, and even though it ended just around the next curve a quarter mile away, I was still thankful for its presence, because what would have most likely taken a half hour on the higher ground only took 10 minutes to navigate on the path.

I then had to crawl up a small embankment to get back onto the "main" road—my nemesis. The fun wasn't over yet, as there was still an unknown amount of muddy slop ahead of us.

Thankfully, we were able to see the road start its descent in the distance.

Brendon and I duck paddled our way through the muck for another two miles as the girls walked down the mountainside, meeting us at every straight section of the switchbacks.

Tired, but determined, we passed the worst of the mud before nightfall and began our descent through the thick fog of the high Andes. I don't even want to think about how much beautiful scenery we were robbed of because of the misty darkness that hid our surroundings.

After hours of intense difficulty, we were finally able to see trees take shape out of what was just previously a blanket of nothingness. As we twisted around a corner, my eyes widened in excitement as I could just barely make out the faint lights in the small village of Vichaycocha. Those lights shined through the mist like a lighthouse to sailors lost at sea.

We were going to make it. Everyone had worked together as a team to get through the worst conditions we had ridden up to that point, and hopefully for the rest of our travels.

As soon as we pulled into Vichaycocha, we stopped at the first hotel we came upon and parked the bikes. The rooms were nothing special, but they felt luxurious after what we'd just been through.

After unloading the motorcycles we met in the restaurant to order a round of congratulatory beers.

"The last two days have been the most beautiful, as well as the most stressful of my entire life," I stated, lifting my beer to a toast. "To many more exactly like them!"

"To many more!" the rest of the gang replied as we clanked the bottles together.

A new friendship had been fused between the Haks and us with a bead of weld thicker than the dried mud cemented to the bottom of our boots.

Prior to leaving on our around-the-world adventure, my imagination had never been abstract enough to have created a landscape equal to those we'd just ridden through. I was thankful that we were all now laughing about the struggles that seemed to be so dire just a few hours ago.

The emotional cocktail of adrenaline, friendship, anxiety, and happiness would be difficult to recreate at home. This was exactly what we had sought from the moment we left Chicago over a year and a half before. We were hooked on a feeling.

About the authors:

Tim Notier was born and raised just west of Chicago, and for the first 32 years, he rarely explored more than an hour away from his birthplace. He loved his motorcycle and cats, but there was always something missing.

Even though she was from the same town, **Marisa Notier** had traveled extensively through Europe, the Middle East, Asia, and Australia while studying abroad. She absorbed exotic cultures and experienced invaluable lessons that taught her of the kindness and warmth of others from every corner of the planet.

Tim and Marisa were once high school sweethearts, but their lives had temporarily led them in different directions. Now they are a team forevermore. They have combined their passions of motorcycling and travel into a two-wheeled journey around the world.

They hit the road in August of 2017, spent two years traveling from Chicago to Ushuaia, Argentina, and then flew their bike to South Africa to continue their circumnavigation.

Before leaving, they questioned if quitting their jobs and selling all of their possessions would be the worst or best decision they'd ever made. But after four years of travel, they can report it has been the most soul satisfying opportunity that has had its ups and downs, but they wouldn't exchange the worst day for their previous lives.

Website: Notiersfrontiers.com
Facebook: Notiersfrontiers
Instagram: @timnotier
YouTube: notiersfrontiers
To date, they are the authors of three motorcycle travel books: *Maiden Voyage, 2Up and Overloaded*, and *Blood, Sweat and Notiers*. Tim and Marisa's books are available as paperback and on *Kindle* from *Amazon*. Marisa is also a contributor to Chris Scott's *Adventure Motorcycle Handbook*.

The Road to Myself

by Christian Brix

"O public road... You express me better
than I can express myself,
You shall be more to me than my poem."

—*Walt Whitman*

It's early afternoon as I ride into Podgorica for a mooch about. There doesn't appear to be much happening as I drift through the city's streets, waiting for some unknown thing to call out at me, but whatever it could be; it doesn't. I find it hot and uninspiring.

I'm on the other side of the city before I know it and stop to consider what comes next. I had planned to stay here for the evening, but the day is still *youngish*, and I still have more miles in me. I consult the map; the only thing I could remotely regard as a guide. I'm heading to meet a friend in Sarajevo in a couple of days, but there are a few ways I can get there and still time.

Time and roads, that heady mix. This trip came from a sign, and I figure another one will present itself at the right place to stop for the evening, so throw my plan to the wind and drift. *Onwards.*

Naturally seeking a high spot to observe the capital, I find myself snaking up the M2.3 in the direction of Budva. I stop at a suitably scenic spot and gaze out over the city beneath me. It looks like many I've seen before and remains uninteresting from this perspective, confirming my initial instincts. I take a deep breath, and fully turn my back to it, continuing onwards into the hills, aimlessly in search of nothing, but technically, everything. The mountains radiate tranquillity in the afternoon sun, as wafts of eucalyptus and maquis carry me on my wayward way. Today, I am in the movie.

Away from people and buildings, in these natural and pure surrounds, my mind returns to a fully open state once again, and in turn, blossoms. It's funny how those pesky humans and their built-up environments always obstruct my natural mental flow. Out here on the road alone, my mind is completely unrestricted, to go wherever it pleases once more.

Climbing further into the mountains, I am surprised by their size and height. As I research unexplored lands on a map from home for the first time, for some reason I subconsciously interpret them as flat. Now that my eyes actually see the distinct features, I'm discovering the physical lay of the land is an act of magic. You might have some idea what's coming, but you never really know a place until you stand within it and have all of your senses engage with its unique characteristics. Just like every human fingerprint is unique, so too is every location.

Some of my happiest memories as a child come from staring at a map of the world and taking in the shapes of the land masses, while trying to envisage standing in their distinct settings. Dreaming of one day being there and taking in the landscape for real. I remember pointing out the most remote place from me that a 6-year-old could imagine—Alice Springs, and wondering what it would like to be there. I also distinctly remember the personal triumph of standing in Alice Springs, aged 21, seeing it in person. *Literally living the dream.*

Eventually, near Cetinje, enticed by the calm and green setting of the village, I come off the main road to reach an elevated flat green expanse, as the land spreads out perfectly flat to the craggy mountains encompassing it. The sky is the perfect shade of blue, and the blanket of greenery underneath it, contains the most splendid and florid shades of green. The two colours playing off each other as the land changes, rouses my subconscious. Grey rock and olive foliage softly unfold in undulating walls, basking in the sunlight. The air is cooler here, providing a respite from the humid city, and it carries the unmistakable enchantment of the Mediterranean. As it has over the centuries, what the land gives, it also appears to take; in a simple balance of existence.

The village is an appealing place, and far more inviting than the capital, but a glimpse of Lovcen National Park off in the distance gently lures me on further, in a calm afternoon of aimless drifting. I'm typically focused on a destination and punching the miles to get there in some mad charge, but today, I am content to simply roam. I'm not taking this road anywhere today; it's taking me somewhere.

Hardy and short windswept shrubs of yellow and orange cling to the low rocky outcrops, as the lower hills harbour a line of pines, before giving way to mountains. Above the trees, sheer rock faces loom, providing drama to the setting. The piecemeal cultivation of the land looks natural and in balance. Locals appear to only be taking what they need, and letting the remaining land remain wild. In truth they are not letting it do anything, this land will always be too wild to be tamed, and it's the land that is allowing the people to live. The road continues to lead me along, as I ramble on, following unseen signs. Having given over to destiny for a few hours, I navigate solely by my senses.

Past the small village of Njeguši, the habitation thins out once again, and I start to ponder more seriously where I will sleep tonight, but still instinctively move forward, pulled onwards by a gentle force of gravity. There is still daylight and there is no danger here. Through another small village called Krstac, I turn a corner and as the land opens out before me, my heart stops, then leaps to life again in a huge rush of elation. Overwhelmed at the scene before me, I pull in to make sure what I am seeing is actually real.

The sun shimmers over the gentle ripples of water on a massive inlet of the Mediterranean Sea. A huge cruise ship gently floats across this magical scene, totally out of place with the setting, and like a spaceship—it seems an illusion. Unlike Podgorica, the landscape is enticing, uplifting and clearly talks to me. *This is the place.* At the inside edge of the basin, I can see a small, old, fortified city, and instantly know that this is where I've been heading. I don't know its name, only that I must go there. *Now.*

I feel like Marco Polo finding new land. Of course, it's always been there, but it's new to me, and as such, it can only feel like a momentous discovery right now. This feeling of unexpected discovery is like sticking my finger inside an electrical socket. The lazy day of drifting abruptly ends. My energy levels are rejuvenated by a clear destination, as this soft world comes into a sharp focus.

The road continues to skirt high above the water, and I stop many times to study the amazing colours and stunning scenery below me, banking this exceptional stretch of land into my memory the best I can. I want to cherish this sight forever. *I will.* Every time I catch sight of the fortified city in the valley below, it sends furore throughout me. The hit doesn't stop, and only increases the closer I get to this mystical place. Louder than any land I have ever heard talk to me, it's singing to me in an unknown melody, seducing me on and I am unable to do anything but follow its call.

Mountains abruptly rise straight from the sea, following no rules or pattern and running capriciously across the earth, then crashing once again into the crisp blue sea. Growth clings to the small spots where the mountains graciously allow it to live. The air radiates an invigorating cleanliness which stimulates my entire body.

Every inch of this roadway is a postcard I would buy. It reminds me of Italy, but this is a wilder beauty. Italy is well known for its charm: you can predict it, but I was not expecting it here. It is unmistakably, unreservedly, and unendingly, Mediterranean. It could be no other place! Human existence is rightfully in its place, as the jagged mountains tower above its tiny patch of occupation. Nature rules here and humans are merely overnight guests in the millennia of evolution that has shaped this superlative spectacle.

To have so unexpectedly struck me like this, the setting carries a heightened significance. I had never read about *The Bay of Kotor* in any guidebook (although it's most certainly in them all) or been told to look out for it. To me, my roving wanderlust alone brought me here, and my aimless drifting is now rewarded in ecstasy. It's an entirely different experience to stumble upon something unforeseen on a journey, as opposed to anticipating its arrival. It's not a discovery per se, but you absolutely feel like you have just made one, or perhaps better put— earned one. My first lesson of overlanding is to never follow a guidebook, but to only follow my nose, as that's when truly surprising things happen.

This landscape is the best stimulant I've ever experienced. You can take all the illegal drugs in the world and combine them together and they won't come close to this perfect, natural high. As I quietly sit in this exquisite spot alone, inebriated by the beauty, my mind churns over a river of new realisations. Disparate thoughts, amassed over years of questioning, begin to come together in a slow hum of an orchestral recital. When I change what I see, it changes the way I see things. I've known this most of my life, but here, I sense the effect more intoxicatingly than ever before. Mentally reinvigorated, giant thoughts fall like dominos as the scene before me powers raw new insights.

All my life, I've naively assumed experience is a one-way process of stimuli flowing into me, but it's most certainly not; it's actually a two-way process. This view nudges my mind beyond anywhere it has ever been, taking old thoughts away as it provides new ones; it's literally cleansing.

I start to feel a fundamental recalibration in the way I think, enabling me to see the world even more differently than before. It's not allowing me to be someone else. The removal of accumulated mental debris enables me to simply be my real self.

I am fully in this moment, yet in another galaxy. I catch a glimpse of the grand game as I have done before, but for the first time ever; I see myself outside of it. *That's why it all doesn't make sense!* I was never really a part of it, I've just been caught up in it. I've instinctively come to ride these roads as I'm truly myself out here, in the places in between civilisation, removed from the messy construct of social conventions and meaningless ideals.

Out here on this bike is the *actual* freedom I'd heard so much about over the years... and for the first time in my life, I am truly exploring it, feeling it, revelling in it, coming to life within it. In a world of confusing nonsense, these sweet days of simple wandering are making perfect sense. I was born a traveller; I can see that now; I've always known it, but on this day; I am confirmed a traveller. Like a fisherman dedicating their life to the sea, I too dedicate myself to this endless road. People will always come and go in my life, but the road will *always* be here for me, just like music. It sets me free, it's my place on this Earth, my destiny. Against conventional wisdom, it's not a place; it is all places. My role in this world is to simply drift between them, to marvel at the grand and absurd nature of its creatures, and flourish in the spaces between, remaining the perpetual traveller.

This nomadic existence carries a sombre undertone while viewed in the common construct. Yet there is no sadness here, on the contrary, there is joy—finally, real tangible joy. A placid, but deep release after years of striving. I've finally found my place, my reason, my rock. I can exist within this emotion, without the need for understanding in the crooked structure of society. I take the first steps to jettison the irrelevant ways of thinking which have been handed down to me, yet never worked to explain the world. I validate my own reality, outside of the groupthink.

Understanding is irrelevant within this emotion. There are no words, no reason... I can go on with my communion with nature and roving this beautiful planet that I am so fortunate to inhabit, without purpose. The road shall be my compass, my map, my partner and the one I love above all. The road alone has become my reason. She can be cruel, and she can be kind, but she is always there, no matter what's happening or where I go. I've always heard her calling to me on the breeze, tempting me, by repeatedly whispering the infinitely enchanting words; *'come and find out'*. By following that call, in this world that makes no sense to me; I've managed to find a personal happiness that is sustainable.

I find my sense of being in a state of flowing motion. Silently, the road gives me an identity, and finally, after years of searching, something I can really hold onto, no matter what the future brings. I realise this truth while staring over the shimmering surface of the Med, as it wraps its comforting arms around my weary mind. My will meets my destiny, giving me a cerebral release, which I know will echo long beyond today, and have me chasing this new feeling again and again in the future.

The small stuff fades away. Life is but this moment in time. I can see the people on earth are not really my people, and the life they live is not my life. It's a joke when compared to the forest floor I see on the side of the road. I was not born in the wrong time, or the wrong gender, I was born the wrong species. I should have been born a tree, on this rocky hillside, to see far beyond this bizarre comedy of human life. Somehow, my mind stops working in *human* years, and transitions to *tree* years.

Trapped within the cities and thick webs of human interaction, I've never been able to talk about the biggest of all the elephants in the room. It's so big that it's nearly impossible to see! Out on this nameless road, outside of prevailing ideologies, I finally feel the space to scream—*Fire!!! The whole world is on fire and I can't bear watching it burn!* Humanity is caught in *the bystander effect* on a global scale, and I see that only in these brief moments of clarity, while pursuing extreme freedom, I escape the pull of groupthink and acknowledge the bigger reality.

Out here, the rarest of all human traits; brutal honesty, roams without boundaries. It destroys any sense of permanence, creating a bewildering state of constant flux. Out here I can connect with the universal reality, the one I know in my heart, but can't see in my society. Here I can finally admit what I've always known but been unable to voice: *I do not accept the world as it is and the conflicting ways in which we inhabit it.* It's not real. What I am feeling now *is* real.

While looking out on this glowing landscape I can see that within nature resides the most complex network of engineering and efficiency. Nature effortlessly contains the mystical qualities we have always been striving for: truth, peace, cooperation and purpose. It's a thousand times smarter than all of humanity, as it silently ticks away under our every move. The greatest advances in human science seem the work of infants compared to the unfathomable capabilities of mother nature.

One forest contains more feats of design, problem solving and cooperation than every city of humans combined. While the greatest psychologists probe our minds for clues to our unhappiness, a far wiser species serenely stands right next to them, simply waiting for them to engage. Since Jesus supposedly walked the Earth, we have been shouting about today and today alone. Nature has been silently overwatching for millions of years and will continue to do so well beyond humanity's time on Earth. Why is that so hard for us to reconcile? Why do we think that nature is stupid and brutish? Why can't we embrace life within its quiet balance?

In this moment, I sever my tie with ninety-nine per cent of humanity who remain stuck within *the bystander effect*, unaware that the earth that they stand on, not only has the answers we want, but is screaming in pain from our lack of awareness. The Earth is the greatest unrequited love story of all time, as it toils under our lack of respect and yet continues to lovingly provide for us. This self-imposed alienation from my species sends a chill through the old me, but I know it's the missing link I've been searching for, and the way forward to break the pointless cycle of human struggle. Detachment enables clear vision. I let the primal voice, not of humanity, but the earth itself, rise up through me. That's what's important. Only standing here in this precise spot right now enabled this realisation to happen. I turn from the person, to the tree for answers, and my comprehension of the universe instantly changes.

I learn more in three miles on this bike passing through unknown places than three years of any school. The open road opens my mind and lures it to a chain of new mindsets. The lucidity it brings is renewing, the effect resolving. The road breaks down centuries of thoughtless existence

180

and blind acceptance. It clears out the junk and wipes the slate clean for new ideas, new thoughts, new energy. Out here on my bike, I swim in an endless ocean of fresh perspectives. Discovery is a new drug, of which I only want more.

Just like there is always another place to discover on this Earth, there is always a new thought that is waiting to be had. I find the revelations that I've avidly been hunting for out here in the flow. Every moment out here on the road counts, every turn has a different weight, and every new way of thinking has immense value. I feel the course of my life changing profoundly as I realise this. An immense but silent and personal detour is taking place in the warmth of this setting sun.

In this moment, I make a conscious decision to pursue travel no matter where it takes me or how hard it is. This dedication to travel will be my real education, my pursuit, my *thing*; my real life. The road is my path in life, and it is endless. Just like the universe, I will never find its edge. Instead of driving me insane, it calms me greatly. I still love the people in my life dearly but must break the web of nonsense that ties us to pointless conventions and ideologies which only make our lives more difficult. The connections in my life need to be real and not born of a false, culturally implied importance. *I am going to do my own thing now.* I shall no longer service the absurd traditions which drive conflict, and like nature, I shall attempt to overstand.

Out here it is easier to see through the lies, manipulation and pomp. On the road, it is easier to see the truth, and having now glimpsed it, it's a perspective I never want to lose.

With a childish joy, I slowly descend through a long series of switch backs, each bringing me closer to earth, nearer to this mystical ancient city that I've discovered by chance in the modern maze of old Yugoslavia. I'm soon outside its significant historic walls, gawping in wonderment, as flocks of tourists flow around me. Still flush with the elation of discovery, I don't notice them.

I can't take the bike into the centre of the medieval village and have to park by the giant cruise ships outside of it. Normally this kind of thing would be annoying, but in this esoteric wonderland it's truly irrelevant.

I chart new ground around every corner inside its stout walls, and each one is an epiphany.

Kotor has been continuously inhabited since antiquity. On the southernmost part of the old region of Dalmatia and has been a world heritage site since 1979. Kotor has witnessed numerous changes in power and religion for centuries and was an important city for the salt trade. It's all but impossible to summarise so much history and I come to feel the city is a bit like a tree; it simply carries on despite the constant change in human activity around it. This must be the eternal vibe that is given off, and how I could sense it from so far away.

Regardless of the faiths or the rulers through the ages, this place reverberates with a sense of endurance and vitality. I am compelled to walk all of its lanes, as I pass through its centuries of existence. If only for a moment, I feel the history pulse through every step of its cobbled pathways.

Sitting outside a café enjoying a pizza and a cheap beer I take in the dramatic surrounding mountains as the sun sets. My wandering sense of curiosity alone brought me here. Through the hours of ache in the saddle, the confusion and the cursing, this is my sweet reward. How did I not know this place was here? Absurd as it is, I only feel that by following my instinct I arrived here today.

What exactly is our fate and what is our will? What will happen if we do nothing, and what happens when we try to do everything? Somewhere in between these two poles, the road stretches out before us, and as we travel down it, our lives play out. Today fate loses, as only I made this moment happen. I made my own destiny as I steered through these enchanting hills and marched into this old city, to see things in a new way.

As I ponder this day of days, a band of high red cirrus clouds give way to a peaceful darkening blue in the skies above. The beer is delightful, and the air is delicious. While there was no war, I feel unbridled victory. Although this city has been here for centuries, I feel that I, and I alone, have just discovered it. *This is why I do it*. New physical ground has opened new mental ground more than ever before. This euphoria is remapping my mind and I know that this feeling will come to change the direction of my life. Despite divorcing myself from my society, standing in the moonlight of these sturdy city walls, I feel a deep-seated contentment.

* * *

Enjoying a coffee in Dubrovnik the next morning I gather my thoughts and prepare to meet my friend, a beautiful Swedish girl called Freja, in Mostar for lunch. As we sit together in the sun, beside the iconic Stari Most bridge, we make plans for Sarajevo this evening, and a new excitement brews inside of me. The road prepares to deliver another carefully placed pulse of adventure, as our arrival into the city that sparked the First World War, auspiciously falls on midsummer's eve.

Apparently in Sweden, everyone dresses in white and walks into the woods for a huge party on midsummer's eve. All are encouraged to drink, be merry, and make love with someone in the moonlight. Nothing is forbidden or frowned upon; indeed, it's all encouraged for this one night of abandon. Whatever happens on this evening, does not apply to the other nights of the year. *Swedish traditions in Bosnia?* Where the road goes, I learn to follow. Sense need not make sense here, only relishing the experience is important.

Freja books us into a posh designer hotel in the Mihrivode neighbourhood. We are sharing the bill, and it has a garage for the bike, so I continue on with the flow of things. The lobby is extravagant and gawdy. The owner is extremely proud and waxes over the many facets of the interior design. One can only feel out of place in such surroundings after living on a motorbike for days and in need of a shower.

Walking up the stairs to our room is like crossing a portal. The walls are stacked glass sheets, throwing off thousands of angles of light, providing an ethereal glow. As the owner lets us into our room, she tells us that it is done in *California style*, with a big open lounge, fireplace and ample balcony overlooking the city. Nice digs indeed.

As we get ready to head out for the evening's festivities, Freya's blond hair hangs perfectly on her shoulders and her blue eyes glint lustrously at me. It's too much for me as she stands by the couch, ready to depart in her pure brilliant white dress. Before we know what's happening, we are locked in embrace and completely consumed by the moment. The preparation for the evening's festivities are magnanimously lain to waste, and the process must start again, albeit while sharing a cheeky smile together.

On the way out, we bump into the overly chatty hotel owner once again, and she enquires as to our thoughts on our room. We say all the things she wants to hear, despite our true impressions. She carries on, longer than required about her love of design, here in her personal cathedral of her life's work. She name drops the fascinating celebrities who have stayed here and how much they all revered the place. She points to a picture of Richard Gere on the wall behind reception, taken in our very room, with a massive smile and two thumbs up, while sitting on the very couch we just had sex on. I chuckle to myself and smile inwardly as she recalls his film titles in her thick accent: *The Second-Best Exotic Marigold Hotel, Miles from Home, Pretty Woman, Rhapsody in August, American Gigolo*, knowing that this will definitely be a travel story I tell one day.

About the author:

The son of a Pan Am flight attendant, Christian Brix was exposed to the world from a very young age and grew up as an outernationalist, which he remains. Learning from different cultures and places led him to a degree in Philosophy and Politics, specialising in radical politics and political philosophy.

Christian's writing has been described as geophilosophical, as he chronicles how new landscapes open up new ways of thinking for him. Often travelling solo, his experiences and writing are influenced by his introverted, observational nature.

In 2016–17, Christian completed a 30-thousand-mile journey across Africa and Asia by motorbike. He wrote about it in two books, the first of which, *The Unseen Walls*, covered his time in Africa, and chronicled how this trip of a lifetime did not go to plan due to fear unexpectedly impacting his experiences.

The second book *East to Zero* covers his time in Asia, where he takes these lessons from Africa on fear forward, to realise that human reasoning is corrupt and unable to solve the world's problems.

He lives in London, still travels a lot, takes part in motorcycle rallies, and occasionally does talks about his travels.

Website: christianbrix.com
Instagram: @christianbrixiii
Facebook: willbrix
Christian's books are available as paperbacks and Kindle and are available from his website and *Amazon*.

The Africa I Love
Chaos and Contentment in Zambia
by Helen Lloyd

"Enjoy the little things in life, for one day you'll look back and realise they were the big things."

—*Kurt Vonnegut*

"Do you want single or multiple entry visa?"

"Single."

"Good. We can only issue single visa at this border." *I wonder why he bothered asking?*

I read the anti-corruption poster on the wall while the Immigration officer completed the visas and stamped our passports.

"Welcome to Zambia," he smiled warmly as he took the crisp $100 note from my hand and returned our passports.

"Thank you. Now, where is Customs?" I asked.

"No Customs here," he replied matter-of-factly.

"But we need our Carnets stamped," I explained, placing the A4 booklet with its distinctive yellow cover onto the desk between us.

"That is a problem. No Customs officer here."

"There has to be. Every border needs a Customs officer."

"Normally two Customs officers, but one was sent to cover at busy border in south and the other is not here... is, er... on training. I cannot help. I do not have correct stamp."

I suspected "on training" meant "at home." At a border with so little traffic, it seemed likely the officers took turns spending time with their wives and families. It was unfortunate that on the one day there was work to be done, the remaining officer had been sent to another border.

I stared into the eyes of the slim, middle-aged officer with his smart checkered shirt, hoping to convey my steadfast patience and resolute intent to not leave without a solution.

"Maybe I *can* help," he offered after a prolonged silence.

He picked up the phone to contact his superior. His superior told him to contact the Customs officer at Katima Mulilo where we intended to exit the country.

He called and then relayed that our unstamped Carnets would be okay, that we should be allowed to export the bikes with no paperwork and no problem.

What could possibly go wrong.

Then he wrote a letter for us to show any officials who asked to see our documentation en route. He seemed happy to have a job to do.

"How long since the last vehicle crossed the border?" I asked casually. The last four-wheeled vehicle we'd seen had been some 100 kilometres back, abandoned where it had got stuck on the overgrown single-track that constituted the road in those parts. It had been there six months.

"A few weeks ago," he replied. "Many cross here, but they are all locals on foot. There is a mission hospital in Kalene Hill, the next village. People from neighbouring Angola and Congo visit it for healthcare."

He neatly folded the signed and stamped handwritten letter and passed it to me. "Okay, good. Now you must pay carbon tax."

"What tax?"

"Yes, carbon tax. To offset vehicle emissions."

"Are you serious?"

He was serious.

"Okay, how much?"

"Five dollars. But you no pay here. Must pay Customs officer and get receipt. But Customs officer not here."

"Yes, we've clarified that already. So... where do we now pay this tax?"

"You must go to nearest Customs office. Which way do you go to Katima?"

I produced the Michelin map of Southern Africa from my tank bag and showed him a route south through the west of the country.

"Ah, yes. Then you must go to Solwezi Customs."

He traced his finger over the map in the opposite direction to mine and stopped over the town of Solwezi far to the east.

"But that's miles out of the way!" I exclaimed. "Can't we just pay at Katima?"

"Solwezi—small detour. You must pay tax. You do not want problem on journey."

Sigh. I explained the irony of making a 500 kilometre detour to pay a $5 tax to offset our carbon emissions. He shrugged his shoulders.

We could have got away without paying the carbon tax. Had we been stopped, a back-handed bribe would have solved the problem, if good old charm and persuasion hadn't. Although I would have liked to see the southwest of the country, our route was unimportant, and I was content to take an alternative longer way that gave us more time in Zambia, so we rode to Solwezi, the copper mining town near the DR Congo border.

We rode past churches on the outskirts of town, then the auto spares compounds with tyres stacked outside and on through the market where vendors set up shop on the pavement. Secondhand clothes and shoes were piled on tables, bright handbags hung from hooks, and stacks of fresh fruit and veggies looked ripe and full of flavour. And there were people everywhere—hundreds of men and women—walking, shopping, talking, laughing, hustling and bustling in this city brimming with life.

Oh, how it reminded me of those crazy, dusty, chaotic towns I had passed through in West and Central Africa on previous trips. And I was happy to be here. I was glad we'd had to make a 500 kilometre detour.

Yes, this is the Africa I love.

We pulled over near the police station and multi-storey council offices. I'd presumed we'd find an office at the border crossing to DR Congo and had expected to see a main road going north, but the only roads in that direction appeared to be side alleys. I looked on my Michelin map; the border was barely a centimetre away on paper though, in reality, this equated to 40 kilometres.

A young man approached and asked if we needed help. He directed us to the government offices at Napsa Hai Telecom. We thanked him, rode on, found the building, asked for the Customs office and were directed to the Zambia Revenue Authority building opposite.

Told to wait by the receptionist, we obediently sat on the plastic chairs lining the characterless cream-painted walls that made it seem like a shabby dentist's waiting room, placed our helmets on the floor and rifled through our tank bags to find our passports and paperwork.

A large middle-aged man greeted us. "Hello. My name is Mr Joseph Nyirenda. How can I help you?" he began, and shook our hands. He had a caring, thoughtful demeanour. I could imagine him as a family man with several children vying for his attention when he returned home each evening.

He thought our coming here was hilarious and laughed in big bellyfuls that we'd made the detour. "But why did you not pay at the border?"

We explained about the official being on training.

Suddenly he seemed serious. "There should always be one officer on duty. That is bad."

I hoped we hadn't inadvertently got anyone in trouble.

He put his hands on his leather belt to adjust his trousers over his paunch and onto his waist. "This is the domestic tax office, not Customs. But I will try to help. Come...."

We followed Mr Joseph Nyirenda down a cream corridor to his office with a large wooden table covered in paperwork and a desktop computer that looked like it was from the '90s. He made a phone call, then looked directly at us. "There is a problem. The Customs officer is not in today. He is on training."

"Everyone seems to be 'on training,'" I commented in jest.

He leant back in his chair and chuckled nervously.

"I'm beginning to wonder if this Customs department is real," I joked.

We all laughed.

"I will see what I can do," he replied.

We waited patiently in reception with only the clock on the wall as a distraction. It was Friday, and as the hands neared 5pm, signalling the end of the working week, I began to fidget. The receptionist appeared to be tidying up, readying to leave.

At 5.02pm, Mr Joseph Nyirenda returned. "Follow me." We walked with some urgency down the cream corridor to another office where we were introduced to a slim, clean-cut man with grey flecks in his short hair, a blue-checked shirt, and trousers that matched the colour of the walls. "This is my boss, Mr. Banda. He will help you now. I must go. I am late for my wife."

We sat patiently as Mr. Banda made several phone calls until he received approval to take our payment and stamp the receipt. He then wrote a cover letter by hand for us to give to the Customs office at Katima Mulilo when we exited the country. We hadn't decided what route to take through Zambia yet, but we were certain which border we would be leaving through.

Travelling south, beyond Kasempa, the tarmac turned to laterite. This typical red clay road eventually petered out after a few villages and then we were riding on a dusty forest trail, cool in the shade of the canopy, peaceful and quiet… but not for long.

Soon tsetse flies plagued us. They followed with dogged persistence. Even with my armour offering protection, they found the gaps and took bites out of me. My jacket, zipped up to the chin, and worn biking jeans posed no barrier. After a hard couple of months of riding rough trails in Namibia and Angola, I'd hoped that Zambia would offer some respite from hardship, but it wasn't to be.

We crossed the river on a pontoon with warnings of lions and leopards on the other side now that we were entering the boundary of Kafue National Park. It was getting late and seemed prudent to camp by the park warden's office.

An A4 sheet of paper pinned to the building listed the park's hunting fees. Every species was fair game, it seemed. The permit for a foreigner to legally shoot an elephant cost a mere $10,000; a lion, only $4,200. The prices were much less for various antelope. Separate prices for local residents were listed parallel. The vervet monkey was at the bottom of the list. Locals were welcome to dispose of them at no charge whatsoever. A wry smile crossed my partner's face when he read that. He was still bitter from when they'd stolen our stove, and he had vowed all-out war after they smeared shit on his side of the tent on his birthday. It was as though the Zambian park authority approved of his personal vendetta.

The following day, there were two more river crossings. The man taking payment at the first one explained that we were supposed to pay 140 Kwacha for each of our XT225 Serows because they had foreign plates. No distinction was made whether the plate was on a motorcycle or 4x4, regardless of the space taken. Ten dollars for a two-minute crossing was extortionate. It only cost 14 kwacha for a local vehicle. He agreed that the price was too much and let us pay the local price. For the final crossing at the far end of the park, the boat captain was less flexible. He knew he had us trapped and took great pleasure in showing us the formally approved price list he had.

Exhausted from the non-stop day with the tsetse fly bites itching to distraction, we checked into a guesthouse, ordered chicken and chips for dinner and drank Zambezi beer in the bar while we waited. I was ravenous by the time the tiny chicken leg and undercooked chips were served three hours later. I devoured it all in thirty seconds, stripping every last morsel of meat from the bone. It did nothing to stem my hunger. There was no point getting angry, so I ordered one last beer before crashing on the bed and falling asleep.

The road to Katima Mulilo was easy-going tarmac and the border exit formalities went without hindrance. There was even a Customs officer not "on training" at the Customs office. The woman behind the counter took the handwritten letter explaining why our Carnets were not stamped and waved us through without a word. I couldn't work out whether she simply didn't care or that we'd caused such havoc that everyone at the border knew about us already.

Across the river in Namibia, we found a lodge with a campsite. While my partner put up the tent and cooked dinner, I made a quick run into town to source beer supplies. Our jobs were done just in time to crack open a Mosi beer as the sun set over the Zambezi River.

I woke up at first light, stepped out of the tent onto the lush cut grass sodden with dew and waited for the sun to rise. I looked forward to the moment when the first rays touched my face and felt their soft fingers of warmth on my skin. The nights were cold now and my lightweight summer sleeping bag poorly insulated.

In that first hour of light, I enjoyed the subtle warmth that swept away the chill of the night, forgotten for another day. Mist floating ethereally above the calm surface of the water soon evaporated and little wavelets, shimmering and dancing in the sunlight, rhythmically lapped at the shore. I spied a kingfisher perched on a branch, tipping its tail back and forth for balance, and a graceful white bird flew upriver so close to the water its wing tips sliced the surface. If we were lucky, we'd hear the happy honking sound of hippos as they returned upstream to their daytime place of rest.

By 9am, the heat was already intense, and I took shelter in the shade of a tree to write in my journal. Everything was still again, the sun shining brilliantly and the river a mirror of calm rolling languidly past. The fishermen in their dugout canoes, having checked their traps, returned to shore, their work on the Zambezi done until evening. Only the ring-necked doves, out of sight, high in the branches of the tree behind, continued to repeat their mantra, "Work harder, work harder." All ignored their call.

In the evening, as the sun inched towards the horizon and the sky burned brightly, the fire of the dying light of day, I heard the distinctive call of the hippos again and saw them swim downstream towards their grazing grounds, their glistening black heads and round twitching ears just above the water, huge bodies submerged and hidden. Four hadeda ibises flew upriver, crying out, "Haa haa-de-dah, haa haa-de-dah," as they went, their prehistoric forms silhouetted against the water.

My daily routine soon synced with the rhythms of nature. The calm riverside campsite was too appealing, a haven of tranquillity, isolated from our journey in time and space.

Besides, we were too tired to leave. Having been on the move almost every day since Windhoek two months ago, it was the perfect antidote. Unlike our ever-changing days on the road, this place had its own regular and predictable rhythm, nature running like clockwork. It was easy to fit into its routine and required no thought or planning.

While on my bicycling journeys, I regularly stopped for several days at a time, my body demanding a rest from the sheer physical exertion of pedalling from one point to another. However, travelling by motorbike did not require such effort, so we didn't stop as frequently. But the daily routine of life on the road, of spending hours in the saddle, finding places to camp, pitching the tent and often sleeping fitfully, still took its toll. After a week, though, we were well rested, our clothes washed, our bikes clean, my journal up to date, and my hunger for devouring good books in one sitting sated.

I was ready to hit the road again, escape from the clutches of ease and comfort, and disconnect from routine. Besides, on some afternoons, if the wind had picked up a little, I had a sense of unease, murmurings of discontent in the wavelets on the water's surface that belied the peaceful setting. For the first time in months, I had instant access to the internet. I had not missed keeping up to date with global affairs but had now become obsessed by two events: the rise of Donald Trump in the run-up to the US elections, and the EU referendum at home. The first was a source of entertainment, the second of little note until the morning of the result. I was in disbelief. How could that be right? But I hadn't been in the UK for most of a year and had little comprehension of the discontent in my home country. As "Brexit" entered mainstream vocabulary, I buried my head in the sand the only way I knew how: pack up and ride.

We spent the day making a loop following the Botswana border. It was late in the day by the time we stopped at the junction re-joining the Caprivi Strip. A couple travelling in their 4x4 stopped to talk and recommended we stay at the campsite at Mazambala Island Lodge, which was worth visiting just for the view. As usual, we had no idea where we would pitch our tent that night, and because it was late afternoon already, we decided to check out the lodge, a few kilometres further on.

From the upper floor of the lodge, wooden stairs led up to a viewing platform, which towered above the wetland delta. The sprawl of tall grasses dried golden spread out for miles below us, almost concealing the water channels, which bring life to this region but were now two feet lower than normal for this time in the season. Apparently, it had not rained here for four years.

The campsite was back up the sandy track next to a small stream winding through the bush. A group of four Afrikaners, two couples each with a Land Cruiser towing an off-road trailer, had their camp already set up.

Originally from Jo'burg but now retired, they split their time between home on the Garden Route and camping in the bush. They'd been here two days. They sat on canvas chairs around a campfire waiting for the bread to finish baking in the potjie, the cast iron Dutch oven wedged in the embers.

Looking up from the meat on the braai, Johan said, "I could spend my life on the road and in the bush and never go home."

"Look at this," Adriaan spoke up, waving his beer can in the air, "It's all we need. Fresh air, good food and beer."

"Ja, but we have grandchildren at home. I could not live without seeing them grow up," Marieke added without looking up from the bowl of salad she was mixing. Ava smiled and nodded.

Johan and Adriaan kept quiet. I think they knew better than to disagree with their wives if they wanted their contented lives to continue.

"You eat meat, ja? Will you join us for dinner?" Johan invited. The aroma emanating from the marinated meat was mouth-watering. It'd beat the hell out of our instant noodles.

"Sure, that'd be great!" I replied quickly.

"Lekker. Adriaan, don't be so rude, get them beer," Johan ordered.

Adriaan hauled himself out of the chair, went to his trailer and returned with cold cans and spare chairs for us.

"Listen," Ava whispered. Marieke stopped mixing and tilted her head towards the river.

"Shhh," she exhaled sharply when Johan kept talking.

We were all silent.

"There," Ava spoke quietly.

A contented grunt from the river disturbed the still air. "Hippo," Adriaan spoke and, as if in reply, a happy *honk honk honk* rippled through the dusk to our ears. The sound, like a deep belly-aching laugh, always brought a smile to my face.

We all stood up and crept towards the bank, and there, on the bend in the deepest part of the stream, the hippo splashed. After a moment, Johan went back to the braai and the rest of us watched in silence until the hippo was a silhouette, then disappeared into the shadow of the tall grass as darkness descended and the first pinpricks of light pierced the black canvas overhead.

When the boerewors and sosaties were cooked and Marieke had sliced the bread, we piled the food onto plates and ate around the fire. Through the darkness, our faces lit up red in the flickering flames, we told stories of our experiences camping and travelling through southern Africa. It was an ancient scene of life in the bush as our ancestors might have lived. I looked up through the clearing at the tranquil sky awash with stars, feeling immensely privileged to know and appreciate such peaceful contentment.

"Do you ever think about quitting?" Johan asked.

"Quitting what?" I asked.

"Your journey," he explained.

I laughed at the absurdity of it. I couldn't quit, this was not a single journey that could be stopped; it was my life. I had chosen to be here, now, travelling like this. I was living exactly how I wanted.

The hardships some saw did not bother me much. The cold mornings and sore hips from a mattress that continued to deflate overnight were a small price to pay for this life of simplicity and freedom because, when the sun rose and I stretched lazily on the banks of the stream, my aches and any worries evaporated with the morning mist. When others questioned my choice of lifestyle, I wished I could transport them to this moment and see if they still failed to understand.

"Why would I want to quit this?" I exclaimed and spread my arms out.

"Very true," he said and smiled.

When morning came, the only disturbance on the glassy water reflecting the reeds and clear blue sky, was a gentle ripple as a small fish surfaced near the lily pads. A little brown bird balanced on a reed tip, swooped down to catch an insect; swifts darted through the air, bee eaters chattered in the branches and a yellow weaver bird perching on the handlebar of my motorbike peered and pecked at its image in the mirror. I sipped a cup of tea slowly, savoring every drop of a new day.

If I could freeze this moment, I would be happy forever.

Yes, this is the Africa I love. This is why I travel.

About the author:

Helen Lloyd loves adventure and travel as a way to learn about and understand the world and the people who inhabit it. Over two decades she has made numerous long journeys by motorcycle, bicycle, on foot, on horseback and on water.

When she's not exploring remote corners of the globe, she lives in her campervan in the UK and earns a living as an engineer. Helen enjoys writing and has published three adventure travel books: *Desert Snow—One Girl's Take on Africa, A Siberian Winter's Tale* and *Iceland Serow Saga*.

The story she recounts here, based in Zambia, was from a 40,000-kilometer journey from Cape Town to Cairo after a month exploring Angola, on her return ride south through Botswana across the salt pans in the dry season.

Website: helenstakeon.com
Facebook: Helen Lloyd
Twitter: @helenlloyd
Instagram: @helenstakeon
YouTube: HelenLloyd
All Helen's books are available as paperbacks and on *Kindle*, direct and from *Amazon*.

The Kindnesses of Strangers

by Michelle Lamphere

"Because in the end, you won't remember the time you spent working in an office or mowing your lawn. Climb that damn mountain."

—Jack Kerouac

We spent the morning bumping from our cloud forest hostel in Chugchilan across a rusty-red rutted road to where the pavement began at Zumbahua. A diminutive native woman dressed in a dark blue woollen skirt, a pale grey crewneck sweater, knee-high socks, loafers and a brown fedora stood guarding a flock of sheep, her gaze following us as we rode past her field.

Built at the base of a giant dome volcano, the road paralleled the narrow footpath that ran along the rim of Quilotoa above us. I'd walked the loop trail around the volcano the day before and had admired the gorgeous, sapphire-blue lake deep inside its crater. As flat gray blankets of clouds had glided by overhead, shafts of sunlight had intermittently pierced the grey, revealing colors I hadn't seen in the gloom. These light beams had drifted across Lago Quilotoa, morphing it into a swirling kaleidoscope of deep aqua blues and greens.

After Zumbahua we began our descent from the cool, mist-covered 12,000-foot mountains to the lush green valley below. Known as the "Avenue of the Volcanoes," the valley ran south from Quito for over 200 miles, nearly to Cuenca. On either side it was fenced in by enormous parallel mountain ranges capped with snow-covered peaks, eight of which were over 16,000 feet. The Pan-American Highway ran along the valley floor.

We joined the highway near Latacunga. The air in the valley had been warmed by midday equatorial sun. But at 9,200 feet it hadn't warmed enough to make for comfortable riding. Truck traffic and tollways made the Pan-Am less than desirable, but we didn't stay on it long.

At Ambato we turned off the highway and followed the GPS through the city to a lovely tree-lined neighborhood with large homes and gated gardens. My boyfriend, Brian, led the way. As we reached our destination, he turned into one of the home's driveways, but was blocked by a tall black iron gate. There wasn't room for me to pull alongside him, so I rode onto the sidewalk to get out of the way of traffic. My back tire was barely out of the street.

Brian climbed off his Yamaha XT660Z, pressed the buzzer mounted to the gate, and waited. After a minute, he tried again, but nothing happened. Apparently, Brian's friend Julio wasn't home. Brian and Julio had met four years previously at a photo stop on the Dalton Highway in Alaska. They'd stayed in touch and, when he knew we were traveling through Ecuador, Julio kindly offered us a place to stay.

A slender older man with salt and pepper hair and a big grin trotted toward us from across the street. His hurried Spanish greeting came out so quickly that I had a hard time catching it. He lived across the street and had been watching for us. He was a friend of Julio's and we were to wait at his house until Julio returned from work.

We pushed our bikes back into the street between bursts of traffic and darted across, following our enthusiastic ambassador. He ducked into a gated driveway three houses up, waved his arms to herd us inside, and briskly locked the gate behind us. He was fidgety and energetic, a bundle of nervous excitement, and I liked him immediately.

We left our gear strapped to the bikes as he ushered us quickly into the house. Our guide shooed us through the entry and into the main room while introducing himself.

"Llamame Pancho Loco."

"Mucho gusto, Pancho. Mi nombre es Michelle," I replied.

I paused for a second to get my bearings, but he kept us moving, tugging at my sleeve to lead us into the warm and homey kitchen. The delicious aroma of roasted meat and vegetables filled the air. Pancho introduced us to his sons, who were seated at a long wooden bar counter slurping soup. His petite, dark-haired wife, Martita, smiled and nodded toward two empty stools as she ladled bowls of warm chicken broth for us. Brian and I took our jackets off and sat down. Without a moment's hesitation, they had invited us to dine with their family.

Both sons finished their soup and were served entrees while we dined on our first course. Martita had made rice with vegetables and tuna and placed a freshly fried egg on top of it all. The flavorful hot soup cured my chill immediately.

Pancho explained that their sons, both grown men with families of their own, worked next door at the family car wash and enjoyed daily luncheons with their parents. Family was the center of everyone's life in Latin America, a tradition I admired.

After finishing their lunch, the sons bid farewell before heading out to finish their workdays. Martita kissed them each on both cheeks and returned to exchange our empty soup bowls with plates heaped with food.

Pancho and Martita busied themselves in the kitchen while we ate. It gave us all a break from my hit-or-miss comprehension and translation skills. Even after speaking mostly Spanish for the previous seven months as we'd traveled through Central and South America, my attempts at conversation were slow. Somehow though, I always muddled through and found a way to communicate, even if it was only with gestures and smiles.

After lunch, Martita took me outside to the garden to see her flowers. I repeated the Spanish names she used for each flower, hoping to commit them to memory. Then I said the plant names in English, which made her smile. We each enjoyed our language lesson. White roses as large as dinner plates strained against their weight to face the sunlight. Bright fuchsia bougainvillea vines exploded with color and covered the stone walls surrounding the garden. Sweet floral scents of citrus and jasmine filled the air.

Late in the afternoon, Julio came to usher us across the street to his home. He greeted us warmly and thanked Pancho and Martita for taking such good care of us.

We rode out of one set of iron gates, across the street, through another iron gate, and down a grassy hill to park in the garden behind Julio's parents' home. Julio's family lived upstairs. They'd turned the basement into a comfortable apartment for visitors.

After settling in, we walked to the front of the house to meet Julio's family. The house was large, even by American standards, three stories high, a perfect cube, and painted a pale shade of yellow.

Julio's mother, Martha, welcomed us with tea and sweets. She had kind eyes that sparkled as she spoke an elegant, clear Spanish that was easy for me to understand. Julio's father, Fernando, arrived a few minutes later, sharply dressed in a suit and looking sophisticated. He greeted us with warm handshakes.

In Latin fashion, the family welcomed us into their home for meals, as well as a beautiful place to stay. We enjoyed breakfasts and lunches at their family dining table, which was round and covered in hammered copper. Martha labored over wonderful homemade meals: fish stew, chicken soup, and humitas, fresh corncakes steamed in the husks, long-simmering sauces, baked plantains and countless varieties of corn and beans.

Julio's KTM 525 XC from his ride to Alaska was parked in the kitchen of the guest apartment and made Brian and I feel right at home. Julio suggested a couple of day rides that would allow us to explore the area before we continued south.

On a clear sunny day, we rode from Ambato to loop around the perimeter of the volcano Chimborazo. Vicuñas, relatives of camels, lined the roadways at the highest altitude. At 12,000 feet, there were no trees, only a windswept golden plateau dotted with scrubby gray-green brush. It was a stark difference from the lush, dark green landscape of Ambato.

A planned "few nights" stay turned into more than a week. Each evening Julio and his parents shared Ecuadorian culture with us. One night his father introduced us to a local drink and winked as he referred to it as "medicine." Each small clear glass was filled with a shot of Aguardiente, a kind of licorice-flavored alcohol. Apparently, every village was known to have its own recipe. It wasn't bad, but I didn't think I needed to try them all. Another night Julio let us watch as he taught a dance class in the studio built into part of the lowest level of their home.

We set a date to leave and planned to combine our two remaining "to-do" items into one outing. Hoping to give Martha a day off from cooking and knowing that a favorite of the family's was roasted cuy (guinea pig), we invited Julio and his parents to lunch at a local rotisserie. We wanted to show our gratitude to Julio and his parents for their generous hospitality.

We enjoyed one last breakfast with the family before heading to the village of Baños. They had been so kind to us and made us feel like family. I was going to miss them immensely. Before he left for work, Fernando gave me a hug, a kiss on each cheek, and a kind smile. Martha told me in Spanish that she wanted us to be careful and that they prayed for us in church that morning. She disappeared into her bedroom and came back with something in her hand that she slipped gently into mine. I looked at what she had placed there and found a small blue glass-bead rosary. She either said to keep it with me always or that she would pray for me always; my Spanish skills weren't good enough to tell the difference. I was on the verge of tears.

From Ambato, we rode to Baños, 25 miles to the east and 2,300 feet lower in elevation. The pristine two-lane paved highway slipped into a deep cleft in the earth. The steady streams of traffic reminded me of the narrow flow of leaf-cutter ants on a jungle floor. We rode less than 70 miles in total from Quilotoa to Baños, yet in that space we'd left the patchwork-quilt squares of green and brown farm plots on the 12,000-foot-high mountainsides, and landed in a dense, vine-covered jungle ravine.

Towering above the southern edge of the village perched the Tungurahua volcano. It actively belched steam and ash skyward and glowed an angry red from lava vents at night. I made the most of the local hot springs, the town's namesake, and spent a day hiking up to a tree swing known for its precipitous perch on the edge of the volcano.

After a few days, we rode east along the Ruta de las Cascadas ("Waterfall Route") and deeper into the canyon to Puyo. We crossed over the continental divide of the Andes and into the headwater basin of the Amazon River. The hundreds of small waterfalls and streams, which were scattered over a few hundred miles, eventually converged to form the mighty river much farther to the east. Along our route, the two-lane highway hugged the edges of the canyon walls, while warm mist rose from the river trench below.

From Puyo we turned south again and onto the flat, wide river plain. This took us riding through miles of sugarcane, coffee and banana plantations. Macas, where we stopped for the night, seemed like a workingman's town, a place where one could stock up on tools and agriculture supplies. With the heat and humidity, I couldn't wait to shed my heavy layers. Wearing shorts and flip-flops, we set out to find dinner. A small café on the central plaza served us with roasted chicken and rice, a South American café staple.

I enjoyed exploring the variety of landscapes in Ecuador, but the roads? Riding the highways alongside the Upano River simply couldn't compare to the steep twists and turns of an Andean road. At Bella Union we crossed back over the Andes and headed toward the town of Cuenca. We'd received a message from some friends who recommended it as a picturesque colonial city with a blue-domed cathedral on the central plaza, charming markets and cobblestoned streets, well worth exploring.

Julio had let his friend Roberto know that we were coming to Cuenca but as Brian and I only planned to stay for a night or two, I contacted Roberto after we had settled into a modern, clean three-storey hostel near the city center. That way we could invite Roberto and his wife to meet us for dinner but wouldn't burden them with having to host us. I sent Roberto a message to that effect, but his reply was firm. We WOULD come to stay with him. Apparently, Roberto wouldn't take "no" for an answer.

We left the hostel after the first night and made our way to Roberto's home, parking our bikes inside their small basement garage. As we reached the top of the first flight of stairs, we were immediately seated for lunch. I had a flashback to Pancho's. Roberto's family gave us a standing invitation to have all meals with them and had a guest apartment waiting for us on the top floor. There was nothing quite like being scooped up by an Ecuadorian family, as we had now experienced three times.

Roberto and his lovely wife, Janeth, had three children who all raced motocross. Roberto was an energetic and happy man with a kind face, wavy dark brown hair and twinkling deep brown eyes. He was shorter than Brian and me but seemed taller because of the way he filled a room with his presence. Janeth was slightly taller than Roberto. She was more reserved and soft-spoken but had the same kind face and sparkling brown eyes as her husband.

Their newlywed 22-year-old daughter, Daniela, escorted us around Cuenca in search of parts and supplies over the next couple of days. Daniela spoke perfect English and was the picture of loveliness with long, dark hair, a gorgeous smile and her stylish way of dressing.

Both bikes needed repairs before the next leg of our journey. Besides the basic oil changes, filter cleaning, and spark plug replacements, Brian took advantage of having a workspace to change his brake pads and do some more in-depth servicing.

I had been debating for some time about what tires to put on my bike. There would be a lot of gravel ahead and I wanted something that would handle well. This was the chance to do something about that.

We stayed a few nights and then planned to ride two to three days south to cross into Peru, taking a dirt road to the border. But as the day of our departure arrived, I was under the weather again. Stomach bugs were getting tiresome. I spent nearly two days sleeping.

One evening after dinner Roberto asked about our travels. I told him I'd had an accident in Canada, just two weeks into the trip. It had left me with a badly broken leg that required surgery and I still got choked up when I told the story.

At the beginning of this journey more than a year before, I'd left my home in South Dakota intending to ride through Central and South America to Ushuaia, Argentina. At the last minute, we detoured into Canada to ride the Trans-Labrador Highway. Getting back and forth to the TLH was to add 7,000 miles to our trip, and a thousand of those miles were gravel.

Newly completed in the wilds of eastern Labrador, the road connected a handful of remote communities for the first time. The TLH itself comprised 714 miles of built-up roadbed and was covered in loose gravel. With only a few settlements along the way, fuel and supplies were only available every 200 miles.

After nearly a week of riding across the US, and the provinces of Ontario and Quebec, we'd crossed from pavement onto the gravel of the haul roads. These led us into the remoteness of Quebec. For the next two days we swam in the deep gravel and camped amid what felt like a series of plagues, with blackflies and thick smoke from forest fires. But finally, we made it to Labrador City and the start of the TLH.

In front of us, miles of scrubby thin evergreens and shrubs stretched across the Canadian muskeg. Long flat stretches of road were only occasionally interrupted by a stream or wide pond. I was ever mindful of the need to conserve fuel and water, and to stay safe.

At Churchill Falls we stopped to check out a satellite phone. This was provided free by the Canadian government to anyone crossing on the TLH. As I had signed the form to accept it, I paused for a moment under the gravity of it all. After having camped for a night at Happy Valley-Goose Bay, a former military outpost, I'd been warned that if anything happened on that desolate road, we'd have to wait for hours for help.

Little had I known that just a few hours later an "anything" would happen: I went down, hard.

First, there'd been the officer who happened upon me and my bike sprawling across the gravel, less than a minute after I'd gone down. And within another five minutes, an emergency medical technician with an empty cargo van arrived. And within the next 10 minutes, another two officers showed up. They helped the medical tech load my motorcycle into his van. He'd also offered to store it for as long as needed.

I needed to be flown to St. John's, Newfoundland, for surgery and afterward had no place to stay. A woman in a local motorcycle community generously offered a guest room for as long as it took to recover. And yet another offered to store my bike in St. John's and would fix whatever needed repaired from the wreck. But my bike had been left over 1,000 miles behind with the medical tech. Word traveled quickly in the tightknit Newfoundland-Labrador motorcycle community and another rider offered to haul my bike to St. John's in exchange for a beer. It was the most overwhelming chain of generosity that I'd ever heard of. I still didn't know how I had been so lucky. But not just then, ever since the start of the trip I'd been the recipient of incredible generosity.

Roberto and his wife, Janeth, sat listening with rapt attention. When I finished sharing my experience, Roberto asked how I was doing. While physically I was well, I told him I was afraid of the road ahead.

We still had 5,000 miles to ride before reaching Ushuaia, and much of that distance was remote and rugged. Ruta 40 in Argentina, the road to Ushuaia, was infamously bad, with a horrible mix of sand, gravel and notoriously high winds. I'd heard stories of trucks being blown off roads in the Roaring Forties and knew my bike didn't stand a chance in 80 mph or stronger gusts. Wind had played a part in my accident in Labrador, which made me fear the winds of Patagonia even more. I explained how in-depth I had been studying tire types and researching how to prepare. I had ridden thousands of miles of gravel since the wreck, but the additional experience wasn't helping to reduce the anxiety.

Roberto nodded and paused for a moment before telling me he understood how I felt. He and his children had each had accidents and had been afraid when they got back on their bikes. But he believed fear is part of everything we do in life, and that life's lessons could teach us to be careful and to respect the risk. But we shouldn't let it control our lives. It was my turn to nod. He was telling me the things my father would have said if he had been here. Roberto asked if I had any thoughts of not finishing the trip. I had not. He smiled and told me to stop worrying. He believed everything would be fine.

After a couple of days' rest, I felt better. After two more, I'd recovered enough for us to continue. But then I found it hard to leave. Perhaps it was a combination of road-weariness and missing my family, along with the generosity and kindness of Roberto and his family. I'd enjoyed my time with them so much that I didn't want to move on yet.

The night before we planned to depart, Brian and I shared a quiet dinner with Roberto and Janeth. During our after-dinner conversation, Roberto paused and said he had something he wanted to share. He started by saying that he had always loved motorcycles and had taught his children to love them, too. His lifelong dream had been to travel by motorcycle, as we were doing then. But he married young and started a family right away. His family meant everything to him, and he had no regrets. But he still held a small version of that dream alive, which was why he welcomed motorcycle travelers to stay.

Roberto went on slowly then, holding Janeth's hand while he spoke. His voice faltered slightly as emotion momentarily overwhelmed him. Watching him, I got a lump in my throat. He said that they'd enjoyed having us, and that we were now dear friends to them. Then he paused, changing the word, and said we were family.

I swallowed hard and blinked back tears, trying to gather myself and translate his words for Brian. But Brian's people skills and Spanish were good enough to have clearly understood the meaning of Roberto saying "familia." We explained how grateful we were for all they had done for us and for their friendship. They had opened their hearts, their family, and their home to us, and it had meant the world to me.

The 150-mile ride south along the Pan-Am Highway had been smooth as it glided through central Ecuador along a rich green valley; tall eucalyptus trees on the hillsides on either side of the highway had filled the air with their pungent, camphor scent. Just after the town of Loja, we turned left off the highway to ride towards the town of Vilcabamba. I'd heard other riders talk about Vilcabamba, pretty and famous for its ex-pat community and yoga retreats. Vilcabamba rests in a valley below a mountain called Mandango, "The Sleeping Inca," who protects the area from earthquakes.

Since we had dirt riding ahead the next day, I voted for a stay in a room at the pleasant Hotel Izhcayluma on the south edge of town. But when we signed online, we found a message from a Swiss friend that said he and three others had ridden the route we intended to take to the Peruvian border. He said the road had been really hard work. There'd been construction for most of the 80 miles between Yangana, where the pavement ended, and La Balsa, where it began again at the Peruvian border. It was a dirt road, without gravel, and a week of rain had turned the surface into a slippery and sticky mess. The Swiss friend had passed through three or four days before, and since then the rain had stopped. He suggested we wait another two days to let it dry out.

I spent the extra days washing laundry in our room's sink and catching up on journaling and sending emails to friends and family back home. It was a quick ride to the town center, where I could stock up one last time on inexpensive groceries and supplies.

Prices in Ecuador had been very good in comparison with some of the other countries we had visited. I could buy a market-sized bag filled with fresh mango, avocado, carrots, onions, zucchinis, tomatoes and bananas for only a few dollars. But those were things I couldn't carry across the border into Peru, so instead I bought staples for my bike kitchen: rice, pasta, canned tuna and dehydrated soups. One afternoon I enjoyed a fresh maracuya juice in the shade of a café veranda on the town's central plaza. I was pleasantly surprised when it turned out to be tart, citrus-like passion fruit.

With two days of dry weather behind us and a forecast for rain the following day, we pushed on. As I loaded the bike in the morning, I noticed something unusual on the front fairing.

A small group of the tiniest pale yellow-green specks were laid out in the shape of a spiral. It reminded me of the Maori symbol, the Koru, which resembles an unfurling silver fern frond. The Koru symbolizes growth and new beginnings. I decided it was a good omen for the dirt road ahead, and my nerves settled a bit. Then I leaned down to get a closer look. Each of the crumb-sized dots hovered a quarter-inch above the surface of the plastic faring by a silk thread, 21 in all. For a moment I wondered if I should wipe them off but left them alone for the wind to take them as it would.

South of Vilcabamba, the two-lane road was paved for a few dozen miles as it entered distinctly jungle-ish country. I noticed a yellow highway sign, not far down the road, warning of bears and wondered if there was such a thing as a jungle bear. Later, I found out that Andean, or Spectacled bears, live in the mountains near where we had ridden.

Our southbound road climbed and curved, leading out to a point where we could see into the next valley. The rolling high hills were cleft in two by this deeply cut river valley. For as far as I could see a jagged red scar slashed into the lush green hillside; it showed where construction equipment had torn open the mountainside for the new road. Our road would turn up ahead and drop to the valley floor to follow the river.

Pavement gave way to gravel, and eventually dirt. Smooth-packed dirt deteriorated into roads with deep, dried ruts, remnants of the previous week's rains. We crossed a few streams and kept moving, eventually climbing up the mountainside.

Around one corner, we stumbled upon the work crew. Two dozen men in dirty yellow safety vests worked at various tasks along the road, operating everything from shovels to backhoes.

Spread out over a two-mile section of the road, they forced us to weave our bikes between the enormous heavy equipment, while trying to be mindful of the steep drop into the valley below. Guardrails were nonexistent in this part of the world, and no one looked out for you. We hit a few slippery spots, where the wet reddish clay created a hazard, and I wondered how bad it had been for our friends the week before. Perched on a ledge on the side of the mountain, I could imagine how easily a rider could slide right off.

We reached a long dry section and saw a few houses perched on the cliff along the roadside. Rusty corrugated tin roofs and thin, gray-painted plywood siding provided all the shelter you needed this close to the equator. I watched small children clad in only T-shirts, no pants, playing in the vegetation at the side of the road.

As we passed one hut, a lean, sand-colored dog trotted up beside my bike, and with little effort, because of our slow pace, nipped my left leg. I gave my horn a little toot as he came back for a second nip. I giggled and kept riding, grateful as always for my heavy boots and pants, even on hot days like that.

The riding got trickier from the small town of Zumba, with the road dissolving into a single dirt lane, with increasing frequency and sharpness of curves. Miles of bumping through the hot, dry, wild land came to a brief stop at a security gate stretched across the road, seemingly in the middle of nowhere.

A slender young officer in a beige uniform waved to us to stop. After reviewing our documents, he noticed the spiral of eggs on the fairing, smiled and said, "Mariposa." Butterfly eggs. I smiled at the thought. We presented our passports, and the guard raised the iron barrier for us to pass.

Ecuador had been one of my favorite countries of the trip. As we mounted our bikes to ride on toward Peru, I counted 21 eggs still clinging to my bike.

About the author:

Michelle Lamphere was born and raised in Sturgis, South Dakota, home of a world-famous motorcycle rally. But she didn't start riding until she was 30. Her love of the outdoors began at an early age, thanks to her parents' weeks-long summer camping trips.

In 2013 she quit her 21-year hotel executive job, sold her home, and hit the road for Ushuaia, Argentina via eastern Canada. What started out as an extended vacation and break between careers turned into a two-year journey across 20 countries and 45,000 miles.

In 2015 she published *Tips for Traveling Overland in Latin America*, and in 2017 *The Butterfly Route*, a memoir of her two-year journey.

Michelle owns and operates a small vintage motel in Custer, South Dakota, and works on projects that support motorcyclists.

She is an unwavering optimist, a hopeless romantic and the beneficiary of farsickness which has taken her to over 70 countries. Her greatest fear would be missing out.

Michelle is a co-host of the *Adventure Rider Radio "RAW"* show.

Facebook: TheSturgisChick
Twitter: @SturgisChick
Instagram: @SturgisChick
Website: SturgisChick.com
Michelle's books are available as paperbacks and on *Kindle* from *Amazon*.

I Still Haven't Found What I'm Looking For

by Travis Gill with Chantil Gill

"It's not possible to experience constant euphoria, but if you're grateful, you can find happiness in everything."

—*Pharrell Williams*

I'm a product of the '80s. Saturday morning cartoons, computer gaming, *Star Wars* movies, the Cold War, and music on CDs. I can still remember the feeling of excitement of walking into a music store, flipping through the thousands of plastic cases, and admiring all the square-shaped cover art. As a high school student, I didn't have much money, but what I had was spent on music. I owned a portable Sony Discman that would skip at the tiniest of bumps. I can still remember the oddity of walking while contently listening through headphones with the Discman delicately handled like a waiter balancing drinks on a tray.

One of the earliest CDs I purchased was by the Irish rock band U2, their 1987 album *The Joshua Tree*. Even after all these years, I still remember the eagerness of removing the protective covering and opening the hard plastic jewel case to reveal the shiny, mirror-like face of the disc. Before playing the CD, I would gently remove the booklet and study each photograph, poring over every word. The best booklets always included multiple pages of artwork and the lyrics of the songs. Unfortunately, *The Joshua Tree* didn't have much artwork, but I vividly remember the black and white photograph of a bristled, oddly shaped tree that looked like something from another planet.

Fast forward to the mid-1990s. I'm now married to a wonderful woman, Chantil, and we have two kids, a good-paying job, a car loan, and a home mortgage—the "American dream." My love of music has grown into video and I have some of the nicest home theater equipment we can afford: a large television, Surround Sound receiver, amplifiers, and myriad speakers placed around a comfy sofa. My collection of discs has also matured; I now have a large collection of laser disks. One of my favorites is the concert release of U2's *Rattle and Hum*. The opening song of that concert is truly one of the best in the history of rock and roll. From the drumstick strikes of Larry Mullen Jr., to the mesmerizing use of the repeated arpeggio and delay effect of the Edge's guitar, to the harmonic bass syncopation of Adam Clayton, and finally, after a two-minute intro, the defining voice of Bono as he fires out, "I want to run, I want to hide. I wanna tear down these walls that hold me inside." It is incredible!

Fast forward again to April 2015, I am in my mid-40s, unloading our first motorcycle, a used 2011 BMW G650GS. The motorcycle feels awkward and really heavy as we manoeuvre it down the ramp from a friend's truck, rolled it off the loading ramp and leaning it on its sidestand in a parking lot. I remember the excitement, but also the intimidation. Even though the G650GS has a seat height well below that of other larger adventure motorcycles, it feels tall. I wonder how on Earth I will ever feel comfortable riding this "monster" of a motorcycle. I idle it awkwardly around the parking lot and then park it for an evening. I even wait until the next day before having the courage to ride it on the street.

It's now November 2016. In a short year and a half, we've added another motorcycle to the stable. This one is also a BMW G650GS but is slightly more off-road and overland oriented with a taller windscreen, longer suspension travel, wire-rimmed wheels, and a larger 21-inch front wheel. BMW calls it a Sertão, named after the northeast desert regions of Brazil. But I call it "Apache," named after the first horse I rode when I was a kid. Chantil and I have also completed two street-oriented motorcycle safety courses, and another off-road-oriented course, as well as numerous motorcycle trips focused on improving our off-road skills. We both feel competent enough to ride on interstate highways and remote trails for extended periods.

For a three-day weekend we plan to ride our motorcycles north from our home in San Diego, California, around the Salton Sea, and into Joshua Tree National Park via a remote off-road trail. We will do some camping and then return home via the desert resort city of Palm Springs. Being late in the autumn season, it is a perfect time to explore the Southern California desert regions; temperatures are comfortable then, and most days sunny and dry.

To get into Joshua Tree National Park, most enter via the paved and heavily traveled access roads at the north and south sides of the park. In the spring and autumn seasons these roads can be clogged with large and slow-moving recreational vehicles. The best entrances to the park are the "secret" remote ones, such as the southwest entrance of Berdoo Canyon Road. The entrance to the park is nothing more than a posted sign that reads, "Roads not maintained. High-clearance four-wheel drive vehicles only." Perfect for a couple of medium clearance one-wheel-drive adventure motorcycles!

It is during our ride on the Berdoo Canyon Road that we get to experience a vast forest of these unique shaped Joshua trees. They don't grow very tall, but their strange shape makes it feel like you're riding through a magical desert version of a *Dr Seuss* book. The dark green leaves of the Joshua tree are a pleasant contrast to the yellow and brown hues of the surrounding Mojave Desert. It is difficult to make progress on the motorcycles, since each turn is another opportunity to park and snap pictures of the wonderful scenery. As beautiful as this unique region is during the daylight hours, the glamour comes alive during the first and last light of the day. Then you can enjoy the silhouette of bristly Joshuas against the panoramic canvas of a rising or setting sun. Joshua Tree still remains one of my favorite places on Earth.

One hundred and ninety miles northeast of Joshua Tree National Park is another well-known desert landscape, Death Valley National Park. On a stretch of road to the southwest of Death Valley there was a lonely Joshua tree that was memorialized on U2's best-selling album. It was during a photo shoot in December of 1986 that Bono had learned about the trees and liked the idea of calling their fifth studio album after these hardy, twisted plants of the American Southwest. That lone tree has since fallen and is slowly disintegrating in the harsh desert environment, but the spot still remains a memorial where U2 well-wishers leave behind mementos. There's even a metal plaque that asks the question, "Have you found what you're looking for?"

In 2017 our son finished high school and left to serve a church mission in the Washington D.C. area. Since we were now empty nesters we figured there was no reason for us not to fly the coop ourselves. We've always wanted to travel Europe and when a job opened up in western Germany, we quickly accepted it. One evening I asked Chantil, "Why don't we make an adventure of moving to Germany?"

For most, uprooting and moving their lives to a new country would be adventure enough; however, we wanted to travel and experience other places along the way. But where should we travel? A cross-country trip of the US via Route 66? Eastern Canada?

A quick view of the globe revealed a country located between the Americas and Europe, a northern Atlantic country no bigger than my home state of Colorado. A country that had recently experienced a boom in tourism—Iceland!

We made plans to sell most of our possessions, load our BMW GSes, and ride them across the United States from southern California to Portland, Maine. There they would be loaded onto a cargo ship to Reykjavik, Iceland. We would then fly back to San Diego to coordinate the last of the moving arrangements and then to Iceland to retrieve the motorcycles. We planned to enjoy 18 days in Iceland, and then take a ferry to the Faroe Islands for another eight days of riding. The final ferry would be to Denmark, before riding into Germany to start work. It was going to be an epic adventure.

The 7,200 miles of riding across the United States, eastern Canada, Iceland, Faroe Islands, Denmark, and into Germany truly was an adventure of a lifetime. We endured some of the worst weather we've ever ridden in: temperatures above 115°F (46°C) in the deserts of Arizona, extremely heavy thunderstorms in Minnesota, and the most cold and miserable rains in the western fjords of Iceland. We suffered breakdowns that included a broken clutch cable, stripped teeth on a front sprocket, a broken clutch lever, and a front fork that leaked its oil. However, we relished some of the most stunning and beautiful scenery we'd ever experienced. Imposing waterfalls, breathtaking volcanic geology, jet black beaches, the softened blue tones of giant glaciers; extraordinary beauty that made me clamor for my camera, only to be disappointed that no picture could possibly capture the expanse of such impressive landscapes. Iceland and the Faroe Islands continue to have a special place in our hearts, with wonderful memories that solidified our plans to travel full-time in the future.

While we lived and worked in Germany, our travels were limited to extended weekends and earned vacation time. But we made the best of it and enjoyed short but memorable motorcycle riding through Germany, the Netherlands, Belgium, Luxembourg, and northern France.

By summer of 2018, I had earned enough vacation time to schedule a trip that we'd been planning since arriving in Europe, a three-week tour of the United Kingdom and Ireland. We spent months looking over places we wanted to see and experience, adding them to our online map. Eventually we had over 100 tiny virtual pushpins; we were going to cover a lot of ground in those three short weeks! And we gave the trip the name, "Left to Live," for two reasons:

1. This would be our first time we'd ever ridden on the left side of the roadway. "Stay LEFT if you want to LIVE!" We even went as far as making a vinyl sticker for our motorcycles' windscreens.

2. Secondly, we only have a finite amount of time in this life. We decided that we would like to have memories instead of dreams, and dreamt of exploring as much of the world as we possibly could.

By late August we were riding our motorcycles from the right side of the road in Coquelles, France, onto the loading ramp of the Eurotunnel Shuttle, and then exiting the shuttle on the left side of the road in Folkestone, England. The entire process was quite spectacular. It was exciting to be traveling on this modern marvel that whisked us from France, under the English Channel at 115m below sea level, and then into a new country in a matter of 35 minutes. And due to the time change between France and England, we even arrived 25 minutes before we left!

I remember the seventh day of our Left to Live tour very well. We'd crossed into Ireland the day before and found a campsite just south of Dublin. The morning was a bit cold and cloudy, but our hearts were warm and bright. We'd just received an email that there were two openings on the boat to visit Skellig Michael Island. Months before, we had tried to get tickets to this popular UNESCO World Heritage Site but were only offered standby tickets. Skellig Michael has been incredibly popular since the movie *Star Wars: The Force Awakens* (2015) was filmed there. Access is strictly limited to preserve the fragile environment and structures of the island, so getting tickets was extremely difficult.

217

After completing the daily ritual of packing our camping gear and putting on our protective motorcycle clothing, we were on our way with an exciting day ahead on our minds. It was during a somewhat mundane stretch of the N11 highway that I remember the powerful feeling of euphoria. During the highway portions of our trip, I often pair my smartphone with the headset Bluetooth receiver and listen to music. The music can be shared through Chantil's as well. Since the phone's screen doesn't work very well with motorcycle gloves, I typically put the music on random play and end up looking forward to whatever the next song might be.

As we were rounding a long sweeping curve and into a stretch of Irish countryside, I was taken aback by the vivid green hues of the surrounding fields along with the fresh aroma of a light rain shower that had passed through just minutes before. The sun's rays were starting to break free from the grey clouds attempting to hold them back. At that exact moment, the next song in the playlist began and it was immediately recognizable from the soothing synthesizer sounds that merge into the distinct six-note arpeggio guitar chords. At that moment it struck me. I was riding in U2's homeland and listening to one of their most iconic songs, *Where the Streets Have No Name*.

The culmination of so many memories and decisions was so overwhelming it brought me to tears. And the already special day of riding a motorcycle along the N11, in southeastern Ireland, was immediately transformed into a powerful and emotional experience.

The music, the memories, and the moments… so many choices and unique opportunities had come together to create this short but powerful moment. My eyes were watering with the joy of being able to experience the reality of my hopes and dreams.

Later that day, I told Chantil about it and how I wished I could somehow contain that moment of elation, to figure a way to bottle and share it with the world. I remarked, "If I could figure this out and market it, we'd be billionaires!"

However, the more I thought about it, I realized it would be impossible to harness the collective thoughts and previous experiences that trigger such sensations. Each of us is going to have to get out there and find our own unique euphoric moments.

Happy trails. I hope that each and every one of you find those moments and answer the question, "Have you found what you're looking for?"

About the authors:

Travis and **Chantil Gill** are an American couple who had always dreamed of traveling the world, but never imagined it would be on motorcycles.

In 2015, and while in their mid-40s, they purchased their first motorcycles. Their first longer adventure outside the U.S. was to Baja. That trip hooked them and the decision was made: they were going to ride the world!

As they traveled, they've produced a series of *YouTube* videos, written for motorcycle magazines, and been guests of *Adventure Rider Radio*, the *Allan Karl Show*, *Bionic Bikers* and *Spain Speaks*. They are "ViajarMoto," so named in honor of their original trip to Baja and the influence it continues to have on their lives. To date, they have explored 36 countries.

Upon completion of their journey, they plan to return to the memorial site of the fallen *U2* Joshua tree near *Death Valley National Park* to answer the question: "Have you found what you're looking for?"

Website: viajarMOTO.com
YouTube: viajarMOTO
Instagram: @ viajarMOTO
Facebook: viajarMOTO
Patreon: viajarMOTO

The Rough Side of Silk

by Simon Thomas with Lisa Thomas

> **"Once the travel bug bites there is no known antidote, and I know that I shall be happily infected until the end of my life."**
>
> —*Michael Palin*

Since time immemorial, the Silk Road (M41) in Central Asia has existed as a trade network connecting Eurasia and North Africa. Contrary to its name, the Silk Road is not a singular road, but a route. Often it's a web of ancient rock-strewn tracks and meandering trails trodden for millennia by travellers, merchants, explorers, armies, and kings. More than 3,000 years of history that includes some of the most striking and dangerous landscapes in the world.

Our dream of riding the Silk Road was now a bone-jarring reality, and we needed to ride and survive the entire thing if we were ever to reach Iran and continue our journey.

We'd awoken in Kockkor-Ata, a small village northwest of Jalal-Abad, Kyrgyzstan. The odour of drying concrete hung in the air. We sat cross-legged around a tattered Persian rug joined by 10 or so construction workers, each covered in paint and sawdust. They watched intently as we munched on stale bread and pieces of fruit. "Ah, breakfast amongst new friends," I had waved a tiny crust of bread and smiled hoping to convey my appreciation and approval. Their grinning dirty faces nodded back on cue. Lisa was already picking up the language and deep in animated conversation with the thinnest and cheeriest of the group.

We'd stopped too late the previous night and had given up finding any kind of accommodation until one of the workers spotted our resignation, whistled and waved us into the gloomy but fenced compound. You've just got to trust sometimes.

Out by the bikes, Lisa was zipping up her tank bag and stuffing a map into its clear plastic sleeve as I handed over the fee for the generous accommodation we'd been offered by strangers: two pirated DVDs we'd picked up in central Russia. It's bloody good that money isn't the only currency when you travel.

The northern Russian town of Novosibirsk, where we'd picked up our Kyrgyzstan visas, seemed only a fuzzy memory. Amidst a growing, unsettled crowd, we'd stood on the steps of the Kyrgyzstan Embassy for three freezing days before a group fight finally erupted, fuelled by frustration. The embassy doors had flung open and armed guards had run out, allowing us to sneak in, put on our best English accents and apply for the visas.

It was midday as we rode southeast around the low-lying Fergana Mountains before turning southwest and entering the ancient Kyrg city of Osh. Market stalls spilled their wares into the streets, selling everything from cheap plastic torches to goat heads; oh, and some toxic green washing liquid called "Spooge." Yeah, I giggled too.

A few domed mosques dotted the city skyline, making the scene feel familiar, almost Moroccan. Riding into the centre of Osh, our cheerful waves of greeting had been received without response by the locals, whose blank looks had left me feeling uneasy. Hidden from view inside a small café we'd devoured a bowl of rice flavoured with the ubiquitous mutton fat. As we ate, locals stopped, stared and finally cracked huge smiles as they pointed and walked past the parked bikes.

By late afternoon we'd made good progress, but my concentration had been pulled by the sheer scale of the landscape around us. The M41 had disappeared from view and reappeared as it snaked its way between layers of orange and caramel mountains. On the horizon the teeth of the Pamir Mountain range raked the sky. I'd glanced at my GPS, which confirmed our destination as Sary-Tash, a small village on the Kazak-Tajik border. We needed to pick up the pace to make it before nightfall.

With investment from China the length of the lower M41 was being torn up and replaced. It would be a delight in a year, but just then it was an accident waiting to happen. Standing up on the pegs for better control over the mixture of tumbling large rocks and loose soil, we rounded a wide bend and were brought to a sudden halt as a half-hearted flag bearer limply waved us to a stop. The scene down through the lower valley where we were about to ride looked decidedly post-apocalyptic. Dozens of eight-wheeled rolling giants belched black diesel fumes into the sky. It was difficult to watch as they clawed and tore away at the already raped valley sides.

"What a mess," Lisa said quietly over the intercom. "How long do you think we're going be stuck here?"

I was already thinking the same thing as I watched the sun sink another degree.

With a nod and wave, we were ushered on and into the work area. Ahead were two of the biggest earthmovers I'd ever seen, barrelling through the gorge and kicking up a storm of choking dust. With a deep breath and fingers crossed we opened the throttles, prayed and plunged into the airborne debris. The maelstrom lasted for all of five seconds before we emerged safely and into clean air. Around us the landscape was painted in shades of yellow and tangerine-red by the sinking sun, the mountains in the distance in sharp relief against the royal blue sky.

The sky was a dark purple at the top of the Taldyk Pass as we pulled off to the side of the track. Looking out across the vast expanse of Alay Valley, we could see the lights of Sary-Tash village in the distance twinkle to life as maybe a couple dozen small generators kicked into nightly action.

"We're not going to make it before dark," I whispered to Lisa, as if it might make the news less worrying. We'd run out of daylight, and still needed to negotiate a route down to the village.

The temperature had plummeted to -9°C as we cautiously made our way to the sanctuary of the village below. The snow-fringed track and slippery switchbacks tugged on our already frayed abilities to concentrate.

Up on the pegs again, Lisa was battling; her eyes have never been good at night and at dusk her vision almost fails completely. The freezing temps made it harder to relax and stay loose on the bikes. The trucks still on the road hadn't slowed their pace and their headlights blinded us as each approached. Lisa pulled up beside me and I could see the real terror in her eyes. As some of you know, Lisa doesn't scare easily but she was beginning to freak, and I wasn't far behind.

By the time we reached the first of Sary-Tash's buildings we were freezing—literally. At the end of a small unlit path, I'd barrelled into a deep water crossing and was nearly bucked from the saddle by the steep rise on the other side, before pulling up in front of a tiny homestay.

In the dark we greeted our host and painfully peeled our stiff bodies from the bikes. We were exhausted, wet and frozen. Inside, the small, stone white-washed walls of the room looked like sanctuary. Flickering orange light danced on the walls lit by a single candle. Piled high against a wall, our host pulled down half a dozen old rugs where she gestured we would sleep. Exhausted, inside our sleeping bags, and under the weight of half a dozen dusty rugs we could barely move. Sleep came quickly.

My eyes peeled open at sunrise. Particles of dust floating in the air were lit by a shard of yellow light that split the shabby curtains. It was -2°C in the room as I checked my mud-stained watch, confirming it was 6am I knew what I wanted: 30 minutes on my own with the camera. Everyone we'd met who travelled this way had given us the same description. "A wall of mountains seemingly without end." I wanted to see *this* wall.

The cold air stung my face the moment I stepped outside as the black mutt puppy that had greeted us the night before bounced around my feet. Across the low, white-washed rooftops of Sary-Tash, I could see the jagged peaks of the glaciated Pamir Alay range on the horizon. Lisa and I had been reading about this expansive valley for years; its size and beauty were near legendary. We'd always known that if we wanted to enter Tajikistan from the north, this was one of our few options. Now that we were actually here I was feeling blissfully overwhelmed. Daft as it sounds, the remote solitude and beauty of this place caught me off guard.

In the early morning pristine air, the silence was deafening. "This is it, the Alay Valley," I murmured out loud to myself while taking a deep breath and exhaling loudly, letting the moment sink in until it was absorbed.

My clumsy frozen hands fiddled with the camera as my lungs took in a full measure of the cold air. I could feel the smile I was wearing. The Alay Range is a 500-kilometre-long seam of mountains that separate Kyrgyzstan and Tajikistan, and apart from a few nutty bikers is normally the exclusive turf of trekkers and mountaineers. Getting there is a feat in itself, and I couldn't imagine climbing in this giant's playground.

I walked towards the mountains for 20 minutes, all the while looking for any signs of a route through or over them. But I couldn't see a damn thing!

I took many photos, changing the settings from time to time in the hope that just one would do this incredible sight justice, but in truth I knew none would. It's like photographing the Grand Canyon; no image can truly capture or convey the sheer size or majesty of it.

I lay on the ground to photograph the golden grass as a forefront to the mountains. Meanwhile, the young black dog that had followed me thought it was a game and nibbled my arms and tugged on my trousers trying to play. I spent as much time trying to push the playful mutt off me as I did taking photos; great fun, and time that I'll treasure for a while to come.

Back at the homestay, Lisa was slurping on a mug of warm tea and deep in serious-looking conversation with the two Israelis we'd heard arrive the previous night and who were heading north. Their warnings of heavy snow and frozen air didn't ease the angst I was attempting to contain.

Outside, with Lisa tightening the last of her bag straps, I paid $25 for the night, which included dinner and breakfast. That may seem expensive but it had saved us from a low of -22°C during the night. The day was going to be colder still.

By 8am we were wearing as many layers as we could find and fumbling to fill both bikes to the brim with fuel from a blue plastic drum, before handing over a fistful of paper thin, dirty notes.

The utter lack of intercom chatter between Lisa and me was noteworthy in itself as we rode the short three-kilometre track to the base of the Alay Mountain range and into the Kyrgyzstan compound. Up ahead, our planned route had become indistinguishable amongst the vast slabs of rock and snow-covered ground.

Inside the small border compound, we'd easily found the modern looking portable cabins and completed our Kyrgyzstan exit paperwork.

Back outside, the thick covering of ground snow had me concerned. Ahead was one of the most beautiful mountain roads on the planet to ride and one of the world's highest borders still to cross. The Kyzyl-Art Pass at 4,280 metres is ranked as one of the most spectacular in the world, and since we'd started planning this route we'd been keen to capture some powerful photographs of the area. Right now, I was more concerned about just surviving it.

We'd read countless stories of the severe weather in the region even in summer, and here we were, with winter closing in around us!

I was sliding my butt onto the frozen seat when Lisa blurted, "Not much traffic along this route, and snow and heavy rain storms have killed people."

"I know," I said, trying to sound reassuring, as though everything was going to be fine.

"Yeah, okay," she replied, "Just saying!"

Strangely for me, my head was swimming with angst and I wasn't sure I was hiding it well enough from Lisa. After a diary entry the previous night, I'd read the Lonely Planet chapter on this region. Now as we rode higher, one paragraph kept coming back to me: "The Pamir Alay range is one of the most remote and rugged parts of Central Asia... but this is one place where you can't just head off with a 1970s Soviet-era map and a handful of Snickers bars."

Shit, we still had to clear Tajikistan Immigration somewhere ahead, I thought to myself as I fumbled the clutch lever and clunked my bike into the wrong gear. I couldn't feel my feet.

We'd ridden high into no-man's land and the patchy tarmac had quickly turned to red clay as we'd climbed higher through the switchbacks in second and third gear. To our left, tall snowy mountains rose steeper and steeper. The snow was now beginning to cover the track.

As we climbed higher, each turn of the bars had required more concentration. We could both feel the thin air leaching the last of the energy from our bodies, while the freezing air gnawed at our limbs and bit our faces.

"Get your ass off the seat," Lisa yelled through the comms as my concentration had wandered. I'd become lazy and had bounced over a patch of loose rock and into an ice-crusted muddy and shallow stream. Higher up the snow had drifted across the track. The entire landscape had become overwhelming. This was truly a giant's playground, and we were just specks passing through. There are a few landscapes in the world that put you and your existence into clear perspective. If you're lucky you'll get to experience one of them. I guess it's the universe's way of saying, "Yeah, you're not the centre of me!"

As I crested another rise, the track had broadened, and the tall, imposing concrete statue of a Marco Polo ram had cast its long shadow over me. I'd been so in awe of the landscape I'd not been watching the GPS as we'd crested the top of the famous Kyzyl-Art Pass. The bright red clay contrasted with the pristine snow and the royal blue sky above us.

I yelled to Lisa to stop, but the freezing temperature had killed the batteries of our intercoms. Off my bike I waved and jumped like a madman, desperately urging Lisa to stop before she crested the summit and the "shot" was lost. Her altitude sickness had worsened dramatically over the last 20 minutes and I knew it would have been wrong to ask her to turn and ride up again.

I quickly grabbed the camera from my tank bag, and almost tore off the zipper in the rush. Lens hood off, power on… power on. "Shit, shit," I yelled as I realised the battery was dead. Lisa was getting steadily worse, as I cycled through five batteries before realising that every one of them was as flat as a pancake, each killed by the sub-zero temperatures we were riding.

Okay, c'mon Simon, think, I said to myself as desperation began to take hold and my imagination began to race. We'd worked so hard to get to this mind-blowing location, we had to have photos. *How to charge the batteries?*

In desperation I started the bike on its side-stand and let it idle while pulling all the camera batteries and balancing them precariously on the cylinder head of my R1100GS. In truth I had no idea at what point the scolding heat would melt the hard plastic cases of the batteries, or if they'd just explode and go off like fireworks.

Still on her bike, Lisa was looking worryingly pale and her lips were blue. We'd agreed she'd ride past me and continue down. Fifteen minutes had passed by the time I'd checked the batteries, one, two, three and four, only to find that battery five had warmed up enough to turn the camera on. One last wave to Lisa and she was off as I knelt by the wet track and pointed the camera.

I managed to ease off five shots before the camera died; the best laid plans. All I could do was hope that I'd not screwed up the camera settings. I desperately wanted to believe I had caught at least one great shot of my wife up on the pegs of her F650GS with the hunched shoulders of a Pamir snow-capped giant in the background. Sure, it sounded absurdly romantic, but there it was.

I slid the lens cover on and walked back to my bike, letting out a sigh just before looking up—when time stopped! Surrounded by the most biblical landscape I'd ever been in, I was suddenly, and palpably aware of my, of our lives. Right there and in that moment nothing else existed. I wasn't thinking of what was over the hill or remembering the struggles we'd survived to reach that moment. I was simply and powerfully aware that we were there and, for a speck of time, we were part of this place, this ancient, overwhelming and majestic place.

What hit me was that this wasn't an adventure, or a story, it was so much better, this was our life. A series of interlocking choices and actions had brought me to that moment of singular joy! Being there with Lisa, experiencing all of it together, made it real. A lump in my throat grew as tears trickled down my chin. I closed my eyes and absorbed as much of the moment as I could.

The bark of Lisa's bike somewhere in the distance brought me back, and a wave of decision making and necessary actions reoccupied my brain, including all the steps needed to reach our next destination. But, those few seconds up there... they are the hard-fought-for glimpses of life we dream of and the very reason why Lisa and I are drawn to travel.

A mile past the summit, the Tajikistan compound came into view along with half a dozen young, bored soldiers, sauntering outside. Each was pulling on a thin cigarette and carrying the mandatory Kalashnikov slung over his back. Two large, rusting fuel containers rested in the red mire and were now in active duty as the passport and Customs offices. I couldn't feel my hands as I dismounted the bike and searched for our papers.

The rattle of a guard's Kalashnikov gave us direction and something murmured in Tajik had me moving, while Lisa waited outside.

Inside smelled like dark and stale tobacco, and a small TV hissed and buzzed in the corner. The ceiling was eight feet high and they'd somehow managed to squeeze a set of bunk beds and a desk in. These guys work and live in this tiny space for eight months of the year and are then cycled out to active duty somewhere else. *Jesus what a way to live,* I thought to myself, smiling as I handed over our papers. A small iron furnace was belting out heat from behind the door.

This was weird, even by our standards. I was hunched on the lower bunk, with a Customs guard practically sitting on top of me. He was still wearing just his piss-stained thermals and scribbling into a ledger with authority, as if everything was normal.

As my eyes drifted to the floor and to the guards' feet, the banjo tune from the movie *Deliverance* starting slowly twanging in my head. Scraping the rusting red metal floor and sticking out from his once-white knitted woollen socks, were the longest set of yellow toe nails I'd ever seen. *Don't stare, don't stare,* I told myself. It was too late.

God! I'm going to get cavity searched, was the thought that flashed through my mind. I'd quickly pushed this ridiculous and intrusive thought to an unused part of my brain, where there was plenty of space.

The guard snorted, snorted again and then hacked something substantial from somewhere deep inside him before spitting it toward the furnace and handing me the completed paperwork. As I thanked him, a globule of spittle formed in the corner of his mouth and then popped.

"Everything okay?" asked Lisa still sitting on her bike.

"Yeah, fine," I replied. I didn't have the energy or time to begin describing what had just happened.

All in all, it had taken us two hours to clear the border. The usual wave of excitement had overtaken us both at the prospect of a new country. Rounding a long, low set of mountains in late afternoon, the view ahead had left us dumbstruck, the scene a "white-out" except for the vast icy blue waters of Lake Karakul. Our route was straight ahead, but how could it be? As far as we could see the land was covered in snow.

We'd skirted Lake Karakul (the highest lake in Central Asia) as the afternoon came to an end. Unbelievably the tar road had stayed clear of snow. As we approached the town of Karakul, I knew we needed to stop; even wearing all our heated gear and with everything set to maximum we were freezing, and our abilities to concentrate had become suspect.

The sight of a lone cyclist coming towards us was reason enough to stop. Ben from the UK looked as sorry for himself and as cold as we felt.

"Hello, good afternoon, wow!" said Ben sounding like a character from *Four Weddings and a Funeral*.

"It's a chilly one," he continued. The longer we travelled the more we appreciated the impact and peculiarity of raw British understatement.

It was -12°C!

Lisa and I finally found the power of speech, quickly introduced ourselves, and set about grilling Ben, the insane cyclist from Islington, for every bit of info he had on the route ahead. Ben's words of "almost impassable" were not the encouragement we'd hoped to hear.

"Bollocks," I blurted for the first time in two years, suddenly feeling very English.

We had hoped to reach the Tajik town of Murghab by nightfall, where we'd planned to pick up fuel. But with darkness fast approaching we knew we'd run out of time to summit the Ak-Baital Pass at 4,655 metres and reach Murghab in daylight.

With the towering mountains behind us casting long shadows, we quickly made up our minds. A quick scan of the small, ice-buried town had revealed a hand-painted sign, which simply read, "Homestay." Twenty minutes later we'd slipped and slided across the hard-packed ice, opened the creaking metal gates of the homestay and parked in its small yard. Inside we made ourselves comfortable amidst small cushions on the rug-covered floor. We sat around a low table sipping on sweet, warm tea and swapped information about each other's upcoming routes as a low fire sat in the grate waiting to be stoked.

By 7:30am the next morning, we had pushed back the half a ton of bedding and managed to escape the bed. Lisa had been awake most of the night with a splitting headache. Worryingly, she was now showing the early symptoms of altitude sickness. Waves of nausea were hitting her thick and fast and I'd grown genuinely worried. The altitude was exacerbating her heart condition and we'd had no time to acclimatise. One day we were in the lowlands and the next we were touching the sky.

The temperature inside according to Ben's thermometer was -2°C. We dressed quickly. With a few "Good mornings" exchanged with our host, we headed outside only to be face-slapped by the frozen air. Within seconds bare skin was icy cold, it was -10°C. The visit to the loo was an unpleasant experience, not good at the best of times but when you're that cold, getting sensitive body parts out while dealing with the acrid stench of ammonia and piss, well, it's a wake-up call for your senses.

Over by the bikes, a thick layer of frost had covered them both, making them glisten in the pristine morning air. Ben was already packed up when we tried to start the bikes. The 1100 had protested a little but then sparked to life. Lisa's F650 was going to be a different story and after 40 minutes of key turning, push starting and finally jump-starting with jumper cables, it sparked to life. It was now noon.

Straining our eyes, we watched Ben become a speck on the horizon travelling north as we began our route south. On the bikes we both felt uneasy with the sheer amount of layering we had to pull on: two sets of thermals, a T-shirt, another long-sleeved top, our heated jackets (on full), our riding suits and then our outer waterproofs over it all. We'd brought out our winter BMW riding gloves and even the BMW balaclavas to cover our faces. The wind chill was indescribable.

Steadily we began our own push to the Ak-Baital summit. We rose too quickly, and at 13,000 feet Lisa's head was pounding and the nausea affecting her balance. Her altitude symptoms were getting worse, which is a deadly concern in this remote location. We had to push on. The fastest way down was up and over; returning wouldn't get us low enough, fast enough. It was -22°C, and 50 feet to our left a seemingly endless fence of wooden posts and barbed wire marked the Chinese border. At 15,000 feet the switchbacks demanded every ounce of the concentration we had remaining. Visibility was a struggle. Even with sunglasses and dark visors the glare was blindingly painful. Three kilometres from the summit of the pass, our progress was halted, as our wheels spun and lost traction in the compressed icy snow that had obliterated the track.

Lisa was feeling worse and a mistake here, a moment's loss of concentration, would have seen her over the edge. I hadn't told her but her lips had turned a scary blue and her eyes had the sunken look of the oxygen-deprived. All I wanted to do was get her over this pass and into a lower elevation.

From over my shoulder the coughs of an ancient Russian 4x4 had grabbed my attention as it slowly chugged towards the summit. I waved it down explaining, "My wife is unwell!" Without hesitation they bundled Lisa inside and promised to deliver her to the top. With Lisa heading up the track I rode one bike at a time, 500 metres, then returned for the other. Short of the summit, the track was clearer and Lisa stood waiting.

As I walked back for the last time to collect Lisa's bike, my lungs were fit to burst. At 15,270 feet I was spitting blood onto the white virgin snow. God knows how far I'd walked going back and forth to ride one bike and then the other. My head was spinning and Lisa's fatigued posture pressed home the urgency of getting lower and pressing on.

We had stopped for the briefest of moments at the top of the pass, as much to take in the view as to video the GPS screen, which read 15,309 feet. We'd desperately wanted to take dozens of photos but we were just too cold.

As late afternoon rolled by, the reduction of 3,000 feet improved Lisa's altitude sickness enough to where we knew she was out of the woods.

Murghab Town was our chance to feel some much needed warmth although it is, at 12,102 feet, the highest town in Tajikistan. It was just below the altitude we needed to get Lisa to, for any kind of overnight stay. Heading to the bazaar, we needed water and somewhere to exchange dollars for local currency (Tajik Somene).

Dozens of small, rag-tag stalls lined the single street. A mix of wooden stands, rust-ravaged shipping containers and 4X4 bodies made up the local shopping complex. The few vendors braving the cold stocked little more than old clothes and out-of-date Snickers bars. One lonely bottle of toxic-coloured shampoo, sitting on a wooden plank, made for the highlight of our shopping experience.

Two days after leaving Murghab we were travelling across the Pamir proper, and riding Tibetan-style high plateaus and then wide remote valleys. Bolivia (now almost four years behind us) had been the last time we'd ridden this high and had felt the same sense of being utterly separated from the rest of the world.

The Chinese call this range the "Congling Shan" (the "Onion Mountains") and it's easy to see why. The entire range is simply layer upon layer of mountains, each taller and more magnificent than the last.

By mid-afternoon we'd out-raced a snow storm that had pushed in from the south across the Alichur Plain, a wall of freezing air and heavy snow that had threatened to catch us up before our route had taken a westerly course.

As the afternoon disappeared we summited the Koi-Tezek Pass at 14,097 feet and were painfully aware at just how cold we'd become; our concentration wandered and waned as our blood had centralised to our cores to protect vital organs.

On the western side of Khorog we'd filled the bikes to the brim with fuel. The plan of reaching Dushanbe in a day had proven to be a tall order, but we didn't have much choice. Weeks earlier we'd had to provide a specific date by when we'd collect our Iranian visa from the embassy there. By mid-morning, our definition of what we thought of as "mountains" had been re-written. We'd slowed our pace, as much because of the onslaught of twisting blind bends as for the sheer majesty of the country around us; yet another travel high.

For two days we skirted the Afghanistan border en route for Kulyab where the Gunt River meets the Pyanj River, where we'd detoured north for 40 miles, before again heading west at Rushan. The tar came and went whimsically, and for the most part we rode up on the pegs.

We had followed the brimming banks of the Pyanj River, its waters flowing fast and full, swollen from the first of winter's heavy snow. On its westerly bank dozens of tiny Afghani settlements clung impossibly to mountainsides. Local Afghans had waved as we'd ridden by. We'd passed dozens of dark painted signs marked with a skull and bones, each denoting a heavily mined area.

In Dushanbe, Tajikistan's capital, we set about collecting our Iranian and Turkmenistan visas, a process that had taken two full weeks.

In Uzbekistan, and on the outskirts of Samarkand, I was waved to the side of the road by a traffic cop who was fumbling with the buttons of his speed gun. He'd done his best to convince me that I'd sped into a 70-kilometre zone at 95 kilometres per hour. He gone on to demand I pay him $50 USD as an instant fine. He'd not even been holding the gun when I'd passed him.

Catching him off-guard I'd shaken his hand proudly, and stated, "I am a policeman in the UK. We are brothers."

"I have GPS," I'd continued.

Tapping my GPS screen firmly, I flicked through the functions and quickly found the "calculator feature" and then punched in the numbers six and three. With a half-smile I'd proudly shown my antagonist that my GPS told me I was only doing 63 when I passed him.

Suitably impressed the officer agreed and the fine disappeared. To this day I still can't believe that stunt worked!

In the chill of early morning, we sat quietly on the tiled steps of the magnificent Registan, in the heart of the ancient city of Samarkand in Uzbekistan. It was slowly sinking in—this is our life. We were living the adventure and already halfway along the Silk Road between China and the West. We were actually following in the historical footsteps of Marco Polo and Genghis Khan.

As we slurped sweet, fresh pomegranate juice, our journey and what it meant to us slowly took form. We had risen to every challenge and been surprised at our tenacity and resilience. As a couple, as husband and wife, we'd grown even closer and I was simply in awe of my wife.

Mmm, it's funny; we're not the same two scared Brits who originally set out. We'd changed, grown and learned. *Most importantly we've never, ever felt better, or more alive!*

About the authors:

Lisa and **Simon Thomas** set out to ride around the world in May of 2003 and have since ridden 500,000 miles, and explored six continents. The pair have ridden, survived, recorded and shared their incredible journey for 16 years, through some of the world's harshest environments, all the while being tested to their limits and beyond.

They've survived a broken neck and malaria in the Amazon, being shot at in Russia, traversing 36 deserts, and threatened with expulsion, having been wrongfully accused of kidnapping a president's son. But, that's another story. They've run out of water, squinted at hallucinations, repaired damaged bikes with scrap airplane parts, dined with Masai warriors and loved each other through every step of the way.

Lisa and Simon have shared their experiences with over 100 live audiences around the globe, authored articles for top travel and motorcycle publications and made over 40 international TV appearances, written a cook book and been the focus of a *BBC* documentary.

Today their reach extends beyond the motorcycle world and the pair have presented and shared their unique insights with corporate clients and industry leaders for brands like *BMW, Boeing* and *Adidas*.

As authors, photographers and filmmakers their work has been seen across five continents and read and enjoyed by millions. It has been said that Simon and Lisa helped define what is now called "Adventure Riding."

Their website has also become a main source of information in the adventure riding community.

Photography: Simon & Lisa Thomas
Website: 2ridetheworld.com
Facebook: 2ridetheworld
Instagram: @2ridetheworld
Twitter: @2ridetheworld
YouTube: 2ridetheworld
LinkedIn: Simon and Lisa Thomas
Their book *Dirty Dining* is available from *Amazon*.

Cycle South

by Daniel Byers

"If you don't take risks, you can't create a future."
—*Monkey D. Luffy*

Waking up in a cold sweat, I sat up trying to clear my head and take in the surroundings. *Where in the hell was I?* The walls and fixtures seemed completely unfamiliar. The intense sunlight streaming through the old, caulk-cracked windows only added to the confusion, making it difficult to focus. I didn't realize my glasses weren't on, making awakening that much more difficult. As I continued attempting to push away the cobwebs, I looked around a bit more, finally noticing the multiple IVs protruding from both of my wrists. A cacophony of Spanish voices echoed into the room from an adjoining hallway, the sounds reverberating off the hard tiled floors and walls. There were several other beds near me, occupied by others seemingly either asleep, or unconscious.

Terrified by the sudden realization I was in a hospital, I started hyperventilating, which quickly brought on nausea. A heavy-set nurse with her dark hair pulled into a tight bun came rushing towards me. She was shouting at me in Spanish and waving her arms wildly but, unable to stop,

I rolled to one side and threw up over the side of the bed onto the floor. I tried my best to take this all in and make sense of it, failing miserably.

This is *not* how I envisioned my motorcycle trip-of-a-lifetime would go. Hell, at the moment this situation was unfolding, I had yet to remember exactly *what* or even *when* it had happened. I knew not the day of the week, exactly where I was, or how I'd gotten there—only that it was a hospital in Salina Cruz in Oaxaca State, Mexico.

My first thought was I had been in a motorcycle accident, although there was no memory of it. Most certainly this was one of those predicaments many family and friends had warned me of when they learned I would be leaving my corporate lifestyle in Ohio to ride a motorcycle through Latin America, with no itinerary or time constraints aside from the limitations of the money I'd stashed away.

Adding to my stress was that none of the hospital's staff spoke English. My Spanish at that time was rudimentary at best, and I was mostly reliant upon Google Translate for extended conversation. Compounding things was that I had neither my cell phone for Google Translate, nor even my wallet or passport with me. And from what I *could* understand from the doctors, I needed surgery as soon as possible, and they needed money. I was terrified and completely doubting myself and my actions more than I ever had. The shit had hit the proverbial fan.

Memories of feeling ill in my Salina Cruz Airbnb apartment began to resurface. My mind slowly pieced together a memory of having been ill enough that I had to be transported to the hospital, but without being fully aware of it. I tried and failed to explain to the hospital staff that I needed to contact the owner of the apartment in order to access my bank so I could pay them.

Finally, on the fourth day in the hospital, Teresa, the woman who owned the Airbnb (and whose son, Freddy, had found me unconscious and taken me to the hospital) convinced the hospital staff we were family, and they allowed her to see me. When Teresa hugged me, giving one of the warmest smiles I've ever seen, something deep inside clicked a little. Barely perceptible, a minute adjustment of my subconscious was being made. A fine tuning to my soul was in process, and slowly my fears and trepidation were being replaced with moments of calm. Teresa had brought my cell phone, a charger, wallet and passport. She also paid the initial bills (which I, of course, repaid later). The world was not going to end, at least not today. The sun would continue to rise daily, and I began to accept my fate.

Nearly a month passed in the hospital. During that time, they continually monitored my lower colon. It had ruptured from a bad infection. I'd thought it was a bad flu and had just started a round of antibiotics the evening before I'd passed out. The hospital staff continued trying to explain that surgery was needed to remove a section of my colon, and that they were hoping the cocktail of different intravenous antibiotics would keep the spread of sepsis at bay. Multiple specialists were brought in. They wanted to remove an 18-inch section of the lower colon if the infection couldn't be brought under control. The delineation between needing the surgery or not was extremely fine, but if the opening in the colon wall was 5mm or larger in diameter, surgery was a must.

Repeated CT scans as well as exploratory surgery revealed my damage was 4.5mm in diameter. So they continued the cocktail of different antibiotics in the effort to keep things from getting any worse. While doing so they were also treating the infection that had spread into the abdominal cavity. I was struggling to deal with all of this, and the language issue didn't help.

Life suddenly started to get more bearable when the medics informed me that they'd found a local English-speaking nurse at another clinic who volunteered to come by daily after her shift. This is how I met the stunningly beautiful Lidia Ruiz, who turned out to be yet another of the most incredible people from my journey. Tall and with an athletic build, she lit up rooms with her smile. And her perfect English startled me when she first spoke. Spending many years in the United States as a child, she'd returned to her home city of Salina Cruz to become a nurse and raise a family.

And with Lidia's help I found out what the doctors had attempted to explain. I knew what they feared and at last I clearly understood my predicament. She put me at ease right away, and unknowingly became part of the mechanism of change manifesting in me. Until that point of my trip, I'd not really been particularly friendly with the locals along the way. I certainly *was* friendly to those I met, but never stayed in one place long enough to develop any kind of real friendships.

Looking back, it took a great deal of courage at the beginning of my journey. I'd quit a great corporate job, sold my belongings, modified a Suzuki DR650 for the task, and left my previous life behind, my family and friends, too. I left everything, not knowing or really caring at first, if or when I'd ever return to Ohio, and I was proud of myself. I'd spent more than a decade working corporate jobs and paying off large debts from a brutal divorce and a custody battle that left me financially devastated. All this made it a struggle to support a motorcycling passion, which continued to grow despite all that had gone on.

All along, I kept telling myself I'd do something to celebrate life, if and when I arrived at a zero-debt point. As 2018 approached, it looked like that was finally going to happen. Plans were hatched and my dreams were spray painted to make them slightly more visible, like trying to mark the Invisible Man. Warnings about traveling the world alone by motorcycle were duly ignored.

Since a young age, I dreamed of riding around the world on a motorcycle. Those early dreams were mainly fuelled by exposure to one of the earliest adventure-motorcycle travel movies, the 1971 cult classic, Cycles South. The freewheeling style of the riders in Cycles South had me excitedly thinking about someday, perhaps, being on the road myself, and how much fun the freedom of exploring new places would be. Some long-distance bicycle touring in my early teens was all part of a growing wanderlust. It wasn't until years later, as my dreams slowly started to become reality, that I found the original Cycles South movie on YouTube. Seeing it again, it rekindled how important it had seemed so long ago in the 1970s.

Many moto-travelers create custom decals for their trips. They're used to exchange with other riders and to tag famous locations where multitudes of riders before them have traveled. I looked at the Cycles South original movie poster and modified it a little for *my* trip decal, and from that moment my trip became "Cycle South."

As the plan for the motorcycle trip began to materialize, of course new doubts formed in my mind about the various *what-could-go-wrong?*

scenarios, but without pause the days counted down to the planned departure date. Remember, I was told by almost everyone that what I was about to do was a crazy, dangerous thing. Non-stop warnings were given as to how I would be kidnapped by Mexican cartels, or worse. These possibilities, these tiny little barbs of warnings, wore away at the battle-hardening veneer I had been steadfastly forming for life on the road. Still, fears and doubts were in the back of my mind as I pulled out of the driveway in Ohio. The excitement and adrenaline of leaving suppressed the worst of them, but they were there, and they weren't healthy.

I had a semi-planned route through the United States to Mexico with multiple defined stops. I intended to stop in Baltimore to see my son, Spencer, as well as in North Carolina to stay and ride with friends through the Smoky Mountains, scheduling my arrival at the time of our annual group get-together.

I also had to stop in Denver, Colorado to meet Woody Witte, of Woody's Wheel Works, to pick up the set of custom wheels he'd built for my motorcycle. I'd named my bike "Thousand Sunny" (or "Sunny" for short) after a ship in a famous Japanese *Manga* series, One Piece. Sunny was surely ready for what adventures lay ahead. But was I? The doubts bubbled. Had my 57 years on this rock provided me with suitable coping and survival skills?

And now, here I was in a Mexican hospital, and very ill. I was relatively certain that my motorcycle trip to Ushuaia had ended. According to the doctors, there were further medical procedures needed within the next six months. When the infection was eliminated, they eventually released me, but only on the promise that I would get the needed surgical work done soon, and certainly within the six-month window. I got back on my motorcycle and headed north and eventually made it back to Ohio. Eventually? Along the way I rode the TAT (the Trans America Trail) west to east. It seemed like a good idea, and as I was free, I rode it.

Upon arriving at my father's home in Ohio, I was in a completely different frame of mind from when I had departed. I was a survivor, and I was still free. Maybe, just maybe, I thought, I could turn things around and have another crack at riding to Ushuaia. This was, after all, the new me.

I began selling what remained from a lifetime's worth of accumulated possessions. More motorcycle parts. Collectible cards. Coins I'd dug up and a number of books from my collection were all sold online. I went nuts on eBay as a seller. Slowly at first, and then with building momentum, the amount of money I raised from the sell-off grew. The moment came when I determined that I not only had enough funds to re-start the journey to Ushuaia, I also had enough for the medical work needed, but certainly not at the typical healthcare costs in the United States without completely depleting the nest egg I had worked so hard to accumulate. I had a Plan B, and with a coordinated effort from friends in San Miguel de Allende, I flew back to Mexico. There I had the needed surgeries and recovered at a friend's villa before flying back to Ohio for the final re-departure preparations.

A few weeks later, and after much last-minute running around, I was back on Sunny and heading south again, this time with an entirely new outlook, and a promise to myself to relax more and take each day as it came.

I set out with this fresh new perspective on life and a better appreciation for feeling healthy. I realized that I was no longer a young man, and that I couldn't continue living my moto-life in the fashion I had been. For one thing, I had never watched what I ate. Being an ex-bicycle racer, I was still behaving as if I could consume anything, burn it right off and come out smiling. Compounding this issue was that I was going through Mexico again, a country that's the home of *many* gastronomical delights and an over-abundance of spices. Before my colon rupture, I ate a *lot* of very spicy foods. I grew up loving spicy foods, the hotter the better. And hydration? I never paid attention to it, but the lack of it, according to the doctors, was a part of the problem on my first trip southward.

Early on in the Cycle South journey, I'd ridden in intolerable heat. That heatwave continued nearly all the way through Mexico. There were several days close to 120°F, and I was withering slowly. Stupidly, I didn't increase my water intake. Quite often I would make the mistake of utilizing whatever water I was carrying to wet my T-shirt for cooling, rather than drinking it as I should have.

To make matters worse, I'd driven into my skull the need to make considerable distances each and every day. This was a habit from many years of riding sport-touring motorcycles around the USA 20-hour day in the saddle was common back then, and those bad habits carried over to my trip-of-a-lifetime. By the time I was close to Salina Cruz where it all went wrong, I was beat, dehydrated and highly stressed out. I already had an unreasonable deadline with plans to meet the German sailboat Stahlratte in Panama to carry my bike and me from Carti, Panama around the infamous Darien Gap to Cartagena, Colombia. There are no roads linking Central and South America.

As nervous as I was about my first border crossing from the US into Mexico, I was 10 times more stressed about the multiple countries in Central America that lay ahead. Simply put, I pushed harder and harder towards that ruptured colon.

As I headed south the second time it all seemed so crystal clear. I had razor-sharp memories of the mistakes I'd continually made, and how they'd combined with the level of needless worry I'd loaded on my shoulders every morning. I'd been doing that, every day, when I should have been celebrating life on the road. Perhaps things do happen for a reason. Perhaps it's our responsibility to recognize when change is needed and to act accordingly. Sometimes it takes a big event to make us wake up and learn.

As I write this, after three years on the road and having finally fulfilled my dream of riding to Ushuaia, I look back to that moment in the hospital and understand its importance. Not just for providing needed guidance for my journey, but also for a new outlook on the world. From that point forward, reinforced daily by even the smallest of victories, things started becoming easier.

Fun was a daily occurrence, and the number of others I met and got to know grew exponentially to the point where I had a hard time believing my good fortune. Border after border fell before me, yet the daily average for kilometers covered plummeted, allowing more time to relax and explore my destinations. Riding south through Central America was a little rushed because, again, I had a deadline to meet the Stahlratte sailboat in Panama. This time I'd not stressed out about that deadline because my long-term plan was to ride all the way back to Ohio. I'd be able to slow down even more in Central America on that leg of the trip. I also planned to stop in countries or points of interest missed on the first attempt.

Arriving in Carti, Panama two days early was perfect timing. I still had time to make friends in Antigua, Guatemala, Honduras and Costa Rica, and I'd relaxed enough to head off the Pan-American Highway. In Nicaragua I'd ridden along a hard-packed beach and had raced with horses running wild. In Panama I'd camped in the jungle, listening to monkeys howl throughout the night. So many fantastic experiences, yet I just knew I would make it to that sailboat in time. I also knew that once Sunny and I were safely aboard Stahlratte, the next step was to disembark in Cartagena, Colombia. There I'd begin the South America leg, and yes, knowing that brought about some fears. I beat them down, like beating the dust out of a large rug strung across a line, and showed no mercy on myself in that regard. These new coping skills would become handy in the next continent.

You might be asking yourself how I can say that one of the darkest, scariest moments in my life ended up being *that* moment when things clicked and started going well for me. We all long for life experiences that will endure forever in our memories. We strive to do things and go places and to relate to others in ways that make us and them happy. The problem is, far too many find their happy places out of laziness and fear. As a result, they relegate their lives to work and evenings on their favorite sofa or Lazy Boy. Their brains shut off the little voice in the back of their minds that's screaming, "Hey! Get out there! See what's around the next corner!" They continually convince themselves that they are happy right where they are, right where they've always been. And the few times they allow that little voice a place at the table, they quickly drown it out with fears of the unknown. For many, that unknown could be as close as the next town, let alone another country or continent.

How we decide to allay those fears is a very personal thing. For me it took the incident in Salina Cruz to open my eyes. For you it might be something like reading stories of travel and enlightenment. Or indulging in the many travel blogs from others that have gone before you.

The things that cause us to open our eyes and minds to the people and places in the world aren't important. What does matter is that one does open their eyes and their mind and try. For me, my newfound ability to remain calm and cool, no matter what the problem in front of me, served very well during the re-start of Cycle South. And it carried on for the next two years of travel that ensued upon my re-departure.

Country after country fell before the front wheel of my DR650. Border crossings, one of the main areas of worry and stress, became not quite enjoyable, but were tolerated. At times I even looked forward to them as so many moto-travelers meet each other during these crossing delays.

As more proof of my change in attitude, in Mendoza, Argentina, I incorrectly installed new front brake pads the day before a planned crossing into Chile. During the ride over the Andes Mountain pass, the brake pads came undone. They locked up the front brake and ruined the rotor! I made it back to Mendoza only to discover there were virtually no Suzuki parts available. Lengthy searches for a cross-compatible rotor also failed. Ordering online could mean a two-month delay, making arrival in Ushuaia in a less than favorable season. What to do? Time to panic? No!! Travel teaches you that things do go wrong, but there is always a solution and sometimes it's the beginning of an interesting new adventure.

Calmly I looked at all online options and finally found a cheap used rotor in Chile's capital city, Santiago. Online I also located another motorcyclist who was heading my way, and they offered to bring it along. Problem solved, and another lifetime friend made. The delay was barely an additional week, enabling my journey to continue. The old me would have folded—I know he would have.

The newfound inner peace served me well twice towards the end of the journey. As I was preparing to leave Ushuaia and ride north along the eastern coast of Argentina towards Buenos Aires, I began hearing bits and pieces in the news about a mysterious new virus. The importance this would play in my near future really didn't register at that time. My mind was intent on where I was, and where I planned to ride in the coming months. I'd skipped Bolivia on the way south so planned to head there, but first I wanted to ride into Brazil where I'd cross at Foz de Iguazu and visit the world-famous series of waterfalls on the Argentina-Brazil border, then ride to Bolivia. From there I'd head towards Peru before carrying on northwards.

After clearing the Argentinian border, I rode across the no-man's land to the Brazilian side. It was surprising to see the traffic backup there but, as is the normal thing for motorcyclists to do in South America, I rode to the front of the line. There, my passport was stamped into Brazil, but when it came time to import my motorcycle, all the Customs computers were down.

I spent nearly four hours in the office of the Policia Federale captain, waiting for the computers to come back up, while remaining quite calm. The captain was a very friendly fellow who spoke decent English and let me wait in his air-conditioned office. It was only there I realized that I had a new language, Portuguese, to deal with. While we were waiting, he received a text message that he shared. It stated that all of the borders in South America were closing in two days' time, due to the pandemic I'd been hearing about.

So began my seven-month stay in Brazil, waiting for the borders to reopen. I didn't worry. I did not panic, though there certainly were some moments of concern as the months dragged on. I rented a small apartment in a closed pousada (motel) in Praia do Esteleiro, Santa Catarina, and became part of the wonderful family who owned the building. Their love and care made that period not just tolerable, but often beautiful. Brazil is such a stunningly gorgeous country to be "stuck in" but, very concerned about the rise of the virus there, I limited my riding to day loops around the nearby mountains.

My room was barely a five-minute walk from one of the cleanest small beaches I'd ever seen. It looked like a scene from a James Bond movie and had me imagining a submarine or small airplane beaching there with Sean Connery contending with the villainess du jour. Time passed slowly, and my imagination had some fun.

Finally, after seven months, I found a way to ship Sunny back to the US This was a difficult decision, but it was becoming increasingly difficult to remain in Brazil. The borders weren't opening, and I was ever conscious of my dwindling funds. I decided that I might as well wait out the pandemic at home. So I booked passage for Sunny on an ocean vessel that normally shipped cars, known as a "Ro-Ro" ferry (roll-on, roll-off) so there was no real preparation needed. Sunny was ridden onto the huge boat in Paranaque, Brazil, and would sail to Galveston, Texas where I planned to retrieve her.

After a very emotional goodbye with my new Brazilian family, I flew back to the US via a series of interconnecting flights. Arriving in Houston, I was reunited with Sunny. Had my funds been in better shape, I most likely would have remained in Brazil and continued to be hopeful of the borders reopening. The bonus was I had a job offer in Denver, working for my friend Woody at his motorcycle wheel-building shop. So that was my next destination. I was taking everything in stride.

Picking up Sunny at the port, I was thrilled when she fired right up, and quickly settled into a nice idle. She had been on the ocean for over a month by that time and I was concerned about corrosion. Putting my riding gear on for the first time in many weeks, it felt absolutely amazing to be underway again. I was heading towards a new city in the gorgeous state of Colorado. Part of the plan included meeting a new friend in Texas and touring Big Bend National Park with him. I'd never ridden there and was looking forward to it, especially with a local motorcyclist who was well-versed on the roads and trails. But, as I'd learned, plans don't always come together in the way they've been imagined.

On the second day in Texas, coming over a rise in Texas Hill Country at about 70mph (the narrow two-lane roads by the Mexico border have a 75mph speed limit) I saw what appeared to be a group of small, dark-colored animals crossing the road about a quarter of a mile away. Knowing I had plenty of time, I did not brake but rolled off the throttle, allowing Sunny to slow down with compression braking, a slight "pop pop" emanating from the exhaust.

Drawing closer I saw that the dark black and brown wild pigs had completely crossed to my side of the road. Slowing right down, I instinctively looked ahead to make sure that there was no oncoming traffic. Seeing none, I crossed over the center line wanting to put as much distance between me and the pigs as the road would allow. This habit had been formed from many months of riding past herds of wild animals in South America. But it ended up a bad mistake. The moment I was about to pass, much larger pigs came dashing out from behind a large sagebrush less than five feet away. Lowering their heads as they charged, the javelina slammed into me, one impacting my front wheel and the other my left leg.

This knocked my left leg off the foot peg, causing it to fly backwards. It slammed into the side of my case and bounced forward again. With Sunny's front wheel suddenly and uncontrollably swinging side to side, she began what's known as a "tank slapper," her handlebars careening wildly.

Somehow I regained control and brought her to a stop on the side of the road, but as I went to lift my left leg off the peg and put the side stand down, I realized I had no feeling in that side of my body. I fell over with Sunny on top of me, trapping the leg. I laid there for I'm not sure how long before a border patrol officer stopped to assist. Again, tragedy had struck. But yet again, aside from the immediate pain and my reaction to it, I remained calm and later had surgery to piece the leg back together in Alpine, Texas.

This accident happened in early November, 2020. As I write this it is now late March, 2021, and I'm still in Denver. The operation was not successful. I'm unable to stand or walk, and with physical therapy showing limited results, I'm awaiting a nerve-reconstruction surgery. If that doesn't work I'll be facing more operations.

I remain positive and know I'll get through this, too. I will be able to walk again and someday ride Sunny once more. I'm sure I can recover enough to be gainfully employed, and then I'll stash away as much money as possible for another few years and get back on the road again. Cycle South... destinations unknown, but now armed with the proper attitude for travel I know it's a wonderful world filled with amazing places and people. It would be a shame to not experience more of it, don't you think?

About the author:

Daniel Byers is a 60-year-old, semi-retired corporate buyer hailing from northeastern Ohio in the US. For that period he had worked in both the automotive and pharmaceutical industries, providing new program product support and contract negotiations for suppliers both foreign and domestic.

Disgruntled by political divisiveness at home, and suffering from a lifetime of intense wanderlust, he sold off his belongings and cashed in a retirement plan to fund his dream of riding his motorcycle around the world. He left Ohio in April of 2018 and reached his goal of riding to Ushuaia in February of 2020. His travels included a long hospital stay in Mexico as well as a seven-month lockdown in Santa Catarina, Brazil due to the Covid pandemic.

Three years on the road later and he is now temporarily residing in Denver, Colorado recuperating from injuries sustained in a motorcycle accident immediately upon his return to the United States. For now, unable to ride or walk, he revels in the incredible places and people he met along the way and works hard at someday resuming his travels.

YouTube: Dan Byers Cycle South
Facebook: Daniel Byers
ADVRider.com Blog: Cycle-South

Alone with the Grass and the Sky

by Geoff Keys

"Travel isn't always pretty. It isn't always comfortable. Sometimes it hurts, it even breaks your heart. But that's okay. The journey changes you; it should change you. It leaves marks on your memory, on your consciousness, on your heart, and on your body. You take something with you. Hopefully, you leave something good behind."

—*Anthony Bourdain*

I had been travelling for seven years, been to many amazing places and met dozens of great people, any of which could have been the subject of this chapter. But I didn't choose a beautiful temple, or any one individual. Instead, I chose a country: Mongolia.

Before reaching there, I'd travelled across Europe and Russia, and visited the Baltic States and Kazakhstan. I'd faced some challenges, but none felt as different, new and refreshing as Mongolia. I'll try to explain why this country is such a special place for me.

Coming eastward the countries changed but they all still had a clearly European feel. To a large extent, Russia was the same. By this I mean that everything a traveller needs was readily available. Urban areas, with their comfortable facilities, were common. Kazakhstan was more challenging and was the first country where I had to contend with desert. But it too had many large cities and towns.

Looking back, the first hint about how Mongolia might be was the road south from Novosibirsk. I left this typically large Russian city and soon found myself on a long, straight road, with very little to capture my attention. This 1,000-kilometre ride, a couple of hundred of which are through mountains and lakes, was clearly very popular with tourists. In terms of distance, it was rather like riding from Paris to Nice, but there were hints of things to come. I passed through some hills where the road had steep slopes on both sides. One was quite green but the opposite was completely bare, just rock and scree, with not a single blade of grass. I guessed that my companion, the scouring wind, took away all means of sustenance and survival on that side, but didn't affect the other.

The real Mongolian flavour came after crossing the border into western Mongolia. To the east were mountains and lakes, a more alpine-like terrain. But I was heading south, keen to experience the open spaces in a region of endless steppe with the occasional lake or river to negotiate. The vista was as open as it could be, nothing but low hills interrupting the dirt road that stretched away in front of me. I'd visualised how it might be, and this was the Mongolia I'd imagined. It looked magical and was everything I'd read about or seen in books, films and photos.

But words and images don't compare with actually being there: seeing the vast blue sky, with clouds scudding across; smelling and feeling the wind-driven air; looking across the brown, grassy plains to the low hills ahead. There were even shaggy-coated, black-haired yaks to greet me, their wide horns seeming to represent Mongolia's welcoming open arms.

251

In my youth it was common to remark on something a long way away by saying, "It might as well be in outer Mongolia". Well, there I was, in outer Mongolia— the blue sign near the border had told me so. I clicked into gear and set off, with even "Doris" the Suzuki seeming eager to explore.

Mongolia is the world's 18th largest country but has a very low population with a mere 3.3 million souls. It is 4.5 times bigger than the UK, twice the size of Texas and only slightly smaller than Alaska. Though it has a population density of just two people per square kilometre, the capital, Ulaanbaatar, is home to 45% of them. It's also the world's coldest capital, having an average annual temperature of 0°C. I rather liked these statistics and had made some loose plans as to where I would travel. Heading south towards the Gobi Desert was key to them.

Lonely trails were what I desired, and I had no trouble finding them. There were a few asphalted roads, too, but most routes were just tracks across the grassland. And, as a track became worn and corrugated, the locals simply started a new one next to it. Very often there'd be half a dozen running parallel. No regulation or planning, it just happened.

Because I had no navigational maps loaded in the GPS, I used paper maps and a compass as much as possible. The problem was that many of the tracks I needed weren't marked. One day I got caught out when one of the many parallel tracks veered off, away from where I wanted to go. It was sandy and I dropped the bike, trapping myself underneath it. I'd decided to cut across the grassland back to where I guessed I should have been; the route denoted by the occasional truck driving past. As I lay there with my leg trapped beneath the pannier I was wondering whether I'd be able to get up, and if I couldn't, whether I'd ever be found! I was being a drama queen but it was the sheer emptiness surrounding me which brought on those thoughts.

At that time, I had a Garmin GPSMap 60CSX, a wonderfully versatile GPS designed to be handheld but which also fit into a bike-mounted cradle and was powered by the bike's battery. Even without maps installed, it had the facility to enter coordinates and allow the compass to guide me there. My plan was to look up places I wanted to get to on the internet when Wi-Fi was available and note the coordinates for later use. I had great fun with this method because it meant all I could do was follow the purple compass line as closely as possible.

Towns presented a flow of new things to see. Very often there'd be a crossroads with a fuel station on two or three of the corners, as if they were making up for their paucity out there in the wild. There were streets where all the businesses were the same: banks, electronics shops, etc. Most buildings were Soviet era, low rise and plain, but occasionally there'd be a newer one reaching skyward. But generally they'd be very utilitarian, although sometimes there'd be a cultural building, such as a theatre. Often there were public plazas, pleasant places with statues and fountains. But newest to me were streets or market areas utilising rows of steel shipping containers. From them, bulk produce such as rice, flour or hardware were invariably sold.

The walled compounds with several gers inside stood out from the mix. A ger is the Mongolian name for a yurt, so common throughout Central Asia. They're round, peaked-roof tent-like structures, covered with skins or felt. The nomadic Mongolian herder way of life involves constantly moving their gers, usually via the ubiquitous pickup truck, out among the hills where their herds of camels, horses, cattle and sheep graze. They use horses or small Chinese motorbikes for getting around, and often have solar panels and even satellite dishes outside their gers.

In somewhat of a contrast to the nomadic ways, the walled-off areas in towns were a reversal of "home on the range." The compounds often had solid buildings of some kind, which I guessed were for storage or ablutions. I learned the herders came in from the steppe to live in these compounds during the winters. Although there was space for animals, most of their herds were sold for slaughter beforehand. This way of life was centuries old, the big changes being the availability of modern buildings and electricity, and of course pickup trucks for transportation instead of the traditional way of moving possessions around on the backs of horses.

At one point I stayed in the town of Arvaikheer, which aptly means "Barley Steppe." It's one of the most central points in Mongolia, and enjoys a mild, but very dry, climate. The town's theatre had recently been renovated and looked quite resplendent for a Mongolian structure. However, the central square was a bit of a historical flashback with monuments from the Soviet era. A striking feature of all the towns was that walking along the main road, and glancing down a side street, I would always see the brown hills in the distance. The lonely land was never far away.

Nearby were some places I visited, including Vulture Gorge. After loading its coordinates into the GPS, I set off following the purple line. The road and the compass were good friends that day. I'd been able to follow a newly asphalted road for a while, before veering off on a track following the compass. It all worked well and eventually I found the gorge.

Sadly there were no vultures in Vulture Gorge—they'd long disappeared. But there was a visitor centre where I could park the bike, and head out to explore on foot. A notable feature was a section of gorge untouched by the sun and therefore had year-round snow. To get there, I walked along a stream, which descended deep into the gorge. Small, furry creatures were darting everywhere, and mountain goats were atop the rocky outcrops, as were signs saying not to shoot them.

I left a stone on each of the Ovoos I passed. Ovoos are piles of stones, slowly built up by worshippers, and used for religious ceremonies. They're usually placed in geographically significant locations, such as next to rivers or hilltops; both local shamans and Buddhists use them. Adding to the piles seemed the right thing to do. Eventually I came to the narrowest section of the gorge, where the sun never reached… but there was *no* snow! Perhaps global warming was playing a role here, too, but the chill in the air was quite something, giving me an eerie feeling.

Sometimes my navigational attempts failed. For example, I wanted to visit the Flaming Cliffs, having read about how the setting sun set them ablaze in a blood red colour. But the road and compass let me down. I took every route I could find but none was correct. The few road signs encountered were useless, pretty to look at with white lines and Cyrillic writing on a blue background, but no help at all.

Part of the fun of travel is those you meet on the road, and in the town of Khovd I bumped into Matt, a young American. He was keen to buy a horse and a packhorse, then travel on his own nomadic journey. It was an admirable ambition, as his goal was to travel like a local and get a better feel for their way of life. I often wonder how he got on.

One day while riding the grasslands and wandering through the hills I came across a couple of young Mongolians. We all stopped to say hello. One was on a bike and the other a horse; both wore heavy woollen deels, the traditional Mongolian coat. In their bright colours, they stood out vividly against the pale grass. Deels are a long coat of a wrap-around style, with a waist belt and several clasps on the right-hand side. They have high collars and the bottom flares out to facilitate riding. Sometimes they're a drab olive colour, but often bright colours such as blue or orange. On the more decorative variations, such as those made of brocade, and those worn by some women out on the town, the belt is replaced by a silk sash, equally bright in colour.

That same night I camped a short way from the track and was visited by three guys, on two Chinese bikes. As before, the men were wearing deels, the most common herders' attire. Again, we exchanged greetings, but this time they seemed to be inviting me to come and stay with them. I declined because my inexperience still made me a bit wary of such things, and it would have meant taking my tent down again, and I'd been worn out after a long day.

I often camped in the wild without concern about the ownership of the land. On the open grasslands it simply didn't seem relevant; I just put my tent up and cooked. But even when I rode well off the road, up around the side of a hill, someone would usually come by to say hello.

One fellow arrived on his bike, pulled out a pipe (that looked very much like a socket spanner attached to a steel tube), sat down and shared it with me. He didn't much like the tea I offered and made it clear he hoped I had some alcohol. I didn't, so he soon rode off and left me in peace. He looked like many I'd seen, wearing a deel but with a cowboy-style hat, just to add a bit of style. All the bikes were Chinese made, with crash bars front and rear. They looked basic but tough, very much suited to the terrain and their riders.

With very few towns and therefore almost no light pollution, the skies were wonderfully clear and filled with starry curtains. One night the usual twinkling peaceful beauty gave way to a howling wind. I'd pitched the tent in a hollow, seeking shelter, but the wind picked up and I lay awake planning the morning challenge of decamping and loading the bike. It was a struggle, but I managed to win the tent versus wind battle. And not long after sunrise it became just another gorgeous sunny day.

I came to love the contrasting effect between land and sky. There was usually plenty of blue above as I rode, but often with a patchwork of clouds on the move, as if each was matching my desire to always be somewhere else. By contrast, the land seemed far more docile, and invariably green but with grey or brown rocky outcrops. That contrast sometimes took my breath away and I'd just stop and stare across the steppe, feeling the timelessness of this land.

I found myself riding along a track that ended at a herder's summer camp but this time I decided to carry on following the purple line across the grass and over the hills. On previous occasions I'd turned back to find a different route but the feeling of freedom here was encouraging me to stretch my normal boundaries. This sensation was both strange and exhilarating, bringing home how different Mongolia was to everywhere else I'd been. Open sky, open land and the freedom to roam.

Encouraged to be more adventurous, I planned a longer trip to visit Khongoryn Els, a large outcrop of sand dunes in the Gobi Desert. The Gobi is a shadow desert, the world's sixth largest. It was created by the sheltering effect of the Tibetan Plateau, which blocks the rain that would otherwise have blown in on the winds from the Indian Ocean. As well as sand there is plenty of scrub. Rainfall is less than 200mm per annum and the temperatures can drop as low as -20°C or rise as high as 47°C. Despite this, the region is somehow able to support many animals, as witnessed by the herders who occupy the area.

The Khongoryn Els dunes lie at the southern edge of the desert. They are sometimes referred to as the "Singing Sands" because of the sound the shifting sand generates as the wind moves it around. The Singing Sands are up to 12 kilometres wide by 100 kilometres long. "Quite easy to find then," I thought. The track there was unsurprisingly very sandy and rough. I "mostly" managed to get through those sections, and likewise negotiate the washouts.

"Mostly"? On one occasion my skills let me down and I communed with Mongolia in a way I'd never intended. After dumping the bike, and in the process of picking it up, I managed to break the windscreen. With no chance of a repair there, I packed the pieces away, hoping to duct tape and cable tie it together later.

As I continued towards the dunes the track became increasingly difficult. I could see them in the distance, close enough for a half decent photograph but I continued to drop the bike too often to feel like tackling the remaining 10 kilometres there and back. So I re-programmed the GPS and found a track that led to a riverbed. The bed was wide and covered in small- to medium-sized rocks that made riding a struggle, but the quirky thing was that there was absolutely no vegetation to be seen. It was as if something had scoured away all signs of life.

As I rode farther, the riverbed took a sharp turn but the compass pointed straight ahead. Following the purple line, I rode up and over the bank and across the grassland, eventually finding a track heading in the desired direction. But I was still in the desert leading to more fun and challenges. The route eventually petered out, having narrowed to single-track, which also faded away. There were more dunes to negotiate and as I tried to ride up one of them, the bike bogged down in the sand and I could smell the clutch getting hot. This was not good but escape was easy in the end. Removing the luggage, I dragged the bike out of the hole, then took a good run at the dune. This time, my faithful little Suzuki, aided by some desperate foot-paddling on the part of its rider, made it to the top. From there I could see in the distance the beginnings of a wider track, heading through more sand.

Perhaps it was the amount of time I was spending on my own, wrapped by this incredible landscape, but sometimes the land seemed to speak to me. Outcrops of rock occurred all over these otherwise featureless steppes, yet one day as I rode through the hills I saw an outcrop which demanded to be photographed. It's hard to pin down why they called out to me. I stopped and took a few snaps, and then as I pulled away, my clutch cable broke. Any sensible biker will carry spare cables and will usually have the spare clutch cable, being the most likely to break, taped in place alongside the original; it makes life easy. All I needed was a 12mm spanner out of my tool kit, but the kit was no longer there!

The tools had been inside a plastic tube mounted low on the bike's frame. The brackets had broken off and the tube was now missing. But

I was able to change the cable using my Swiss Army knife pliers. As I worked, I recalled having heard a very loud *crack* as a larger than usual stone was kicked up by the front wheel. Thankfully that hadn't been far back, and retracing the route I managed to recover the tool tube.

I saluted the outcrop as I rode past it. I couldn't help but feel that if the rocks hadn't called out to be photographed, it could have been many kilometres farther on before the cable broke. By then I might not have been able to retrace the path to the missing tools. I was very grateful to that pile of rock, or perhaps it had actually been my Guardian Angel at work.

My Guardian Angel looked after me on other days too. Once I'd stopped at the top of a hill for a drink, a snack and to enjoy the views. As soon as I pulled up at my destination 60 kilometres later, I realised that I no longer had my backpack. I'd taken it off where I'd stopped, and then left without it! 60 tense kilometres back, with the amazing luck of finding exactly the tracks I'd ridden, I found it sitting where I'd left it. My all-important journal was inside; losing it would have been a disaster.

Mongolia is a Buddhist country that was under the Stalin regime for many years. As a result, most of the temples and monasteries were demolished as part of his attempt to eradicate religion. It had been outside one of the few remaining, the Erdene Zuu Monastery in the town of Khakhorin, where I realised the backpack was missing. This temple was largely intact because Stalin, in an effort to convince the world he wasn't so evil, retained some religious buildings. Although the large temples in the compound were gone, the smaller remained and were worth seeing.

In town I arranged to stay at the Family Ger Camp. Aimed at tourists, the camp had a modern ablutions block, but I stayed in one of the traditional gers. There I met Theo, a young Frenchman and he joined me as pillion to visit the monastery and the site of Karakorum, the ancient Mongolian capital. No buildings remain, just an empty site with a diagram showing where this centre of power and culture once was. A nearby museum displayed a scale model representing how the city may have looked. A surprise was to see all the churches, mosques, Buddhist temples and other religious buildings. Chinggis (Genghis) Khan ran his empire as a meritocracy that demonstrated his civilized side by including all the religions within it. Another display traced the Khan Dynasty and the massive amount of land their empire had conquered. It was his grandson, Kublai Khan, who expanded the empire to its greatest extent. At its peak it was the largest contiguous empire in the world.

Karakorum had been built on humble beginnings. By the end of the Jin Dynasty in 1235, it was little more than a town of gers. A wall was eventually constructed around it allowing it to become, over the decades, a place of international politics and fabulous building structures. At less than four square kilometres, it wasn't a large city, but it sat on the east/west route of the Silk Road, which made it one of the Mongolian empire's most important trading cities. It survived until its destruction in 1388 during the Chinese Ming Dynasty. A curious fact is the nearby Erdene Zuu Monastery was built from stone salvaged from the city's ruins.

The family who owned the ger camp were constructing a swimming pool and sports facilities for their visitors. Clearly they were modern Mongolians, but when it snowed, the water supply froze—so much for modernity! We ate in the family ger and none of the food was all that challenging. But a challenge did come from trying to breathe while sleeping in our ger. There was a small wood stove but, because the lid fit so poorly, much of the smoke seeped into the ger rather than escaping through the chimney.

At camp I also met Andy an American guy and the three of us made a day trip to see the nearby Tovhkon Monastery. We hired a 4WD with driver and enjoyed the road as it wound around wide rivers and lakes and through valleys and hills. For me, not having to concentrate on navigating or determining what the road was going to demand of me next, was a refreshing change.

We walked up to the monastery through a woodland, the first I'd seen since arriving in Mongolia. The buildings weren't spectacular but the view from the hilltop certainly was. Low hills were scattered across the horizon and were covered in trees displaying their autumn colours. A rare pleasure, as I'd seen few trees on my travels across Mongolia. Fir and larch were the dominant species, providing a colourful contrast to the various shades of brown of the higher hills further away. Along with the green river valleys we'd driven through to get there, it all made a pleasant contrast to the sand, rock and grasslands I'd become so accustomed to. It felt as if Mongolia had put on her best gown to greet us.

My time in the country was drawing to a close and the route back to Russia first took me to the capital, Ulaanbaatar. My first view of the city was atop a hill a few miles away where there was no mistaking the severe pollution that hung over the capital. The dense smog was a by-product of the days of Soviet occupation and how they'd constructed the district's heating grid. From that vantage point I could see the tall red and white chimneys rising up from the coal-fired furnaces that provided heat to the many tower blocks.

Another holdover from Soviet days was the city's name. Finding the correct spelling is a challenge but the *Encyclopaedia Britannica's* is the one I'm going with—the accepted translation of the Cyrillic spelling. But the Soviets? The modern city gained its name after the Soviet-backed Communist revolution of 1924. It means "Red Hero." Before that it had several names as well as over 29 locations. Indeed, at one time it was a monastery in the form of a tent that was moved around on wheels, hauled by yaks.

As I rode into the valley there were plenty of working folk riding cheap motorbikes and driving pickups past the rows of factories and workshops. As I got closer to the city centre those kinds of transport gave way to smart 4x4s driven by elegantly dressed women. I realised I'd arrived during the school run. The children were being collected in "Chelsea Tractors" (or "Ulaan Batterers," as I christened them). The contrast to the Mongolia I'd just come from and to the poorer people on the outskirts, was immediate and unmistakable.

There's a famous overlander base on the outskirts of the city but I gave it a miss. I wanted to be right in the city itself, so I sought a hostel, finding one just off Peace Avenue, the city's main street. It was cosy, with comfortable beds and a pleasant lounge area, and was run entirely by women. I was puzzled by this at first, but the owner said it's often the way in Mongolia. She told me that men aren't really interested in business. They'd rather find a labouring job, just to get some money so they can drink and have fun. I know that isn't true of all men, especially the herders, but I'd definitely gained the impression that the people like their vodka.

While there, I visited Ulaanbaatar's various places of interest, including the very large and famous Gandantegchinlen Buddhist Monastery. The name translates to "The Great Place of Complete Joy." It was established more than 200 years ago and managed to survive the Stalinist destruction of religious places. Its temples are renowned for their grand designs.

In contrast, I also visited the State Department Store, another Soviet holdover. There I bought a few items and, as happens in Russia, the system for payment was complex. It involved taking my items to an assistant, who wrote out a chit, taking that to the cash desk to pay, then taking the receipt back to the assistant who wrapped the goods and gave them to me. I suppose it's a method of employing the maximum possible number of people, if nothing else.

The most spectacular sight I saw in Ulaanbaatar was the memorial to Chinggis built near the city. "Massive" just doesn't do it justice. The statue is of him on a horse, gazing towards his birthplace. The site is alongside the Tuul River at Tsonjin Boldog, 54 kilometres from the city. Legend has it that he found a golden whip there. The memorial is 40 metres high and made from 250 tons of stainless steel. It sits atop a museum building, which itself is 10 metres high. The statue gleams and glistens in the sun. It was absolutely stunning, especially when riding over the hill and seeing it for the first time.

Inside the statue was a lift, followed by a passageway through the horse's chest and neck and onto a viewing platform. Looking back towards the statue I was overpowered by the enormous head of Chinggis. In the opposite direction was a spectacular view across the countryside towards another tourist complex dedicated to Chinggis' mother. Her statue faced him, ostensibly welcoming him home. Not all of the buildings were finished but I marked that up as a good excuse to return one day to see the finished job.

The contrast between city life and the herders' nomadic ways was brought home to me even more while sitting in the department store having a coffee. There was a group of teenagers nearby, chattering away and playing with their smartphones. Their facial features looked much finer than their country cousins, paler too. As they laughed and joked I couldn't help but wonder what that young man I'd seen on the back of a horse, wearing his deel and helping his family with herding duties, would have found in common with these smartly dressed and sophisticated city kids.

Perhaps the confluence of these two groups lies in the post-Communist awakening. Tourism brings the modern world to everyone but doesn't seem to have spoiled this country and its people. Long may it stay that way.

It was time to head back to Russia. The road was smooth asphalt, probably Chinese built. The Chinese might not know much about democracy, but it seems they know how to build highways. Perhaps it was fitting to ride out of a country that is still very much attached to its historic ways of living on such a modern road.

It's not possible to travel Mongolia without feeling the spirit of the land. This spirit wraps itself around you when you're out there, alone with the grass and the sky, riding where the mood takes you. You are constantly reminded of the connections the people have with the land that sustains them. I found it impossible to ignore the spirituality within the connections I myself made with this unique country. I fell in love with Mongolia.

About the author:

Geoff Keys is based in the UK. He is retired from the *Automobile Association* where he worked for over 31 years, always involved in the delivery of breakdown services to members. An experience that helped

him to hone the valuable ability of dealing with any situation life threw at him, particularly on the road.

He was inspired to travel by his love of motorcycles and his innate wanderlust, fed by books by other travellers, especially motorcycle travellers. But his biggest influence came from a friend who had left the army in 1990, bought a Honda 650cc Trail Bike, and rode to Australia to visit his brother. It was the adventures he described that sealed the decision.

He has visited 30 countries so far, having ridden across Europe, Russia, Central Asia, Japan, Oceania and Southeast Asia, a journey that continues as he is currently in India.

Geoff writes a blog, telling the stories of where he has been and what he has found, with a focus on the people met along the way.

When will this journey end? Nobody knows.

Blog: www.motopangaea.com
YouTube: Geoff Keys
Facebook: Geoff Keys
Twitter: @KeysGeoff

The Road in the Sky

by Michnus Olivier with Elsebie Olivier

"All you touch and all you see, is all your life will ever be."

—Pink Floyd (Dark Side of the Moon)

After more than a decade exploring the blue marble we call home, this one accidental discovery, an old dirt road in the sky, led us to an experience that truly hammered home what motorcycle adventure is all about. The essence of why we sacrificed so much to see the world, to experience the beauty of this globe and its cultures, and our decision to explore it on two wheels. This is the story of reaching that road, and of following instincts.

In the planning stage for our South American peregrination, the more famous countries regularly popped up as those to explore at length. Peru, Chile and Colombia are three of the better-known destinations with their unadulterated landscapes, fascinating cultures and the sheer fun to be had.

Bolivia seems to be one of the last to be mentioned, almost as if for some it's a pass-through country simply to add another passport stamp to one's collection. We heard and read stories of the Salar de Uyuni, the biggest salt lake in the world, the expensive fuel prices foreign vehicles have to pay, and then the dash through the Lagunas route to Chile or Peru. We heard brief stories of a stopover in La Paz, but never much more.

That left us curious, and later we discovered just what a unique city La Paz is. At 3,600m above sea level, La Paz nestles between sandy, rocky, multi-coloured mountain cliffs. At that altitude the city is the highest capital in the world. It's home to a cable car system, which is the world's longest and highest; the ride is famous for the intense stomach-turning views over the steep-sided city. Even the cemetery is fascinating, like a one-of-a-kind outdoor art gallery. We heard little more than simple descriptions of the steep, cobbled streets and almost nothing of the cholita ladies and their history. These women, with their high bowler hats and brightly coloured polleras, or skirts, puffed out by layers of petticoats, have a quite unique look and are a flamboyant part of street life. They have a dark past, though.

Many were Indian women who migrated from rural parts of the country. They worked as maids and street vendors and as such were considered "unsavory." For a long period of the city's history these women were banned from the more public areas, areas where the wealthy might wish to wander. Now, cholas—or cholitas—are very much a visible force. All, it's said, are proud to be cholitas and some have gained such wealth that they have bodyguards to protect them and their proudly displayed jewellery. All of which contributes to make this city a marvel, but we heard little of this beforehand.

In fact, during our five years of crisscrossing South America, very few overlanders spoke of Bolivia with anything remotely like a burning passion or a sparkle in their eyes. In part that's why it took us such a long time to make our way to the country. There were just too many other more famous places and "must-sees" to explore first; we prefer to travel gently, too.

Our own modus operandi for travel is to go slowly, to see and smell what is next to the road, rather than chasing borders. We'd long before decided that if we end up seeing only a part of the world, that will be okay. At least the countries and regions we will have explored, will have been done with vigour, along with more meaningful, deeper understandings thereof. The single most alluring objective is to snatch every opportunity that hints of something new and interesting. We love exploring with a see-where-it-leads-us-to attitude. Overlanding on motorcycles provides the perfect opportunity to travel this way.

Often those spontaneous, opportunistic moments turn out to be the stuff of personal legends and evocation. On countless occasions we've taken unconventional routes and ended up with epic experiences. These moments are the mental pension for old age. When memories of normal life fade away, we have no doubt these colourful stories will remain vivid.

Lady Mary Montgomerie Currie penned in a poem, "All things come to those who wait." This came true for us in Bolivia. Not that it was planned; pure dumb luck played the biggest role. The day we entered Bolivia from Paraguay on the southeastern border would have tied knots in many superstitious hearts but, luckily, ours are not. The crossing started well but didn't continue that way. Stamping out of Paraguay was such a quick dash that we started to think the border was going to be a breeze. We'd tempted fate. But as it turned out, trying to get into Bolivia was like running into a brick wall.

It's a small border post where we suspected that little happens for much of the year. The building is farm-like, with a zinc roof that includes an under-roof parking area for both the Paraguay and Bolivian Customs officers. Dogs were the only creatures to greet us, lazily lifting their heads and not even bothering to get out of the way on the road. Tumbleweeds literally blew through the parking lot; some hitting the dogs on their way out of Bolivia.

We were the only travellers at the border post. The Customs lady decided there were problems with the visas issued to us in the city of Santiago just a few months before. She was not impressed by the work of the Bolivian embassy workers in Chile. This was now, somehow, our fault. We'd begun to wonder if she thought we'd faked the visas, but decided we'd better not comment.

The atmosphere grew more tense and, as it did, we became even more concerned. Eventually, after an hour of abrupt, meaningless questions and explanations, she slapped our stamped passports on the table and turned around as if she simply couldn't be bothered with us anymore. She continued ignoring us, and started scrolling away on her mobile phone. But we were stamped in, that was all that mattered. Trying not to disturb anything or anyone we eased out of the office and headed back to our bikes.

During the time she'd been questioning us, thundering black clouds had formed, and cold air had rolled over the savanna and into the surrounding thorn tree forests. As we started out along the dirt road, the mother of all thunderstorms dumped a sea of water onto the hot, humid landscape. The road turned into a challenging rocky, muddy river; the going was very slow. By late afternoon, with the rain still hammering down, we rode into the small town of Villamontes. The day had been just a taste of things to come.

It didn't take long to find out just how unpredictable and challenging Bolivia would be to ride, especially in the rainy season. Though a significant number of roads had been upgraded over the last 10 to 15 years, there were many that hadn't been touched. Most of Bolivia is rural, with either mountainous or Amazonian-type terrain, and there's little infrastructure. The roads that exist are predominantly a challenging and frequently precarious mix of dirt, rock and gravel. People throw the term "death roads" around quite liberally but, in Bolivia in most instances, those words actually mean the horror they're supposed to portray.

Do a Google search for "dangerous roads" and the Yungas Road, just outside La Paz, will feature prominently. It's described as being the most dangerous in Bolivia, and one of the worst in the world. The reality is that the Yungas Road is now a tourist trail with steep drops and beautiful views but isn't used by regular traffic anymore. There are many lesser-known roads currently in use that are far worse and still being braved daily by Bolivians.

The following morning, no more than 10 kilometres out of the town on the road to Tarija, we had our first taste of Bolivian rural road hazards. The road hugged the river with some terrifying drop-offs, and some sections had been carved out of the rock, creating natural overhangs. When we got to the first landslide, we found locals with old, oily, knackered, dirt-covered, earthmoving machines frantically working to try and clear a landslide that had destroyed parts of the road. Much of that day was spent loitering and kicking stones around while watching men clear the rocky debris. Elsebie also kept busy by scrolling her phone's offline maps looking for routes to the Salar de Uyuni. We had a couple of options of how to try and see everything we wanted to in Bolivia, and timing was crucial thanks to the three month visa allowance. The challenge was to plot a route in such a way that we could traverse as much as possible within the allotted time.

Late that afternoon we got going again. The road workers partially opened the way with a tiny space for motorcycles to pass between a stuck truck and the vertical drop to the river 400m below. No other traffic would be using that route for at least a few more days.

The receptionist at the hotel in Tarija asked if we were there for the day of "Compadres." We had no idea what she was talking about and looked at each other with confused expressions, yet it sounded like a party or celebration of some kind, for which we'll always have time. This is, after all, a big part of the reason we spend our lives roaming the world. You can learn much about a country from its celebrations.

"Compadres" and "comadres" are two pre-Carnival celebration days dedicated to something truly special: friendship. The traditional big event of compadre and comadre takes place in Tarija and involves the giving of special gifts to close friends and family. We learned that it also included the enjoying of regional food, drinking, colourful decorations, parades, singing, and dancing. It's celebrated throughout Bolivia, but it's a really big thing in Tarija. How fitting that with pure luck we'd arrived in the city a few days before the spectacle took off.

The words "compadre" (male) and "comadre" (female) are used by parents in a respectful way to distinguish the godparents of their children. Even those without children usually use these terms to refer to someone whose friendship they expect to keep for a lifetime. When a person officially becomes the compadre or comadre of someone, it's a must to give a gift called a "canasta."

These gifts, traditionally, are cane baskets of seasonal fruits, vegetables, local bakery goodies, and regional drinks. The baskets are decorated with balloons, flags, serpentine, and flowers. But the main ingredient of the canasta is a large, traditional, incredibly sweet bread known as "torta," intended to sweeten the life of the recipient. Now, we all die of something, and if it's by a sugar bread gift from a friend that's also good, I guess. Finally, to finish off the basket, there's a bit of dirty-minded fun. An essential gift in the canastas is a pumpkin for men, and for women a big fresh cucumber!

The first day of celebration on the calendar is for compadres. That's on the Thursday a week before Carnival. That day, the men meet in the main square of the city or in a place they call "Campo de Los Compadres." Later, after copious amounts of alcohol and fun, they join their closest friends to prepare a barbecue, or a traditional dish called "chancho en cruz" ("pig on a cross"). This is a full-size pig or sheep barbecued around an open fire on a cross-like grid.

Local Singani is a must-have and is consumed throughout the weeks of celebration. Singani is a type of brandy or grappa. It's unique to Bolivia and ranges from a soft, easy, drinking brandy to an extraordinarily strong homemade moonshine. The party truly kicks off the moment a guitar and a legüero bass drum can be heard. Compadres love singing, and like pro performers they pull out their entire repertoire of songs. The action does not stop until sunrise. The comadres is a week later. With the men partying like that, they need a week to recover.

The following Thursday (the beginning of Carnival week), comadres is celebrated with even more gusto, with the women out to show the men how to properly party. That day the central market of Tarija is not only flooded with *canastas*, but also the flowers that will decorate women's hair. Bright orange Rosa Pascua and Comadre are the local flowers used in this festivity. Known locally as the "Easter Rose," tradition has it that the carnation-like Rosa Pascua originated in this area of Bolivia.

Nearly 10,000 lavishly and colourfully dressed comadres take over the city, singing and dancing and parading in the streets. Dressed up with typical cholita chapaca costumes, their bright vibrant colours, with frills and elaborate patterns, sometimes makes the women look like human-sized partying flowers. It's a weekend of massive barbeques, with bands playing throughout the day and spontaneous dancing, a 24-hour, non-stop wonderfully exuberant celebration.

Leaving the inhabitants to party on, Tarija disappeared in our rear view mirrors. Our next stop on our way to the salt lakes and the Lagunas route was the small town of Tupiza. The dirt road from Tarija to Tupiza was the stuff of dreams. This is why we ride adventure bikes, we can reach and explore places where tourist buses never venture, and we have the freedom to pause.

Riding over the mountains at more than 4,200m altitude, we were travelling an endless dirt road pass with inconceivably mesmerising views towards the mountains in the far distance. From the top we could see the road snake up the side of the mountain with multiple hairpin turns. Stopping for a quick photo and a sip of water, we ended up spending nearly an hour sitting in a roadside field letting our eyes float over the views, listening to the sound of the wind, and watching vultures drifting in the sky above that magical spot.

The festivities were still in full swing for comadres as we rode into Tupiza. The roads were packed with local families waiting for the parade to kick off the afternoon's partying. Booking into a small hostel on the outskirts of town, the owner shoved a room key into my hand and told us not to waste time booking in. "You can come and do that later," he said with a big smile. We dropped our gear in the room and headed to the main square to spend the rest of the afternoon and evening drinking in the culture. The mood was loud, unadulterated party fun, with vendors walking around with homemade carts selling all kinds of food and drinks. Kids' party foam spray cans were in 24-packs stacked ceiling high outside the shops. It was clear the Tupizians were not joking around! It seemed that Bolivians took their partying seriously.

The kids were having a blast spraying anyone moving with jets of foam. Water balloon fights, with adults as collateral damage, were just part of the fun; mothers reprimanded their children with smiles on their faces. The cheerful vibe was intoxicating, the entire town having fun.

We walked, taking photos of the children and adults having the time of their lives. We were wet, and my camera was wet too, as they doused us with water and foam spray, perhaps because we were foreigners and they wanted to make us a part of the fun. It was incredible to observe that anyone can be this sociable. I am not sure that this kind of partying, where total strangers and children were having this level of fun, could happen in many First World countries without someone getting upset over some consideration or another.

The parade, as usual with timing in South America, started later than planned. And by the time the parade was in full swing most of the participants were in good spirits. Singani, and whatever else got mixed in, had a kick. Every group had their own band, while others made use of pickups with mega-blaster speakers and generator-powered rigs to blast music to the world. Kids sprayed parade participants with foam and bombarded them with water balloons. Often, when I took up position in the middle of the street to take photos, the entire parade, full of laughter, would come to a standstill to pose. The homemade moonshine, that could take the hairs off a donkey, was shared with others lining the roadsides in soft drink plastic bottles. Basically, anything with alcohol got mixed into bottles, and you couldn't refuse. Just take a sip, smile, say, "¡Gracias!"

There were no apparent rules or regulations and no police to keep people behind lines and out of the way of the parade. Everyone did whatever tickled their fancy and it was fine. That saying, "When in Rome…" so we partied hard, too!

Our plan was to leave on Monday, aiming to reach the Lagunas area on the altiplano close to the Chilean border. This was right across the country. We were starting at the bottom just inside the border of Bolivia above Argentina and would head west across the country towards the border of Chile and the most southerly point of Bolivia. That would be our turning point to head north to Uyuni and the salt lakes.

Reserva Nacional de Fauna Andina Eduardo is tucked away in the southwestern corner of Bolivia and is the park that borders Chile and Argentina. Created in 1973, it's home to vicuñas, James's flamingos and the yareta plant, all of which are globally threatened species. That entire area is usually referred to by overlanders as the "Lagunas Route," and most mutter discouragingly about it.

This is an inhospitable area at 4,000–5,000m in altitude. The temperatures are extreme. There are no trees, just open plains with vicuñas roaming around, and pink flamingos that feed off the shallow, vividly pink-coloured lakes. There's nothing else other than a few villages here and there outside the park, and that's about it. We even wondered if we should go there at all; the comments from other overlanders sounded so extremely negative.

The photos we'd seen hadn't helped, either. They'd shown a cold desert with a few lakes and cartoon-like rock formations, and shitty places to lodge. After speaking to a few adventure motorcycle riders we knew personally, who had been there and whose opinions we trusted, we decided to go and see the area for ourselves. We needed to make up our own minds.

In fact, we surprised ourselves by paying attention to the naysayers. Historically we adore exploring these kinds of harsh, remote places. We like miles of open spaces in out-of-the-way areas where few go, where nature can be both at its best and its hardest. There can be huge rewards from seeing such parts of this crazy world, places where it's still as it was a millennium ago.

Often, venturing into areas like these is not the easiest thing to do, but we've frequently found that doing so is incredibly rewarding. We decided on a complete loop of the area, riding sections lost to many by their remoteness and reputation. Hopefully our decision would gift us with spectacular views and the kind of fun, challenging off-road riding we both love.

Dreams and plans don't always work though, do they! Every afternoon, from our hostel's roof, we could see the rain dumping an ocean in the mountains. This then turned normal rivers into raging torrents. Eating breakfast one day, the hostel owner asked what our plans were. We said we'd seen on Google Earth a track that led straight from Tupiza to the lagunas area, and that we were considering taking it.

His eyebrows lifted while sipping his coffee. "This is not a good idea," he said. "The rain will make that route near impossible. Furthermore, that road is not a well-used route. It's in very bad condition and not maintained. The only vehicles going that way are a few tour operators in the dry season and they take four to five days to get to the park. Some locals with 4x4s occasionally use it to take food and supplies to the few villages, but that's it. You will have to make a plan for fuel as there is none, and even the big fuel tanks you have on your motorcycles will not be enough." He went on to say, "It's nearly a 1,000-kilometre loop to get to the lagunas area, and then out to Uyuni. One or two places sometimes sell fuel from cans, but you can't depend on that."

We listened carefully but couldn't help wondering if there was another way to get to the Reserve. We used Open Source Streetmaps to look for tracks, and Google Maps in satellite mode to slowly drag the route we'd picked as a maybe. Eventually, after a few hours of staring at the map set, we were able to make our own track through the area, which allowed us to feel more optimistic.

Meanwhile our kind hostel owner had asked a local tour operator from Tupiza if they'd be able to take fuel for us to two villages along the route. The company, a few days later, would be escorting tourists heading for Uyuni. We hoped that 50 litres at each point would be enough. In addition, we would still have to carry extra fuel in Coke and water bottles if we were to cover the distance to the fuel drop spots. The riding would be between 4,000–5,000m altitude, and the DR650 Suzukis consumed more fuel at that height.

We've never carried specialised fuel containers on our trips. They eventually leak regardless, cost a fortune and are carried all the time whether they're needed or not. Our hack is to use 2–3-liter Coke or water bottles, filling our tanks from them as we go. We'd throw them away later. They cost nothing and in the last 15 years we've never had issues.

The challenges didn't stop. The next was to decide when to leave; every afternoon it poured rain and our hostel owner said, "Just wait until tomorrow morning, we will see."

Eventually, three days later, having sat on the roof of the hostel watching rain clouds move over the area where we intended to ride, we decided to throw caution to wind and give it a go. What's the worst that could happen? If we came to a flood, we could turn back; we'd have enough fuel for that.

Some packs of cookies, four litres of water and a few extra cans of Spam, and the next morning we were ready to go. We were loaded to the max with 10 litres of additional fuel each and could carry no more. Tupiza lies between two mountain ranges at 2,850m. Just 30 kilometres outside of the town we were already riding at an altitude of over 4,000m. The dirt road started just outside of town with an insanely beautiful, multi-hairpin mountain pass. This area in southern Bolivia and northern Argentina is home to massive, beautiful, crimson, pink, red and orange rock walls which are sculptured into hoodoos that tower into the air like nature's own La Sagrada Familia. These hoodoos are spire-shaped rock formations, carved from years of wind and water flowing over and sculpting the soft sandy rock.

The day gifted us with the perfect temperature for riding. Clear skies above, with the dirt road hard-packed from the rain... but that surface didn't last long. Due to so few cars navigating this route, the track gets washed away and the surface becomes saturated with water, making it a snotty, muddy ride. We were grateful that the really boggy stuff was only in sections. Otherwise we were able to keep a good pace; we hoped to cover around 300 kilometres that day. Well, that was the plan. This roughest of roads carried on through a breathtaking, colour-saturated, almost Martian-like landscape. Snowcapped stratovolcanoes and mountain peaks soared in the distance. Between us and them were rolling hills covered in a short grassy carpet. At this high altitude, the clean, crisp, cold air made for vivid, sharp images wherever we pointed our eyes.

Our pace was good, but slow enough to be kind to the bikes, and if one of us fell it wouldn't be a show stopper. It was tiring riding, though. Non-stop on the pegs all the time, the track simply wasn't in a good enough condition to sit and ride. Besides, it was kinder to the bikes not to have our arses on the seats. The first of several river crossings was also the biggest, and for a moment while riding next to it looking for a place to cross, it seemed we'd have to turn back.

The track's normal course to the muddy brown, near 200m-wide waters, disappeared into a deep quagmire. It was the kind of mud that sucks vehicles in, and from there they just die slow deaths. Bear in mind that, happily, we were at least half acclimated to riding at altitude, but it was still extremely hard work. And trying to drag the bikes out of mud at over 4,500m would be absolutely exhausting. Lower down the river we found another track that was an old crossing that looked less muddy. Through our headsets we debated whether to give it a go; all sorts of shit could go wrong. We might get one bike through, but not the other, or get stuck in such a way that we wouldn't be able to get a bike out at all. Or drown one and not be able to recover it.

The only thing to do was get off the bikes and start walking into the river where it seemed to be the shallowest. My boots sank into the mud, but underneath it felt firm enough that with a handful of throttle we could possibly make it.

Back on the bike I took a run up and nailed it down the short, slippery bank into the river. The engine immediately complained about the drag from the water and the soft mud on the river bed, and whacking open the throttle did little. At that altitude an old carburetted DR650 breathed like an asthmatic mouse through a tiny straw. Luckily, halfway across, the mud firmed up with rocks and pebbles and I made it to the other side.

Elsebie took the path next to mine, not wanting to use my disturbed track. Unfortunately, she went straight into a patch of deep, sticky mud. In an instant her bike bogged to its axles.

Fuck! This was not good; we couldn't even move it from side to side. We unpacked the bike, and then dug into the soft mud with our hands. An hour later, heaving with shortness of breath, Elsebie climbed back on and, opening the throttle wide, spraying a curtain of mud behind her, she pulled free and ploughed across the river.

We were shattered and couldn't help wondering if the next river would be worse, and if it was, would we have to cross this once again coming back? You never know whether you ride yourself deeper into trouble or have some luck and things will turn out okay.

Our struggles with the river crossing and the challenging track soon faded as we rode past a mirror-surfaced pink and turquoise lake with a volcano as its background. At this altitude, the clouds seemed to be a low hanging carpet reflecting off the lake's surface. I am at a loss for words to describe the magic this sort of scene plays on the mind. It gave me the feeling that my brain didn't know which way was up.

The road got dryer as we rode onto the altiplano. Up on this tableland the roads were rutted, sandy tracks and veined with deep corrugations. Shock absorbers must be allowed to cool down often when the corrugations are that extreme. This is the kind of road that will kill a shock in no time. But it turned out that the cooling-down sessions were a bonus. They allowed us to stop often and enjoy a silence where only the breeze spoke to us. Every time we got off the bikes and sat taking in the surroundings, we had the sensation we were in the middle of a surreal experience. It felt as though our senses were fully alive as we looked closely at the ground for small flowers, took in the smells, and felt the breeze against our skin. We had the feeling that all the impressions were being stored in our minds, each an important part of the bigger memory.

Nearly nine hours later we rode into the wind-blasted and desolate village of Quetena Chico. There were a few hostels with dorm rooms and shared showers, and our first fuel drop was with a local family here. The owner of the hostel we chose was a friendly, short, stocky man and he was quick to bring us coffee as we dropped our tired bones down at one of the canteen's tables. He looked at us with disbelief. "You came from Tupiza today?"

"Yes," I said. "Why, is there something wrong?"

Over the last few days, they'd had severe rainstorms to the north. The huge quantity of water was coming down, destroying roads and cutting off most of the smaller villages.

"How did you manage the road?" he asked.

"It was bloody hard work," I replied with a big grin.

He just shook his head, smiled and said he was going to find the person we needed to collect our fuel from.

Not knowing what was in store the next day, we got up just before sunrise to pack. The hostel owner had showed us a route around the back of several volcanos where we could find more lakes with flamingos. He warned us that the road would be brutal and severely corrugated. Hopefully, the scenery would make up for it.

He added, "By the way, no one uses this route so you'll need to take real care and please, go slowly."

An hour later, fuelled from the dirty cans that had been dropped for us, we turned onto his track.

We rode into a world of incredible, vividly coloured lakes and volcanos with snowcapped hoodies; each more spectacular than the last. But it was bitterly cold, and breathing the thin air was difficult, as the cold burned our nostrils. The track took us past volcanos and lakes with names like Laguna Hedionda, and the Uturuncu volcano, which peaks at 6,000m. We then rode into the Desierto Salvador Dalí. This red sand, surreal, stark, and barren desert valley has a landscape that resembles several surrealist paintings by Salvador Dalí. Those familiar with the Spanish painter's work would be flabbergasted by the similarities. We felt as if suddenly we'd ridden onto one of Dalí's canvases—views to be remembered for a lifetime.

Incredibly, they found silver in this region. Backdropped by the beautiful snowcapped Cerro Lipez Mountain, Pueblo Fantasma, an abandoned mining town, is now very much a ghost town; mining was stopped in 1960. At 4,700m one can only imagine the determination and hardship endured to live here and make a living. There is literally nothing around except the views; winters must have been extreme.

Our turning point was Termas de Polques, a hot spring at Laguna Salada on the route between Chile and Salar de Uyuni. At that point we were really looking forward to soaking our cold, shaken-to-hell backbones in the hot spring that had a reputably unique and unforgettable view. There were only two places to stay. One was an overpriced ramshackle building asking Manhattan hotel prices, and the other a hostel. The hostel was open in spite of it being low season and, as it was midweek, we were able to secure an entire dorm room for ourselves.

No time was wasted before grabbing a few beers and heading to the hot spring. Lady Luck allowed us a good two hours soaking, with a lonely juvenile flamingo filtering food just a few metres away. This hot spring is around 29°C and that was luxury compared to an outside temperature below 0°C. Early that evening we briefly had a spectacular view of a star-filled sky from the steaming spring. I was hoping to get some night-time long-exposure photos. As there's no light pollution, you can see the Milky Way in all its grandeur, but unfortunately that came to nothing. It started to rain.

The next day's ride was going to be another long stretch, but getting out of bed pre-sunrise in a bitterly cold room? It took us some time to dress and pack our gear. I peeked through the dirty, foggy window as it started to get a little lighter outside. I could not believe my eyes! The view in the distance hit me. I hurriedly finished dressing and, grabbing my camera and tripod, jogged down to the thick, muddy, salty mix that formed the edge of the lake.

The previous night, the rain had frozen on the mountain behind the lake. The entire mountain was covered with a mind-meltingly beautiful white blanket. That morning was the calm after the storm. No wind, no sounds, just an eerie silence. Adding the dimmed shades of orange and yellow from the sun as it started its rise to the pink colours of the lake made for a soft, dreamy, pastel-coloured painting. Every second, as the sky turned lighter with the slowly rising sun, the scene changed with a new set of colours. It was truly indescribable; I am struggling to do the scene justice with even these words. I could only try and take photos of the world of pastels that was unfolding before me, but I doubted that even my most carefully taken photos could portray the reality of the scene.

That morning, standing outside taking in the day that was starting to unfold, reiterated the reason Elsebie and I headed out to explore and experience the world. We are hungry and eager to see incredible landscapes, to meet people, to become part of social interactions with foreign cultures, and to widen our perspectives.

The weeks we took to ride this section of our journey were extraordinary. Many times we've found good luck in our years of travel, yet that luck was enhanced dramatically when we opened ourselves to opportunities and were willing to grab them enthusiastically with both hands. Sometimes it's good to follow the voices of one's gut feelings. For us, Bolivia was the best kept secret, and gave us a lifetime's worth of rich experiences.

About the authors:

Michnus Olivier is a GenX'er—born and bred on the southern tip of the beautiful African continent. These days he and his much better half **Elsebie** are global citizens, being semi-permanent, motorcycle-round-the-world adventurers.

Their first passion for everything travelling was kick-started in the early '90s during a remote, off-the-grid tour of southern Africa in an old *Toyota* 4x4 pickup.

After that enlightenment, they abandoned their corporate careers and made the big move away from the comfort groove by becoming entrepreneurs and shrewd property investors. This enabled financial freedom and eventually elevated them to a position where it became possible to travel on a more permanent basis.

With a new motorcycle luggage brand, *TurkanaGear,* in production and partners to help, they are able to see more of the world on motorcycles.

Sometimes, known not to follow or believe his own advice, Michnus loves to share stories and inspiration to anyone with an open mind and an interest in hearing about his views on the real world.

Website: pikipikioverland.com | turkanagear.com
Facebook: PikiPikiOverland
Instagram: @pikipiki_overland_blog
Instagram: @pikipiki_overland_photography
Please check the *Turkana Gear* website for purchase options.

When Life is Full of Firsts

by Sam Manicom with Birgit Schünemann

"Travel. It's all about collecting moments."

—Anon

The mass of people moved slowly, quietly and sleepily down the steel staircases between the different levels and onto the vehicle decks. There, the bunched-up passengers divided and made their way between the close-parked ranks of cars, vans and campers, dodging mirrors as they went.

Hangovers showed on the faces of some passengers; total concentration on others, but in the air was a tangible sense of anticipation. Car doors were opened and, moments later, clunked shut, with their loads of luggage, drivers and passengers in position and ready to go. They sat staring from their glazed boxes at the static, fluorescent-lit world that surround them.

Along the side walls, the thirty or so motorcyclists moved speedily. Their first task was undoing the large orange ratchet straps that tethered their bikes safely to D-shaped steel loops protruding from the decking.

They then milled around in the growing warmth, checking luggage straps, slotting keys into ignitions, pulling on gloves and helmets, and trading grins in the fine sense of camaraderie. As I turned my bike's fuel taps to the on position, she gave off her usual scent of petrol.

The sound of the ship's engines increased and the green-painted metal plates beneath us throbbed and shuddered as the ferry slowed. As the ship pulled to a halt, drivers took it as the signal to start their engines. With the huge bow doors still closed, the air of anticipation was joined by the rich, greasy scent of diesel and petrol fumes. We'd been here before so I knew that the red and white stripy lighthouse on the sea front would be keeping watch over us.

It was early May, and just after dawn we were released to begin our journeys. The bow doors had eased open to reveal a sky that was a soft pale grey, but to the west was a hint of darker blue-grey warning. Thankfully we were riding east.

We decided that before hitting the road in earnest we'd treat ourselves to a coffee or two at the nearby railway station café. The Dutch know how to make great coffee. As I pulled to a wobbly halt, I was amused that even though we'd only been on board the ferry a single night, I felt a slight disconnect with the land; either it or I was swaying. I pondered the thought that I didn't have this sensation when I was riding. As I turned my bike off, my helmet filled with new sounds.

The magnetic electronic echo of a friendly-voiced woman gave warning of the next train to depart for Rotterdam. She did so in a crisp, precise way that told me she'd already had her coffee. Her voice joined the screeching of the seagulls lining the platform roof like living gargoyles, or swirling overhead watching for the unwary and their breakfast rolls.

She made her announcement, first in Dutch, then English. The Dutch speakers seemed to ignore her, yet the foot passengers who'd just disembarked lifted their heads. Their eyes swivelled towards the speakers as if doing so was going to make her instructions clearer. More sounds filled my helmet as a woman passed, her roller suitcase wheels rumbling over the cobbles and clacking over the joints between pavement slabs.

The coffee was black, steaming hot, rich and strong and, as I sipped, I pondered its ability to give the world some clear-cut lines and thought some clarity. This was a great way to start the day; a new country, motorcycles, no rain, coffee and an adventure just beginning.

We weren't using a GPS or a phone app so had pulled out our map of the Netherlands from a clear plastic wallet on Birgit's petrol tank. Spread out on the table and held in place by coffee cup saucers, we reviewed, yet again, the route to the border with Germany that we'd highlighted. Sadly it was going to be a blast along the motorways. We'd ridden in Holland enough to realise that the backroads around the many cities we needed to pass would be hectic as rush hour impatiently jolted into full swing. It was *that* time of day.

Another train departed; it was a nudge that we really ought to get a move-on. We had a six-hour ride in front of us, and wanted to make it to Birgit's parents in Germany with plenty of the day still remaining. The Dutch motorways were busy but ordered. Trucks drove too close to each other as if they were linked by invisible couplings. The road signs were clear, and corresponded nicely with the list of names marked on the pieces of paper we both had on our petrol tanks. Birgit was in front; she likes to ride there, but we work as a team. I enjoyed our riding rhythm as flat fields, stands of trees, the occasional windmill and plenty of the inevitable black and white Friesian cows flitted past at the periphery of my vision. We were moving quickly so I was fully focused and ready for whatever games the traffic might want to play with us.

By the time we were about to cross into Germany I felt as if I was flowing through the day. Libby, my motorcycle, sounded and felt as if she was enjoying the ride too. We reached the spot where the border checkpoint once stood. The land remains unused and we eased on through a space that had the feeling of time left standing still.

I laughed at myself with this thought. Perhaps I was feeling a little tired? We'd taken the night crossing to gain more riding time, but I don't think either of us had slept well. Excitement at being on the move? Anticipation of seeing Birgit's parents; it'd been a while. Or perhaps it was the buzz at the thought of riding into two countries we knew little about. I hope I never lose that sensation.

The countryside from the coast of the North Sea right through to the city of Bremen is flat. Nature doesn't recognise the historical and political lines drawn on sheets of paper. Visitors to the area around the city are often surprised to find canals, locks, windmills and as many bicycle users as they would in the Dutch countryside.

Birgit's mother and father had killed the fatted calf for us, and it felt very strange that our plan was to ride on early the next morning. We were up with the dawn again and soon riding through the tidy city suburbs. We'd decided to ignore the autobahns. Germany's network of backroads is excellent in much of the country, and it certainly is between Bremen and the Denmark border. Once in the countryside I had the slightly surreal feeling of riding through a watercolour land where there were few vibrant colours, just shades of grey, browns and greens with an occasional flash of white. I rode trying to recall the name of the artist whose work had sprung into my mind.

Stands of silver birch and dark evergreens lined the roads, as did cycle paths. Small towns have retained their historical buildings, survivors. Red brick is king but dotted at regular intervals are farms that look as if they have changed little for hundreds of years, their dark wood timber frames supporting whitewashed uneven plaster walls, and the sagging weight of weather-worn terracotta tiles. Each reflection in the small square panes of ancient window glass showed variations of a very strange world, rather like the hall of mirrors in a fun fair.

We were making good time despite a few wrong turns. I like travelling with Birgit because a wrong turn is no drama, it's an opportunity to see something unexpected. The outskirts of the smaller towns gave us a mix of traditional brick houses and purely functional structures that have apres-war written into their DNA. These stood alongside modern cubist houses with clean white lines, large, probably triple-glazed windows, and stainless steel anywhere it could be used with elegance and style. Every one of them looking as if it should have won an architectural award.

We were watching the time but not riding fast. German police don't hold speeding motorcycle riders with much respect on roads such as these. That's fine with us. Other than the occasional need to dash to meet a deadline, the reasons we ride are the freedom the bikes give us to travel where we like, at a pace that allows us to see what's happening around us. I like the opportunity a gentle pace gives for my mind to wander, too. If

I'm a typical male then I'm supposed to be rubbish at multitasking. Years of travel have at least taught me how to ride and think at the same time. It's one of the things I love about travelling on my motorcycle. The inside of my helmet is thought space.

Far to the east in the Czech Republic, the river Elbe begins its 690-mile journey to the North Sea. By the time it makes it to the city of Hamburg, it's a wide, ocean-going ship-navigable, fast flowing river. From Hamburg it splits the countryside between Lower Saxony and Schleswig-Holstein on its final run towards the sea. It's a river that's many things to many people; our interest was the small ferry that runs from the village of Wischhafen across to Glückstadt. My mind and rubbish ability with the German language couldn't help translating that into "Lucky Town." A good omen? I never turn those away.

The ferry runs every 30 minutes, but we'd been warned there could be a long wait. We didn't mind, as taking the ferry would allow us to carry on off the autobahns, and in particular the rather busy stretch around Germany's second largest city. It would also allow us to carry on meandering across the countryside on the way to a shopping date, just before the Denmark border. We were guided to the front of the queue to join four other motorcyclists and two cyclists. Heads were nodded all round but no conversations kicked off. That was fine. Sometimes it doesn't feel as if a chat can add anything to an already full and interesting day. Several large trucks bright with advertising, a couple of anonymous white caravans with exotic names, two expedition-style camper vans with grid-wire headlights, spare tyres and jerry cans, and a string of cars waited patiently in the queue, too.

Large, black-stained wooden pillars are embedded in the ground where the road meets the water's edge. These posts are home to a mechanism that raises and lowers the ferry ramp according to the level of the tide. Some time ago someone started a rubber duck tradition on the wooden cross pieces of the pillars. Perhaps as far back as 1992. Remember the container that had fallen overboard in the Pacific and had burst, sending 28,000 yellow ducks bobbing around the world? I'd read that some had even made it to European waters. Perhaps one of these ducks was well-travelled. Over the years, those taking this route had added to the ever-growing collection of yellow ducks. Birgit grinned at the sight. Her riding companion, besides me, is a yellow duck. She'd been gifted this character by a chap at one of the Horizons Unlimited meets in the UK. Cable-tied to her bike's bash bars, the yellow feller has travelled with her ever since.

I hadn't realised there'd been an air of tension as we'd waited for the ferry. But as soon as we were on board for the 20-minute crossing, smiles broke out and conversations began between strangers. Birgit and I don't have many photos of us together so I was delighted when the cyclists offered to take a shot.

The open black and white ferry gently chugged its way across the river. As a very much lower-class water citizen, every boat of size was respectfully allowed to head up or downstream without us getting in the way. The diesel throbbed smoothly beneath us and the fresh breeze was scented with a seawatery tang.

Once the ferry had docked we let everyone else get off first. The deck master looked at us as if to say, "You aren't doing what's normal for motorcyclists." Suddenly, the expression on his face changed. It was as if he'd realised that rather than have drivers on missions chasing us down the road, we preferred to ride in the peace that followed them.

After all the years of travel I can't help but look for potential wild camping spots as we ride. I automatically did this with greater seriousness as we rolled through the mid-afternoon. Wild camping in Germany is technically illegal and it's not easy to find spots to hide away in. Most of the land is fenced or edged by deep ditches, but I knew that with ingenuity and eyes wide open, a spot could usually be found where we'd trouble no one. Of course, a lot of hassle for those who aren't shy disappears by simply asking a farmer, "May I put my tent up for a night? I'll leave nothing behind me except for my tyre tracks and some flattened grass."

Not for this night though. In Denmark, foodstuffs and alcohol are expensive in comparison to Germany. I'd read of a huge discount supermarket just near the border. Danes crossed the border for their weekly shop, and the likes of us would stop to top up before heading north. We were heading for Norway, just a day's ride and a ferry crossing away. We'd been warned that Norway is one of the most expensive countries on Earth for its food, alcohol, fuel and accommodation. We treated ourselves to a special offer motel from one of the comparison sites; the nearest campsite was an hour away and we knew that we'd be camping from this point on. It might be the last chance for hot showers and clean sheets. Do I sound as if I'm trying to persuade myself the expense was justified?

The supermarket lived up to its reputation. We left our bikes firmly locked to each other, after all it is close to a border crossing and habit dies hard. Ridiculous? It was, but peace of mind is a fine thing and some habits need to stay on autopilot. To me it's like not filling up with fuel because I still have a third of a tank left, and then spending the next hundred miles wondering if I'll ever see a petrol station again.

Tins of tuna, packs of soups, sticks of salami, bags of whole wheat pasta, and a couple of bags of couscous went in the shopping trolley. Tomato paste, a couple of bulbs of garlic, a tin of beef stew that Birgit wasn't impressed at the thought of, cans of sausages, and a couple of packs of bratwurst. We were already carrying curry powder, mixed herbs, powdered milk, salt, pepper and hot sauce. The shopping list ticked off with more motorcycle travellers' long-lasting food, and was topped off with bars of chocolate, fresh brown rolls, lettuce, gherkins and slices of ham. They would do for dinner and breakfast, and as we weren't fussy, lunch, too. I couldn't help but grin at the thought of Monty Python's *Spam* song.

A mug of tea each and yes, a roll with ham, our trusty thermos full of fresh coffee and we were off. The bikes had made it through the night; we laughed at ourselves, but our bikes are old friends. Denmark is a rolling, low-lying land; the highest point is just less than 560 feet above sea level. Most of the countryside seemed to be farmed in as orderly a way as in Germany. England had once been called a "green and pleasant land". That fit here, too. With the entire day in front of us we meandered across what felt like a multi-shaded green patchwork quilt that some giant had thrown across the setting. The more I saw, the more I knew I'd have to come back to this country, with the time to devote just to it. I'd read comments from other travellers who'd described Denmark as being "as flat as its nature, uninteresting, and bland," but that's not what I was seeing. It's that old thing of horses and courses I supposed. We rode the cobbles of the older towns and villages, and I grinned at the thought we were still riding in the dry. Those clouds at the Hook of Holland had carried on west after all.

When I'd told a friend we were heading for Norway, he had five things to say: "It's a long way to Noord Cap, watch for the speed cameras and if a cop catches you speeding you may have to pay up to £1,000 on your credit card. The fuel is really expensive. Pretty place though." He'd then gone on to ponder just how big the country would be if someone took a huge rolling pin and flattened it. He'd read that this small, long and narrow country would be one of the biggest in Europe. An interesting concept.

The Fjordline ferry from Hirtshalls to Kristiansand, Norway requires booking in advance. If you miss your booking it can be a long wait for the next that can fit you aboard, even with only a motorcycle. That night, fully stocked up on fuel, we went to sleep with the phone alarms set to provide plenty of time to break camp, load, deal with the unexpected, and get to the ferry on time. It was a good job we had.

The next morning a bakery drew our attention. The scents of freshly baked bread crept in under our visors and the trouble began. The car park was gravel. Birgit parked her bike and headed inside the shop. I waited, watching my watch, and waited.... Deciding to find out what the delay was, I put my bike on its side stand and had the instant sensation that it was sinking into the gravel. I heaved it upright; as a second longer and it would have crossed the point of no return. Puzzled, I couldn't see where it had sunk in, just a shallow hollow from the broad foot on the end of the side stand. *I must have been imagining it*, I thought to myself as I attempted to put the bike back on the side stand, only to have her speedily, and actually quite gracefully, lay down on the gravel. What!? Fortunately I managed to step away, but at that moment Birgit returned. Her smile of satisfaction at the pain au chocolat hunt she'd just been on changed into an expression of, *What has he done this time?* This look rapidly morphed to a body scan check to make certain I wasn't hurt.

The two of us could lift Libby upright without unloading the tins of tuna and bottles of whisky, but there was an unhappy sight. At the point the side stand fitted to the bike there was clearly a crack in the metal under the powder coating, and this had rusted unseen. After a moment's annoyance, I couldn't help but be happy this hadn't happened on a road or in a busy car park where she might have laid over on someone's pride and expensive joy.

We'd taken the gamble of the much cheaper non-transferable ferry ticket option. That meant there was no time to get the stand replaced or welded. I'd just have to get in the habit of parking where I could lean her against something. I'd get it sorted in Norway. No worries.

Sometimes the decisions a traveller makes are quite simply wrong. In my mind was that we'd find a welder in Norway, or I'd be able to order a replacement and pick it up along the way, or we'd be able to swap a mounting off Birgit's bike. And it just so happened that she'd recently fitted a Surefoot side stand and we'd not had time to take her old side stand off. As both were BMWs, there was just a chance.

Over the next days we found that the mounting from Birgit's bike didn't fit, and that on many of the surfaces it wasn't possible to put my fully loaded bike onto the alternative centre stand on my own. We needed to eat more weight off her. To add to the niggle, there wasn't always somewhere convenient to lean her. Then we found out that BMW Norway would need three weeks, at least, to get a replacement and the price was eye watering. The two welders we talked to about it, very apologetically, quoted around £300 for the job. All they needed to do was to clean the crack to bare metal and make a one-inch weld.

I rode on with my eyes split between the views, the traffic, potential wild camping spots and leaning posts. Tucked in the back of my mind was a tug of annoyance that I'd not replaced the tubes of liquid metal repair, like J-B Weld, I usually carried in the panniers.

The bonus was that wild camping is legal and perfectly accepted in Norway, so long as it's no closer than 100 metres to anything manmade, except a road or track of course. The conditions include keeping the noise down and leaving absolutely nothing behind. I'm very happy to live with those rules. Freedom and courtesy can fit very nicely together.

All the warnings we'd had about Norway's prices were spot on. If you were going to eat out then you just had to hope for a very large portion. Supermarkets were expensive, but not if you bought whatever was on special to supplement your supplies. The extremely high standard of living that Norwegians have comes with an equally high labour cost.

Petrol was eye-wateringly expensive, especially for an oil producing country. But then it clicked that with speed limits being low, our bikes weren't sucking so much fuel. At anything over 65 miles per hour, our old BMWs were like a couple of lushes out for a party! At 50 on main roads, and either 30 or 20 mph in built-up areas, we were on winners. I have to admit that I found 50 mph extremely frustrating for the first couple of days. Norway is a country of very few straight lines and it felt as if the twisties were designed to be ridden, not cruised.

Just about every country in the world I've been lucky enough to ride has a rule or two that I've found are either illogical or simply frustrating. For sanity's sake, I prefer to look at them as cultural quirks. The joy for open-minded overlanders is that the fascinating things always far outweigh the negatives. It's also part of why we travel—to learn, to be challenged, and to allow the curious sides of our natures to fire on all cylinders. And anyway, we can usually ride on out of a country if certain rules or circumstances become too much like mental gravel rash.

Within the first two days we realised that Norwegians and visitors alike take the speed limits very seriously. Culture? Respect for a law well policed? You know that in a 50mph zone, you'll never find anyone going faster, and the zones were always clearly marked. Once this certainty had grown, I began to appreciate that long, wheel-rolling stares at views to take them in were fine. With few places to stop in the more dramatic sections of the coast, quality sideways stares were worth so much more than our usual snatched glimpses.

We had a month to play with. Back when we were planning this stage of the journey we'd realised Norway was going to require us to adapt our travel mind-set. Good. You never have the chance to become a mental slug on the road do you?

Birgit likes to go to the end of things. It's not a case of ticking boxes, but more that she likes to see what's there. That's why we rode to the end of the southernmost road in South America, turned around and headed north for Alaska. But how could we reach both ends in the time that we had for Norway? We'd be scooting past the things of interest, the cultural quirks, the chance to sit and chat with locals and wouldn't have the opportunity to see where side roads went. To top and tail the country we'd have to stop our rather random style of travel. But that's where we are happiest. We wake up in the morning, knowing what we could do, head out and let the day lead us. Sometimes we don't go very far but still have a full day exploring and learning. A slower pace also allows more time for laughter and the "for us" moments. I am happy to travel as an opportunist.

We decided that we were going to concentrate on the southwestern region. The inland central north-south strip of the country looked interesting, and northwestern coastline would easily consume a month in itself. This time, Birgit could still go to the end of things by going upward! There were plenty of trails into the mountains, and we like to get off our bikes for a hike now and then. Where better than Norway?

I wonder what you think about going to a country's "must-see" places? I used to steer clear of them as much as possible. The cynic in me said that everything was going to be overpriced, crowded, jaded, kitsch, and crowds who wanted no more than to buy postcards or snap selfies but had little interest in learning. Much of that is true, but one day I gave myself a serious talking to. Just because another doesn't travel the way I prefer doesn't mean they are wrong. They may be travelling in a way they feel physically or even mentally able to manage; in fact, they may be stretching themselves. And few who travel can fail to absorb at least some of a culture and its colour. I became a firm believer in the thought that it doesn't matter how one travels, only that they do. Of course, motorcycles are best!

The southernmost tip of Norway was accessible and was going to tick a second Birgit box. She's a total fan of lighthouses. When we first met she used to call them "Lightfires" and I loved that. She's from Germany and I am always in awe of her ability to take on another language. That had started in New Zealand where we'd first met, and had grown during our time riding in Africa, South, Central and North America. She's a determined sponge, loves the challenge of learning, and soaks up all sorts of language nuances. She does slip out with some gems though. A few weeks earlier we'd had a significant storm and she told me that it was "blowing a hooligan." Brilliant. We never have storms now, but weather hooligans. But I digress.

The southernmost tip of Norway is west from Kristansand and on a peninsula that ends just after the small village of Lindesnes. At the very tip, is Lindesnes Fyr—a quite beautiful, red-topped, white-walled, round tower of a lighthouse. The area is set up for tourism, but out of season there were just a few others scrambling over the pale, almost sandy-coloured granite rocks. Being so quiet also gave us the chance to climb inside the lighthouse, which has been restored to its historically correct design. Fist-size nuts were holding forearm-thickness bolts in place through the heavy steel walls. All fittings and door handles were of well-weathered, highly-polished brass. Up on the red railing walkway that surrounded the lights themselves, the wind was at hang-onto-your-hat, you can lean into me strength, the power of nature on a gloriously sunny day. A seagull fought the wind next to me for a few moments. I like to think that his stare had no cynicism in it at all, rather that he was curious as to what this human thing was doing at his altitude, behaving like a big kid.

Because of the way this area is carved up by fjords and mountains, many of the smaller roads are dead ends and it was these regions that started our time in Norway. I was once told, "Never go back." The guy who told me that meant two things: never go back to a country you've been to before and, it will have changed and is usually a disappointment. I don't agree as I'm always fascinated by how a country has developed, both the good and the bad. He also meant that as much as possible travellers should ride circles or loops and ignore roads that mean you have to go back on yourself. I didn't agree with that, either. Doing so means I get two very different perspectives of the scenery. On the way back I can stop and enjoy things I might have ridden past the first time, either because of the viewing angle, or I was eager to explore what came next.

For much of the way, the road before heading back inland had us weaving close to the shoreline. Small groups of brightly painted wooden houses, some on stilts, clustered the shoreline, and boats bobbed on the deep blue, wind-enthused waves. The boats ranged from dinghies and yachts to fishing boats, many of which looked as if they had been battling nature for decades. Nothing looked decrepit, and litter in the streets? Not a thing.

There's a bit of schoolboy in me, so place names sometimes make me chuckle. I often get sideways glances from Birgit when I let the inner kid show, and I usually deserve them. The town of Veggjeland had me drooling over the thought of a steak, but not the right kind of drool you want in Norway if you are riding on a budget traveller's wallet!

The 460 is a road that I'd recommend to anyone planning to visit Norway. It took us on a gentle cruise further inland past small towns, villages, lakes, and rivers, all of which were surrounded by green farmlands, with mountainous peaks in the distance and a blue sky overhead. Cornflower blue. We knew that Norway could be grey and damp so we made sure to fully appreciate the perfect sunshine and how the colours of absolutely everything could be seen at their vibrant best. I know I'm edging on the poetic here, but this is the land of inspiration.

Rustic stone bridges looked as if they had spanned rivers for centuries, and perhaps many of the Huttas had been around that long. Huttas are brightly coloured single-story wooden cabins; rusty reds, blues and greens seemed the norm but a few were painted a stark black. Perhaps for contrast, but I wondered if they were warmer in winter as their darker colour technically should attract more heat from the sun. Many are single-room structures, but they also can be found with two or three rooms. At one time, and I guess some still are, they were family homes. We'd found that many were available to rent, even on a night-by-night basis. We had our eyes on them because if the weather did turn, then every now and then we might be glad of somewhere to warm up and dry out.

The southwest is a land of lakes; some are huge yet many are no more than large ponds. All reflected a deeper tone of the sky's shades of blue, giving a vibrant addition to the ground level kaleidoscope of colours. It was almost as if Norway had put on its best frock for us. Up on the tops, snow added a new contrast and most of the lakes had small gleaming white icebergs floating in their crystal-clear water; the visible parts of their undersides showed through the water as a bright, almost unnatural, turquoise. We couldn't help but marvel at a tiny flowering plant that grew from the skinniest of cracks between the rocks, their flowers adding little exclamation marks of crimson to the scene.

We vaguely had the town of Lysebotn in our minds as a destination but let the day ease on by without a sense of haste. We rode past a stream of potential wild camping sites on the smaller roads. So many that, as we headed into the later part of the afternoon, I began to feel it was a mistake to ride on past them. Usually if we found a great spot, we'd tuck ourselves into it, even if it was early. That would allow for journal writing time, bike tweaking and the opportunity to make kit repairs, or simply the chance to go for a long stroll. But the flow of spots had made us confident that we'd find more.

The road down from the tops into Lyseboten, which is at the head of the Lysefjord, is a motorcyclist's gem. The Lysevegen road hairpins its way for 18 miles as it drops the 2,099 feet to the valley floor. Let's put it this way, the 27 hairpins made certain we were wide awake, and our brakes were more than warm by the time we got to the bottom. But not a wild camping spot down there anywhere. No worries, there was a camping site with an amazing view, just a short distance from the ferry we aimed to catch the next day.

This was our first positive cost surprise. If all camping sites in Norway were going to be this cheap, our budget was going to be happy. Tent up on soft but well drained grass, in a spot where we looked down the length of the magnificent fjord walls, a hot shower and a cooked meal, and all in daylight. That was a latitude thing; we were much further north already.

Water transport is the norm in Norway, in part because there simply isn't anywhere to put a road at the base of many fjord walls. Boats are the traditional way of getting around and many traditions still make sense. Birgit and I love watching life go by, so even though the first ferry wasn't until later in the morning, we were down on the jetty early. Sitting in the sunshine watching life is a brilliant thing to do for strangers in a strange land. From our side-saddle perches on our bikes, we watched a battered, red-hulled tug pulling a barge loaded with dredging equipment behind it, and an empty bathtub of a barge behind that. All wore a matching mix of red paint, rust and dents.

A white baker's van stopped off, with one of the skinniest bakers I'd ever seen making the deliveries. Suited office workers came and went from the port buildings, Saabs and Volvos seeming to be the vehicles of choice. A Czech-plated camper van arrived, its occupants never stepping outside into the sunshine as they too began their wait. A mother with three children burst out of a maroon-coloured VW camper van, shrieks of freedom from the four of them joining with the seagulls' calls. Then cars, a green work truck with its open-backed bed full of tools and reels of wire, a couple of vans, and the clock ticked on round.

The ferry was small with a black hull and a white superstructure. As it approached the jetty its jaws opened, rather like the visor on a crash helmet. Inside we could see a full load of trucks, cars and 4x4s waiting to depart. The crew docked with the swirling elegance of practice and skill, and the vehicles shot off as if they were starting a race.

It only took moments for us all to board, for tickets to be checked, and then with a growing throb and rumble from the big diesels, we were all heading down the fjord. It was a beautiful day and a sense of joy eased in, making me smile. This was us, sailing down a fjord, in Norway. We were in the craggy, majestic scenery, a part of it.

I've always liked boats but never been on one like this; time to explore. Thankfully Birgit is a likeminded soul and having wandered we found ourselves seats at the railings. We settled down to watch the small clusters of steep-roofed, white-walled houses in places where no road would ever make it to, the craggy walls of the fjord, and the small ports along the way where supplies were being delivered. Far below us schools of orange, yellow and red kayaks gracefully eased across the deep blue water, some obviously looking for a bit of fun in the ferry's wake. We people-watched the other passengers as they too were enthralled by the moments.

We were also on the watch for "Pulpit Rock." From water level it looked small but all the same this three-sided, straight-edged section of rock stood proud against the skyline at just over 1,900 feet above us. I could see why it had its name and my imagination conjured up the thought that it looked as if some mythical Norse giant had sideways sliced the raggedy edge of the cliff with an axe and had stood back thinking, "Ja, straight, square, that looks odd enough."

We like to get off our bikes and spend a few days hiking here and there as we travel. We both were bicycle travellers in the past, though Birgit was far more serious than I ever was. Travelling like this teaches the value of going slowly and the importance of keeping fit. As we'd ridden our motorcycles around the world, our hikes had taken us to places we'd never have made it otherwise. Keeping fit had helped deal with the sections of gnarly roads and harsher weather conditions. We also knew that in being physically fit, we were mentally too. That meant we were much more likely to see opportunities, and to be able to take advantage of them.

As is so often the case with main attractions, Pulpit Rock, or Preikestolen, though touristy, was a place well worth visiting. The estimated hiking time was one to four hours. By the time we'd done it I was sure that the "one hour" estimate related to those who jogged up, and the "four" to the extremely unfit. We enjoyed a two-hour stroll up the thousand feet along the narrow but very well laid-out track. In part, that was due to the simple point that we started early and had shared the track with few others. Returning was an eye-opening experience; some hikers were completely ill-equipped with heeled party shoes, no water, no cold weather layer and so on. It had been cold up on the pulpit. It was also a humbling experience as many on their way up hadn't seen a hiking trail in perhaps a decade or more. I admired their determination but couldn't help but wonder how a heart attack victim would be brought down.

The weather hooligans were out that night. We'd treated ourselves to a campsite; a shower was in order as the hike had been quite a sweaty affair. The campsite was a really good value again. Less than many campsites I know in the UK and excellently equipped. Birgit and I had been particularly aware of the change in the colour of the sky as we'd hunted for a spot to pitch our tent; we'd lost our gorgeous blue and the sun was long gone. Shelter provided by some low trees seemed like a good idea, but the ground seemed nastily flat! If a storm were to roll in then we wanted to be raised up a bit. We've slept in walled waterbeds too many times. *Ahh,* just the spot and we could, using my large tyre iron, get the tent pegs into the rocky ground.

The breeze began to turn into wind just as we'd finished the pegging and though no one else seemed concerned, we added four extra guy lines before heading for the showers. Power showers rock! Birgit took a side path on the way back and arrived at the tent with a big grin and a loaf of handmade brown wholemeal bread. Moments later the rain started, with the wind now leaning trees and tents before it. By dawn, out of the 40-plus tents that had dotted the campsite like multi-coloured mushrooms, ours was one of three left standing. Sometimes we get it right. The morning calm was eerily quiet.

The weeks passed far too quickly. Every day was a riding or hiking day. The one night of storms was the only time we had bad weather. The blue skies stayed with us as we wild camped or stayed at camping sites; those away from the larger towns and the cities were the best value. All had hot showers, drying rooms, and fully equipped kitchens that were free to use. Some had lounges too.

We also linked up with friends who'd booked to use a Hutta for their summer holidays and that gave us a chance to step back in time. Once this had been a family home and was filled with the family's history. Black and white and sepia photos of its members through the ages hung from the walls. Hand-knitted and quilted fabrics covered furniture and beds. Pottery displaying the patina of time stood on the mantelpiece, bookshelves and windowsills, or hung on fabric strips from the wooden walls. The air was scented by wood smoke, some sort of herb, and the faint but rich aroma of smoked fish, all the touches providing a good idea of how it might have been to live in such a home. Cosy, but harsh in winters.

Fjords were homes to oblong floating fish farms upon which were a warehouse, a workshop, a small house, a courtyard and usually a battered yellow forklift. Behind, as if the concrete islands were towing them, were strings of circular netted fish enclosures. I later read that these enclosures were usually up to 160 feet in diameter and could be the same deep. The bigger nets would hold up to 200,000 salmon! To that I thought of one word: grim. But I felt a little better when I'd gone on to read that 97.5% of the space in the nets must be water and that the farms can only be placed in situations where there is strong water flow. Better than the miserable footage I'd seen of battery chicken and pig farms, but I was reminded to look for labels that purported to be "wild salmon."

The other thing that struck us in the early days, before it became a thought norm, was that Norway is the land of tunnels. I'd read there are over 900. How do you get from one fjord valley to the next? When possible, straight through those stone walls. Every tunnel was very different from the next; not only in length, height and width but some were asphalt and others gravel. One was even a spiral. Several were full of dripping water that when landing on my visor would spangle whatever light was available and momentarily confuse my senses. Quite a few weren't lit at all. Those caught us out the first times. Brilliant, gorgeous sunlight and then suddenly pitch black, which wasn't helped by the point that we'd been riding with sunnies on. I have no idea how Birgit didn't fall off the first time this happened. She must have clicked into instant bat mode; for sure she couldn't risk stopping as she knew I'd be right behind her, and almost as blind.

We ride with our headlights on, but they were pathetic when tasked with the deep instant darkness. It was one of those moments when you know that the gods of motorcycling, or in my case a hard-worked guardian angel, had been on hand. I was the lucky one. Birgit has wide reflective strips on the back of her panniers and at least my headlight was catching them, whereas she had nothing to focus on. Later on we rode the Laerdal Tunnel and what an amazing thing that is. At 15.2 miles it's the longest road tunnel in the world, and it really is a bit like riding onto the set of a science fiction movie. The walls are lit with shades of deep pink and purple, with an occasional dash of yellow to break things up a bit. Absolutely wonderfully bizarre!

This is also a country of waterfalls and at this time of year, with snow melt still happening, it was fascinating. If you can think of a shape or a size for a waterfall, you'll find it here. Well, perhaps not Victoria or Niagara Falls, but you get my drift.

Another attraction we wanted to fit in was to visit at least one of the "Stave churches." Hundreds of years old, these wonderfully shaped wooden churches used a particular type of wood treated in a way once unique to this region. They are filled with classic-style wall paintings, beautiful wood carvings, and peace. They prompted respect on the out-side, and the interiors inspired awe.

We often shared the snowy landscape with sheep so laden with dense wool that they looked rather like fluffy snowdrifts heading across the slopes in slow motion. I'd never ridden alongside skiers before. Some were bright flashes of colour scooting past us on the snow and others were hiking, skies on shoulders, back up to the tops again. A couple of skiers I talked to were calm, confident, tanned and looked incredibly fit. Both spoke fluent English and answered my request for directions with friendly precision. The snow brought out the big kid in Birgit, too. At a stop to soak up the view she collected smiles by jumping onto a snow bank and making snow angels.

Many of the dirt tracks weren't marked on our maps but if there were no gates or property signs, we went exploring. The tracks took us meandering through some of the most beautiful scenery I've ever been surrounded by. The mountains with their snowy peaks high in the clear blue of the sky, white water rivers, huttas bright red against the snow, and the marshy levels covered in the flickering white flags of marsh cotton plants. On many days we saw absolutely no other vehicles at all.

As soon as we rode down onto busier roads I joked with Birgit that she had better relearn how to overtake. We happily stayed within the speed limits and on several occasions were glad we had. Police were out with speed cameras. Many times they were tucked into spots where there was no chance of seeing them until it was too late. No problem for us and we enjoyed grins and sometimes even a wave from a bored police person.

Over the next weeks we hiked to, on and from glaciers. We trailed our hands in the opaque turquoise of glacial water and soaked ourselves in the spray of thundering melt water. Sometimes, when the falling water hit rocks on the way down, the subsequent spray would form wavering white feathers in the air before falling into the valley as mist, that mist then catching the sun to form perfect rainbows. Why do I travel? I love it when life is full of firsts.

We shared tales of the road with other motorcycle travellers and met human-sized wood carvings of trolls. We ate smoked fish and drank whiskey. We grinned at the concept of parking in laybys called "Pause Parks" and had marvelled at the way the mirror-like fjords really did reflect perfect images of the trees, flowers and buildings along the shore.

We discovered that Norwegian street art is a thing and that there are Banksy fans in Norway. We rode miles of what I think of as being motorcycle magic and wandered the backstreets of the city of Bergen. We drank excellent coffee in the street cafés and explored the secondhand and junk shops—where better to find out about a people and their culture.

Just as we were running out of time, the weather changed. Within a day the blue skies disappeared, to be replaced by too many shades of grey and rain. The chill we'd been riding through in shadows and shady areas for the past weeks turned into a biting all round cold. We pulled on our extra layers and travelled on, knowing the sudden contrast was a fine thing in itself. Perspective equals value. Travelling with no side stand? That was a laughter-making chore, all part of the adventure.

About the authors:

Born in Africa, **Sam Manicom** has been travelling pretty much since he was 16 when he completed his first solo trip outside of the UK by bicycle. He subsequently travelled using various forms of transport including sailboats and trains. He has hitchhiked and hiked in many parts of the world.

Wanting to travel in a completely different way, Sam learned to ride a motorcycle. Within three months of starting to ride, he set off to travel the length of Africa. This planned one-year trip turned into an eight-year journey exploring 55 countries around the world.

He now works full time in the world of adventure and overlanding travel. He's a keen advocate of motorcycle travel in particular and when not writing books, magazine articles and conducting multimedia travel presentations, is very much involved with travel-related organisations.

Birgit Schünemann is a geographer and works as a nautical chart compiler. She still has her 1971 *BMW R60/5* from the round the world trip but now rides a 1984 *BMW R80ST*.

Sam is a co-host of the *Adventure Rider Radio* "RAW" show. He has also been a guest of numerous radio shows including *BBC Radio's* "Drive Time," and the *BBC* travel show "Excess Baggage.'"

In 2017 Sam was awarded the *Overland Magazine Spirit of Adventure Award* for his contribution to overlanding. Birgit and Sam are currently based in the UK and they travel together at every opportunity.

Website: Sam-Manicom.com
Facebook: Sam Manicom
Facebook: Adventure Motorcycle Travel Books by Sam Manicom
Twitter: @SamManicom
Instagram: @sammanicom.author

Sam is the author of four motorcycle travel books that take the reader travelling across the six continents which made up his journey around the world. *Into Africa, Under Asian Skies, Distant Suns* (Southern Africa, and South-Central America) and *Tortillas to Totems* (Mexico, the U.S. and Canada) are published as paperbacks, on *Kindle* and *Audiobooks*. You can order signed and dedicated copies via his website, and all are available from good bookshops, *Amazon* and *The Book Depository*.

"When you see someone putting on [their] Big Boots, you can be pretty sure that an Adventure is going to happen."

—A.A. Milne

Collecting Moments

"We do not remember days,
we remember moments."

—*Cesare Pavese*

This multifaceted, challenging, surprising, unpredictable, and sometimes frightening world of ours is an intriguing place, isn't it? It's too easy to forget that within this mix are joy, laughter and love. Travelling the world, either from the pages of a book or on the road itself, reminds us that the world is both incredible and beautiful, and that it's filled with fascinating places, ideas, and people.

At the beginning of *The Moment Collectors*, I asked the question, "Who are Overlanders?" Pointing out that though they tend to be a slightly rebellious lot, that's not the key characteristic, and most weren't so different from anyone else when they set out.

It's a fact that you don't have to be a special type of person to travel the long road. You do need to be yourself—an individual—and to allow your curiosity and senses to lead you. Exploring the world on the back of a motorcycle is an excellent ambition.

Making a big trip happen is usually not an easy thing, but starts with making plans to deal with responsibilities, getting funds together, and changing one's mindset. Looking for new ways to do things replaces the perhaps more obvious reasons why something isn't possible.

303

The long road allows you to boundary stretch, live, learn, have fun, notice the quirky and to love the freedom that motorcycling makes possible. If you open yourself to the opportunities, you will have extraordinary, unexpected and enthralling moments along the way.

"Stop and smell the roses," is an old saying with good reason. You'll likely have realised as you've read these pages, that *moments*, be they challenges or delights, are the reasons why every long-distance international traveller is who they have become. And why they keep heading back for more.

Perhaps a little perversely, travellers of the roads of the world return far more comfortable with reality, having realised that for civilization to work, we must do so together. At the very least, it takes respect and understanding. Even if you're a two-wheeled hermit, you'll be reminded of this over and over again.

If for a multitude of reasons you can't head out quite yet, remember that dreams are where adventures begin. And you can keep them alive by diving into the spellbinding worlds that planning opens up.

Whether you aim to travel or not, I suspect you have read *The Moment Collectors* because you understand the value of curiosity, you love tales of true-life adventures, and you are kindred spirits. We hope that the moments from the road we've shared have surprised, intrigued and perhaps at times made you laugh. Ours are tales of the reality of the world.

Regardless of where your road and dreams take you, we hope to see you out there one day. At home or away, may your curiosity and an open heart bring you opportunities to collect your own spectacular moments.

All the best,
Claire, Geoff H, Spencer & Cathy, Shirley & Brian, Ted, Lisa & Jason, Mark, Graham, Tiffany, EmmaLucy, Tim & Marisa, Christian, Helen, Michelle, Travis & Chantil, Lisa & Simon, Daniel, Geoff K, Michnus & Elsebie, and Birgit & Sam.

A Request
from Sam

THE MOMENT COLLECTORS

TWENTY TRAVELLERS' TALES
FROM AROUND THE WORLD

SAM MANICOM AND FRIENDS

We hope you've enjoyed the tales of the road in *The Moment Collectors.*

Travel has and will continue to have amazing influences on our lives. If we'd not ridden, survived and enjoyed such travels so much, I'm sure I wouldn't be here typing this request.

Independent authors/publishers like us truly value your help, as those seeking books like this often check reviews before picking up or downloading a copy. With your help we can share, and have the opportunity to encourage more people to head out and experience the incredible for themselves.

If you've enjoyed this book, I would be grateful if you'd take a few moments to post a review on *Amazon* and *Goodreads.*

Thank you for reading *The Moment Collectors* and thank you for your help.

All the best,

Introduction to Inspiration

Why are you finding advertisements from companies involved in overlanding and adventure riding at this stage of *The Moment Collectors?*

These are all companies who are highly recommended as having excellent products and quality service. I'm enjoying the opportunity to guide you in their direction.

If you are planning adventures of your own, be they two weeks, a month or two years, I know you'll find some inspiration on these next pages of equipment, travel organisations, books and more.

You'll also find some worthy causes that we are keen to help out.

In the second section you'll find a list of what we think are wonderfully useful links and contacts.

D.A.R.T.
DRAGOO ADVENTURE RIDER TRAINING

BMW–Certified Off Road Instructor:
BILL DRAGOO

Balance, Control, Judgment and Attitude.
These are the four cornerstones of adventure riding.
Possess them all and even if one fails you,
the rest will get you home again!

*Our mission is to provide quality
off-road training at a fair price
for all who wish to learn.*

**Classes are located in Central Oklahoma
and across the United States.**

More information at billdragoo.com

(405) 830-6630 | dragooadventuresllc@gmail.com

HIGH QUALITY EQUIPMENT FROM GERMANY FOR YOUR NEXT JOURNEY.

For over 30 years, Touratech has been manufacturing equipment for your motorcycle trip in the Black Forest, Germany. Aluminum and stainless steel are handcrafted into pannier systems and vehicle protection. More than 350 employees design, produce and distribute products from Niedereschach in Germany to make your trip safe.

CLOTHING

PROTECTION

LUGGAGE

SUSPENSION

NEW IDEAS FOR MOTORBIKES

TOURATECH

Made in Germany

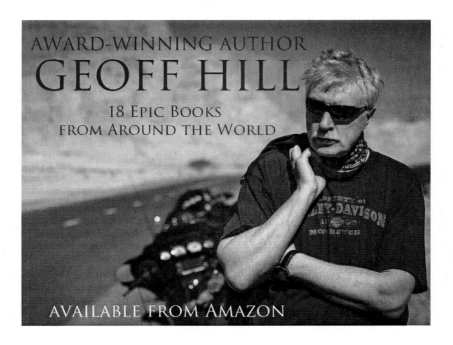

The Japanese-Speaking Curtain Maker

SPENCER JAMES CONWAY
Adventurer | Author | Radio/TV Personality

Available on Amazon, Kindle and
www.spencer-conway.com

African Motorcycle Diaries DVD
www.dukevideo.com

Coming soon 'The Zimbabwean
Psychiatrists Hat'

spencer james conway
spencer james conway

R&G GLEAM.

MOTORCYCLE DEGREASER · **CHAIN CLEANER** · **SILICONE SHINE** · **DISC BRAKE CLEANER** · **DRY CHAIN LUBE** · **EVERYDAY CHAIN LUBE**

★★★★☆
RATED BY MCN!

CLEANING & PROTECTION, EVERY STEP OF THE WAY

NANO BIKE WASH.

1 LITRE

- QUICKLY REMOVES ALL CONTAMINANTS.
- SUITABLE FOR ALL COMPONENTS.
- BIODEGRADABLE.
- FRUITY SCENT.

£8.99 RRP

WWW.RG-RACING.COM

f @crashprotection   🐦 @RnGRacing   📷 @rg_crashprotection   ▶ youtube.com/c/RandGTV

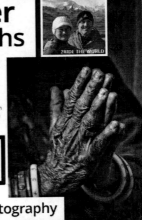

ATLAS
THROTTLE LOCK

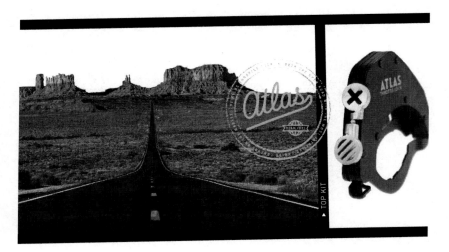

Cruise Control Alternative

The ATLAS Throttle Lock is a mechanical cruise control that allows riders to relax their grip, shake out their hand, adjust their gear and log more miles without the threat of the dreaded arm pump. The ATLAS was designed after a 15 month Round-the-World trip on a paint-shaking KTM 640 Adventure where the need for some wrist relief was real.

The ATLAS mounts to most any motorcycle throttle tube between the grip and the throttle housing. In a matter of minutes you will have added a completely new function to your motorcycle. It's simple, safe and intuitive.

When the ATLAS is engaged, a friction pad presses against the throttle housing to hold your throttle in place. The term "throttle lock" can be misleading because the ATLAS doesn't actually "lock" the throttle of your motorcycle - it simply holds with friction. To adjust your speed, manually rotate the throttle and it will hold any position you leave it in, until you turn it off.

The ATLAS Team
Adventure Touring Leaves All Signs

⊘ atlasthrottlelock.com

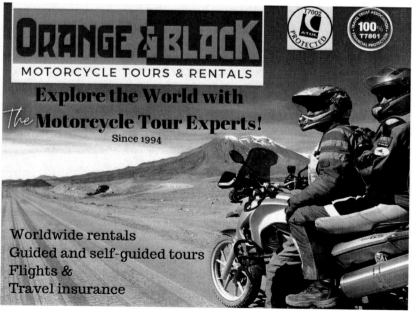

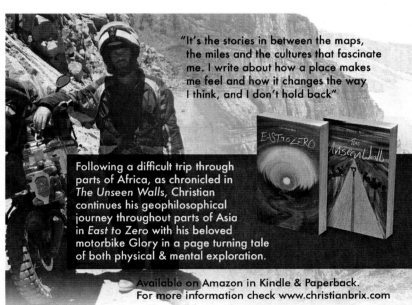

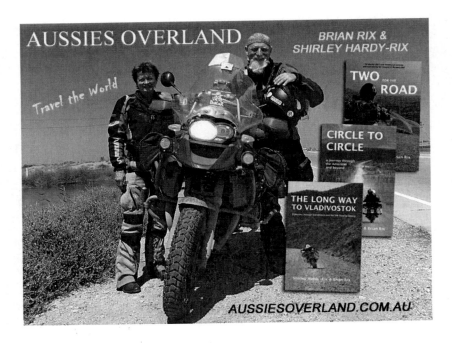

The Orginal ADV Moto Podcast Since 2014

THE VOICE OF MOTO TRAVEL

ADVENTURE RIDER RADIO

RAW

Download Anywhere Podcasts Are Found

"Simply the best motorcycle podcast." Muzakmon

-

"Your podcast is outstanding, informative and fun." J Lesser

-

"I anxiously wait for the next shows appearance in the podcast lists." B Bridges

-

"Best show ever." G Smith

-

"Topics that come up are so pertinent" "You inspired me." G Guenther

-

"Great show." R Steiger

-

"The quality and quantity of information you all share is astounding." M Gebhard

-

"So inspiring and interesting." J Gillihan

-

"What you're doing for travelling bikers is fantastic." D Lilwall

-

"Always interesting and the stories inspiring." D Tsotsos

-

"Jim is hands down one of the best interviewers out there. " Mattylife

-

"The show is fresh and interesting every week" ITAdminUSMA

World's Most Downloaded Show of It's Kind

OVERLAND
EXPO

Get outfitted. Get trained. Get Inspired.
The world is waiting!

Overland Expo® is the world's premier event series for do-it-yourself adventure travel enthusiasts, with hundreds of classes for 4-wheel-drive enthusiasts and adventure motorcyclists, speakers & trainers from all over the world, and a large expo featuring vendors of adventure travel equipment, camping gear, bikes, vehicles, and services.

Find us at overlandexpo.com

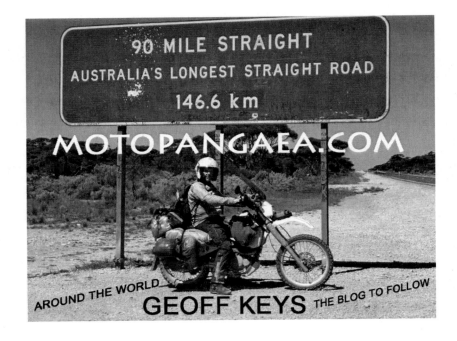

90 MILE STRAIGHT
AUSTRALIA'S LONGEST STRAIGHT ROAD
146.6 km

MOTOPANGAEA.COM

AROUND THE WORLD GEOFF KEYS THE BLOG TO FOLLOW

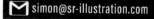

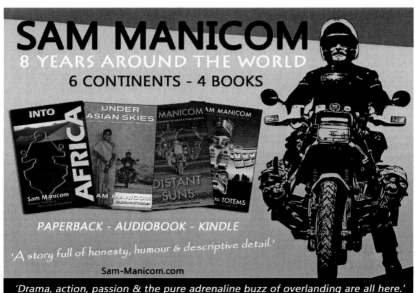

Helpful Links and Contacts

We know you'll find plenty more inspiration in these next pages. Those listed below are just some of the clubs, books, websites, podcasts, and organisations that are enthusiastically involved with helping people to travel long distance. They are sources of information and fascination and are peopled by kindred spirits.

All have been suggested by the 20 authors. Please note, they are listed deliberately in random order.

Publications, Online Shows, and Travel Information

RevSisters.com: *Three fantastic motorcycle film festivals per year. All aspects of motorcycling.*

Backroads Discovery Route (BDR): *Ride the U.S. off the beaten track. Take a look at this organisation and their amazing films.*

Caravanistan.com: *Very useful for central Asia, with info about routes, border crossings, visas etc.*

iOverlander.com: *A database of places for overlanders and travellers. Including camping, hotels, restaurants, mechanics, water, propane filling and may other categories. Details are listed for each place, including amenities, photos, date last visited and GPS coordinates.*

HorizonsUnlimited.com: *The world's motorcycle travel site. Questions answered about paperwork, routes, places to visit, ways to link up with locals and so much more. Detailed motorcycle, 4x4 and bicycling travel* *information from around the world, which is kept up to date with info and tales shared from the road. The "Go to" site for overlanders.*

AdvRiders.com: *Provides adventure motorcycle riders with their own dedicated online community. The site was debuted as an adventure riding forum and has grown to become the most visited website in the world for motorcycle enthusiasts. A site of top tips and fascination.*

AdventureRiderRadio.com: *The world's most downloaded adventure motorcycle podcast. Weekly shows packed with stories, adventures, rider skills, interviews, industry pros, tech, tips, and much more.*

AdventureRiderRadioRAW: *The monthly partner podcast to ARR. The well-travelled panel are sent in questions by listeners. The round table discussion of those topics includes varied and detailed tips and ideas gathered from the road. There is always laughter!*

AdventureBikeTV.com: *Bike reviews, road challenges, interviews, gear tests, laughter and much more.*

TeapotOne.com: *TeapotOne—Bru Time. After riding a Superbike 74,000 miles solo around the world, Bruce Smart produces weekly videos and the Bru Time podcast. These always reinforce his mantra of "Live Your Life!" We get one life, so fit as much in as you can.*

ADMotoLive: *The podcast from ADVMoto Magazine. Top news. Interviews, chats, ideas, new products and more.*

Horizon.BMWmoa.org: *Podcast. News and information from across the motorcycle industry, including motorcyclists (and motorcycles) of every make, marque, model and vintage.*

MotorcycleMen.us: *Podcast sharing the roads, the people, the destinations and everything that goes along with it. Interviews with authors, travellers, manufacturers or someone with a good story.*

Ride and Talk: *The BMW Motorrad podcast. From moving interviews to exciting stories the podcast is all about the bikes and the people.*

The Late Apex PT: *Feeling the need to get fit for the rigours of the road? Talk to this man. The Late Apex PT provides functional strength and fitness coaching for motorsport, adventure travel and the over 40s.*

GlobalWomenWhoRide.com: *An ambitious project that aims to interview one or more woman motorcyclists in every country on this planet. The typical interview encompasses riders' bikes, favourite rides, gear, stories, and somewhat serious stuff like their thoughts around community, female friendship, activism etc.*

XT225.com: *A very friendly and helpful forum for riders of XT225s.*

Angelfire.com: Go to the /sports/serowpages/ for XT225 technical info, mods, repairs and more.

4x4Community.co.za: *Excellent info on travelling the trails of southern Africa.*

DangerousRoads.org: *Tough/beautiful roads around the world.*

MotorcycleralliesAustralia.com: Travelling Oz? Then this site gives you a great chance to link up with other motorcyclists and delve into the kindred spirits within Australian motorcycling.

SheADV.com: *Inspiring, celebrating, promoting, and helping women pursue their adventure motorcycle travel dreams.*

ExpeditionPortal.com: *For motorcyclists, 4x4 and cycle travellers. Forum, articles and more.*

TripAdvisor.com: *Compare and book deals, cheap flights, best places to eat, and hidden gems.*

LonelyPlanet.com: *Around the world travel guides since 1972.*

Bradt-TravelGuides.com: *Some very useful general info—not budget travel but a stack of useful ideas woven in.*

FootprintTravelGuides.com: *Travel guides specialising in South America but also reaching into other parts of the world. Motorcycle friendly.*

Adventure-Motorcycling.com: *Chris Scott desert specialist; books, routes and much more. Look out for the Adventure Motorcycling Handbook.*

MotorbikeNation.com: *Riding Australia? Riders with a special emphasis on touring this country by motorcycle. The site aim is to provide all the necessary information any rider will want when planning a ride; road conditions, availability of essential services, motorcycle friendly establishments and more.*

BestBikingRoads.com: *Fantastic routes across the globe. Also accommodation tips, motorcycle rental and....*

GetRouted.com.au: *Specialists at shipping motorcycles from Australia to Europe.*

B&M Logistica: *Need help shipping out of Brazil? Highly recommended.*

AWE 365: *Adventure travel and outdoor activities worldwide. With 70+ activities in 5,000+ destinations, AWE365 has a huge range of ideas to help you plan.*

Stanfords.co.uk: *UK's best one stop shop for travel books and maps.*

The Hospital for Tropical Diseases London: *Dedicated to the prevention, diagnosis and treatment of tropical diseases and travel related infections. Offers pre-travel advice, e.g. inoculations.*

Berndtesch.de: *Books, survival training, equipment and overland enthusiast.*

Grimaldi Lines: *Travel between continents by freighter. With their RoRo opportunities, your bike travels too.*

Mediterranean Shipping Corporation (MSC): *Travel between continents by freighter.*

The Cruise People: *Freighter cruises worldwide.*

Dakar Motors: *The home of overland motorcycle travellers in South America.*

Jupitalia.com: *Ted Simon author of 'Jupiter's Travels', 'Riding High', 'Dreaming of Jupiter' and many more. Is frequently called 'The Godfather of motorcycle overlanding'.*

"Give Me Gratitude or Give Me Debt" by Glennon Doyle: *Recommended by several contributors. This is an example of not getting caught up in the consumerism that keeps a lot of people from reaching their dreams. Modern slaves are not in chains, they are in debt. It takes a change in perspective and having gratitude for the simple things.*

"Stay Alive in the Desert": *K. E. M. Melville, ISBN 0-903909-11-1. An old book but full of relevant information.*

Roaddog Publications: *Publishers specialising in motorcycle books.*

Kahuku Publishing: *Specialising in adventure motorcycle books from independent authors.*

National Geographic's Destinations of a Lifetime: *225 of the World's Most Amazing Places. This book could inspire travel wanderlust for life!*

Motorcycle Travel Organisations, Clubs, Forums and Facebook Groups

WIMA International: *An organisation for women riders globally; spread across 40 countries.*

ABR Forum: *A very enthusiastically supported forum covering all things adventure bike riding.*

Horizons Unlimited FB: *Inspiring, informing & connecting Overland Adventure Travellers since 1997. Trips, blogs, questions, advice; anything members wish to share with adventure travellers.*

Ulysses.org.au: *Over 40? Riding Australia? Join these guys for social meets, rideouts and much more.*

Adventure Bike Riders FB: *Community for adventurous bike riders. Stories, photos and members tips on where to go, what to see, what to ride and what to take with you. It doesn't matter what bike you ride just that you ride.*

GS Giants FB: *Adventure motorcycle enthusiasts of all brands welcome. A very supportive group who enjoy adventuring with friends, chatting about riding and good times; stories, pictures and events.*

Motorcycle Touring FB: *A community is for owners of all kind of motorbikes and for all who love bike travelling, bike adventure and like to share their stories, photos and / or technical advice.*

GSclubuk.org: *BMW GS CLUB UK—Enthusiast's Club.*

UKGSer.com: *BMW 'GS' Enthusiast's Forum.*

Minimalist Motorcycle Vagabonds FB: *Bringing people together who love to adventure by motorcycle, from the beginners to the experienced.*

International Brotherhood of Adventure Riders FB: *Promoting friendship and awareness of all forms of motorcycle riding across the globe.*

TheBMWclub.org.uk: *BMW Owners Club.*

BMWMoa.com: *BMW Owners Club.*

International Motorcyclist Touring Club: *Touring the world since 1932, the IMTC is one of the oldest and most experienced touring clubs in the world.*

Arabian Knights Riders, Cairo: *The first cruiser motorcycle club in Egypt was started in 2010 for the purpose of enjoying the motorcycle riding experience within the brotherhood attitude. Very welcoming to overlanders.*

Overland Club: *The Overland Club—bringing together motorcycle travellers and those who dream of travelling by motorcycle to share experiences, inspiration and good times. The Club hosts meet-ups, gatherings and events and throughout the year and throughout the UK as well as exclusive online content.*

GlobeTrotters.co.uk: *Travel club for independent travellers.*

Women Adventure Riders FB: *A group open to all women who love motorcycling, women who love the thrill of taking the road less travelled.*

Global Motorcycle Adventures of Women Riders FB: *A central location where women motorcycle enthusiasts from across the globe can share their travel stories, triumphs, challenges, and experience.*

Motorcycle Camping FB: *Group for folks who like to motorcycle camp. If you have a bike and a tent....*

Motorcycle Tours FB: *Every week the group has a different motorcycle travel topic which members contribute relevant stories to.*

Pan-America Riders Association FB: *Tips, suggestions and tales of the road from the Americas.*

Pan-American Travellers Association FB: *Open to all travellers along the American continent. Sharing experience or providing some hindsight into future expeditions, no matter the medium of transportation.*

Mental Health Motorbike FB: *A UK based group to support the Mental Health wellbeing of group members through peer and MHM team members support.*

ADV-Rider on Facebook FB: *ADV motorcycling, routes, equipment, and anything that contributes towards the ADV community.*

ADVRiders/fb FB: *A group dedicated to adventure travels with motorcycles.*

Motorcycle Adventures FB: *Where bike-minded travellers come to connect and create their next adventure.*

Motorcycle Explorers FB: *For those with a passion for motorbike travel near and far. Dedicated to helping riders get out there and explore.*

UK Adventure Riders FB: *Sharing information, knowledge and experiences related to members' global moto-adventure riding on all makes of bikes.*

Chunky Tread Motorcycle Adventure Club FB: *Sharing links to members adventures on two or four wheels. "If your treads are chunky and your story adventure...."*

Overland Motorcyclists FB: *Displays two-wheel experiences around the world; sharing pictures and videos of member's journeys.*

BMW Airheads FB: *For owners of the older BMW Airheads to share information, show off their bikes and post information about projects. Swap ideas, parts and accessories.*

Yamaha XT660Z Tenere FB: *Photos, discussions and an excellent "file" section.*

Yamaha XT660Z Ténéré FB: *Prepare for adventure with the XT660Z Ténéré...*

BMW Riders Association Clubhouse FB: *A community of fun and adventurous BMW motorcycle riders focused on the machine, the marque and the company that makes it all work.*

XT225 FB: *For all those that love the Yamaha XT225 and XT250 Serow models.*

Airheads BMW Motorcycle Riders FB: *An international group dedicated to the riding and maintenance of traditional air-cooled BMW Boxer motorcycles.*

KLR 650 FB: *For those people who own or appreciate the Kawasaki KLR650.*

Kawasaki KLR 650 Owners FB: *Quoting the page, 'Do you own a KLR 650? If so, you should be here!'*

Overlanding Africa FB: *Shares travel information, on and off-road routes, visas, carnet and temporary import, camping spots, wild camps and any other useful information.*

Overlanding Morocco and West Africa FB: *Group for those travelling, overlanding and touring West Africa and Morocco. All countries from Morocco to Angola.*

Overlanding Asia FB: *All countries from the borders of Europe, Turkey / Russia through the Middle East, the Indian Subcontinent, The Stans and all other countries to East (China, Mongolia).*

Bunk a Biker FB: *A worldwide community of motorcycle riders who voluntarily provide accommodations to travelling bikers; promoting the togetherness and support of a motorcycle-enthusiast community.*

Acknowledgements

This book has been created with true traveller's spirit. Everyone contributed, shared and helped everyone else. That's made my work on *The Moment Collectors* a real joy.

Thank you to all the contributing authors. They have been fun to work with and I really appreciate how generous they have been with their time, thoughts and with sharing their experiences and photos.

Huge thanks to Paul H Smith for designing the layout and all of his editorial advice. We have been very lucky that he agreed to work on the project with us.

Thank you to Susan Dragoo who has been wonderful with her editing work and with making sure that none of us have made any blunders!

Grateful thanks to Jill Boulton for proofreading. She has an eagle eye.

Thank you to Simon Roberts for all the amazing illustrations. He has been excellent to work with. If you've not come across him before, you should know that besides being an artist, he is also an overlander and an author.

Thank you to Fil Schiannini who created this super cover and has been involved with aspects of the book layout. As always his advice and enthusiasm is much appreciated.

I'd like to thank Dan Collins of Fresh Tracks for his friendship, inspiration and encouragement.

Thanks are very much due to my partner Birgit who has been the best sounding board a person could wish for. Her guidance is part of why this book is as it is.

And finally, "*Thank you*" for risking buying a copy of our book.

TIME TO RIDE

DREAM + MOTORCYCLE + WORLD

'Let's get lost!'

"When a person travels, they discover who they really are and how incredible this world of ours is. As soon as a person's senses are brought alive, an adventure starts to be a success. So go, ride, get lost, explore, collect magnificent moments."

—*Sam Manicom*

"Travel changes you. As you move through this life and this world you change things slightly, you leave marks behind, however small, and in return, life and travel leave marks on you. Most of the time those marks on your body or on your heart, are beautiful...."

—*Anthony Bourdain* (*June 1956–June 2018*)

FOR MOMENT COLLECTING

"We travel, not for us to escape life, but for life not to escape us."

—*Anon*

MONDAY

TUESDAY

WEDNESDAY

THURSDAY

FRIDAY

SATURDAY

SUNDAY